Reading Theories in Contemporary Fiction

Also Available from Bloomsbury

Reading Theories in Contemporary Fiction

Lisa McNally

BLOOMSBURY

LONDON • NEW DELHI • NEW YORK • SYDNEY

Bloomsbury Academic

An imprint of Bloomsbury Publishing Plc

50 Bedford Square	1385 Broadway
London	New York
WC1B 3DP	NY 10018
UK	USA

www.bloomsbury.com

Bloomsbury is a registered trade mark of Bloomsbury Publishing Plc

First published 2013
Paperback edition first published 2014

British Library Cataloguing-in-Publication Data
A catalogue record for this book is available from the British Library.

ISBN: HB: 978-1-4411-6409-4
PB: 978-1-4725-8972-9
ePub: 978-1-4411-0954-5
ePDF: 978-1-4411-9026-0

Library of Congress Cataloging-in-Publication Data
A catalog record for this book is available from the Library of Congress.

Typeset by Deanta Global Publishing Services, Chennai, India

Contents

Acknowledgements   vi

Introduction: Telling Truths about Reading   1

1   Composition   29

2   Traces   61

3   Deconstruction and Ethics   87

4   Tact   107

5   You   141

Coda: Desire   167

Notes   171

Bibliography   187

Index   199

Acknowledgements

Huge thanks to Clare Connors, Nicholas Royle, Rebecca Beasley and Ros Ballaster for reading so attentively and patiently.

Thanks too to Claire Waters for thoughts on my Traces chapter.

Thank you to my anonymous reviewers and to David Avital and Laura Murray at Bloomsbury.

Thank you to the AHRC and to St Catherine's College for the financial support which made this project possible.

Thank you to Oxford University's English Faculty, in particular Emma Smith, Kirsten Shepherd-Barr and Stefano-Maria Evangelista.

Also thanks to Sarah Wood.

Thank you to Aoife, Ellie, Helen, V, Claire and Will for all the cups of tea.

Thank you Dad.

And Mum. In very loving memory.

Introduction:
Telling Truths about Reading

Timothy Clark, Nicholas Royle and a number of other theorists – whom we might loosely group as 'those thinking after Derrida' – have recently suggested that the RAE (Research Assessment Exercise, now the Research Excellence Framework or REF) is a governing force central to today's university; for Royle, it casts its 'eerie shadow' 'over everything' (Royle 2003, p. 112). The RAE's presence is, Royle's description suggests, sinister. '[E]verything in the RAE', Royle explains, 'has to do with counting, with disavowing the unaccountable and uncountable' (p. 112). Clark complains similarly that it demands a 'compartmentalising and neutralising professionalism' (Clark 2002, p. 103). J. Hillis Miller, who, as a subject of the US system, does not write under the spectre of the RAE, nonetheless observes analogous developments; he argues that the university, as it becomes ever-more 'technologized' and 'globalized', finds increasingly that its 'mission' is 'to produce an educated workforce to make the region where it is located "competitive in the global economy"' (Miller 1999, p. 57).

Thus, for these writers, the university of the RAE is a closed system centred around attainable and tightly delineated objectives. However, they describe the actual work in which academics are involved – thinking, teaching and reading – in very different terms: as strange, often unquantifiable and sometimes difficult to identify.[1] Royle, for example, argues that 'reading entails something unreadable, in reserve, something that resists being understood *now*' (Royle 2003, p. 57; italics in original). Peter Schwenger, in an essay entitled 'Uncanny Reading', suggests that it is a practice characterized by 'strangeness' (Schwenger 1995, p. 340). Sarah Wood suggests that '[r]eading . . . has something in common with the dream' (Wood 2009b, p. 66).

Miller, too, writes of an 'excess intrinsic to reading' (Miller 1999, p. 485). In *The Ethics of Reading* he asserts that

> Reading itself is extraordinarily hard work. It does not occur all that often. Clearheaded reflection on what really happens in an act of reading is even more difficult and rare. It is an event traces of which are found here and there in

written form, like those tracks left in a bubble-chamber by the passage of a particle from outer space (Miller 1987, pp. 3–4).

Miller claims that reading is elusive: 'hard work' and difficult to describe. He aligns it with that which is too far away ('outer space') or too small ('a particle') to be seen clearly or known fully. Moreover, the final phrase of this passage arrests the attention. In an otherwise direct and authoritative academic text, Miller's use of simile and his invocation of 'tracks left in a bubble-chamber' and 'outer space' strike the reader as whimsical; the phrase 'here and there' is conversational and vague. This sudden shift in tone performs the affront 'reading' constitutes to the 'written form' of Miller's work.

Reading, just one of the tasks in which academics are involved, is, these texts stress, an event which leaves only traces; I may 'trace' but cannot capture it. Wood therefore announces that 'reading and writing' are neither 'forms of production' nor 'reducible to knowledge' (Wood 2007, p. 138). Forbes Morlock points out that 'reading yields no quantifiable result'. It can, he admits, 'of course, be measured (as in: have you done the reading?), but quantities of pages and books read make for deliriously bad performance indicators' (Morlock 2007, pp. 5–6). Bill Readings declares that 'Thought is non-productive labour, and hence does not show up as such on balance sheets except as waste' (Readings 1996, p. 175). The work done by academics sits uneasily in relation to the aims prescribed by the RAE; the 'non-productive' and trace-like quality of much academic pursuit cannot be captured by the 'balance sheets' with which the institution attempts to justify itself. For Morlock, 'one of the features of the infamous "Research Assessment Exercise" (RAE) in the United Kingdom is that it seeks to create competition (ultimately over financial resources) in areas of endeavour which are, although hardly uncompetitive, not best organized on a competitive basis' (Morlock 2007, p. 5). Clark stresses that 'there is a tension' between 'institutional values' and this non-productive reading and thought, which he labels 'literary force', but which, as we will see, adopts a variety of names: the trace, *différance*, reading, writing and the Other, to name but a few (Clark 2002, p. 92).

Clark, Miller, Royle, Morlock and Readings all describe the above tension as a contemporary phenomenon and particular product of the RAE. Of course, in some ways, the RAE of today's universities is in fact an (particularly visible) instantiation of a far older dilemma. Jacques Derrida writes that '[a]s far as I know, nobody has ever founded a university *against* reason. So we may reasonably suppose that the university's reason for being has always been reason itself, and some essential connection of reason to being' (Derrida 2004c, p. 135; italics in original). Derrida points out that the university and the notion of reason are intimately twined, and always have been; yet the activities that take place within it are in many ways unreasonable, resistant to reasoning.

The debate in which Clark, Miller and Readings engage may well be especially pronounced today; the current scarcity of financial resources renders the pressure to quantify and to compete acute. However, it is not new; it gestures towards a paradox by which 'literary study' and 'literary criticism' have always been marked and from which they cannot escape. Clark begins his essay with a vignette in which he imagines what would happen if 'the ghost of, say, James Joyce or William Blake' came into the room as he was preparing a lecture or seminar on *Ulysses* or *The Four Zoas* and asked what he was doing. Clark wryly leaves it to us, his readers, 'to imagine their response' to the answer: '"I'm teaching it as literature . . .".'. Clark concludes: 'My point is this: why does this answer, so obviously truthful, seem so inadequate and reductive, almost as if the main effect of studying, or teaching, something "as literature" were to contain or to curtail it in some way' (Clark 2002, p. 91).[2] Studying – and the necessity of classifying what one studies – is an institutional operation which limits the force of the literary. Thus, any criticism or study we might produce inevitably compromises the literary quality which inspires it; we are destined from the outset to fail, likely '[m]ost of the time' to 'forget the strangeness of reading' (Schwenger 1995, p. 340).

There will never be a properly *literary* study. Any account of the literary will say something other than that which it wishes to say; much as it might desire to capture the quality of the literary, it is destined always to betray it. One might conclude, given this sorry state of affairs, that it might be best to give up on literary study and criticism and look for an alternative with which to replace them. Catherine Belsey certainly seems to think so; she announces, perhaps hopefully, that '[w]e are witnessing the end of literary criticism' (Belsey 1999, p. 123). However, such a conclusion is too hasty; the apparent impossibility of literary study might, in fact, be something with which we would do well to work. In a roundabout way, the quality of the literary is made *most* apparent in our failure to capture it; in our inability to give an account of the literary, its non-accountable nature becomes evident. Thus, the paradoxical and impossible nature of literary study offers a unique, if counter-intuitive, possibility; my project here, in this book, is to explore and to perform it.

My book takes its prompts and its inspiration from the situation I have just outlined (the situation in which it is, itself, written and read) and is fascinated by a group of texts that cultivate reading's power – and its weaknesses – in particularly marked ways. The texts I examine force us to consider reading's un-trainable power; they permit me to think a new dynamics and ethics of reading.

Representations of reading

The twentieth-century 'school' which most obviously addresses questions con-cerning the nature of reading is the reader-response theory of Norman Holland, Stanley Fish and Wolfgang Iser. The first section of my chapter will consider it alongside literary works in which, as Gerald Prince writes, the 'narrative text is partly constituted by the result of various reading operations it performs on itself' (Prince 1980, p. 234). Prince refers to texts that contain self-conscious or -reflexive moments – 'reading interludes' – which he elsewhere labels 'metanarrative signs' and which we might simply call 'metafiction' (Prince 1980, p. 237).[3] It might seem strange, especially given that I have already invoked Derrida and more recent theorists who are keen to continue his project, that I should choose now to exam-ine the two theories just outlined, particularly reader response. Although, as I just claimed, it seems the most 'obvious' place to turn for a theory of reading, it is hardly in vogue and it is surely possible already to imagine a more 'sophisticated' theorization. Criticisms of reader response have been well rehearsed and it per-haps seems inevitable (and tiresome) that my chapter will simply repeat them.

This is, however, exactly what I wish to avoid. I believe that there is something provocative to be read in these accounts, an experience of reading at odds with what their authors ostensibly claim. To demonstrate this, I must begin by adopt-ing at the outset a slightly adversarial position and suggesting some of the flaws in both these accounts. As I will show in the paragraphs that follow, the theorists both of metafiction and of reader response realize that we cannot uphold classi-cal notions of objectivity. They propose instead a more honest and self-conscious mode of criticism or fiction. However, they fail to enact it. This is not a reason to dismiss them; we should not stop here. I will show that, when approached in a certain way, their work points to a yet more profound dilemma, which I will explore in the second and third sections of my chapter. I am, in these final sec-tions, forced to consider the attitude I should adopt towards these accounts; my examination of reader response thus provokes questions of reading, of ethics and of responsibility. These dilemmas will recur throughout my book.

Fish claims to practise 'a brand of criticism whose most distinctive claim was not to be criticism at all but a means of undoing the damage that follows in criticism's wake' (Fish 1980, p. 6). Holland, in his book *Poems in Persons*, interviews readers and '[tries] to get them to *avoid* literary analysis and to talk instead about their feelings and associations to the literary works' (Holland 1973, p. 61; my italics). Both theorists claim to shun and to move beyond literary criticism.[4] Fish and Holland alike echo in their work Belsey's desire for the 'end of literary criticism'.

In doing so, Holland and Fish frame literary criticism as damaging and undesirable; they evince dissatisfaction with the way in which it typically proceeds. For them, criticism is, most specifically, as Andrew Bennett points out, a 'distortion', an 'artificial, supplementary, or even parasitic defacement of reading' (Bennett 1995, p. 13). Criticism fails to capture what actually takes place when we read. The rationale behind this grievance becomes apparent, for example, in Fish's *Is There A Text in this Class?* At one point in his text, Fish considers Plato's *Phaedrus*. When talking about the text Fish writes that it 'challenges' certain assumptions 'or, to be more precise, forces the reader to challenge' them (Fish 1980, p. 41).[5] Fish's initial claim is made in a form frequently employed by literary criticism. In it, the text is the subject of the verb challenges: Fish announces that the text challenges certain assumptions. This phrase gives the impression that the text acts and has an existence all of its own. Criticism frames itself as an impersonal and objective account.

Reading, as Barthes points out in *S/Z*, is typically framed as 'nothing more than a *referendum*'. The reader 'is left with no more than the poor freedom either to accept or reject the text'. The 'literary institution', Barthes explains, maintains a 'pitiless divorce' 'between the producer of the text and its user' (Barthes 1974, p. 4; italics in original). It depicts the reader as passive recipient of the text. Barthes argues, however, that 'reading is not a parasitical act, the reactive complement of a grammar which we endow with all the glamour of creation and anteriority. It is a form of work' (p. 10). He describes it a little later in his account as a 'labor of language' (p. 11).[6]

Fish concurs; his further comment – 'or, to be more precise, forces the reader to challenge' – revises and qualifies his initial statement. 'To be more precise', Fish points out, we ought to include the reader in our formulation; the poem's 'challenge' does not in fact have an existence apart from him/her. Thus, the objectivity claimed by literary criticism is 'false'. Fish writes that 'the choice is never between objectivity and interpretation but between an interpretation that is unacknowledged as such and an interpretation that is at least aware of itself' (Fish 1980, p. 167). Holland, too, argues that 'no critic can do anything' other than '[work] explicitly from his transaction of the text'. He claims, therefore, that 'all criticism is at least de facto transactive. It becomes de jure transactive when the critic explicitly builds on his relationship to the text' (Holland 1980, p. 363). Like Fish, Holland points out that the choice is not between a 'transactive' and a non-transactive account, but between an account that is explicitly transactive and one which is not.

Criticism is always 'an interpretation'. Reader response, echoing for literary theory the realizations effected for philosophy by Husserl's phenomenology, realizes that meaning and perception (or interpretation) are inseparable. Iser formulates this yet more explicitly. He tells us that reading is a creative process and that '[t]he convergence of text and reader brings the literary work into existence' (Iser 1988, p. 212). The work does not exist until it is read; the text is realized by its reader.

It is therefore imperative, Fish and Holland suggest, that we render our interpretations – and their possibly idiosyncratic nature – apparent. Holland declares that we must '[recover] reading as a personal transaction' and thus 'restore stories to their rightful owners' (Holland 1980, p. 370). To acknowledge the inseparability of interpretation and s/he who performs it, we must turn our attention to the reader and accord him/her 'joint responsibility for the production of . . . meaning', as Fish writes in his 1980 preface to *Is There a Text in this Class?* (Fish 1980, p. 3). Holland promises to do so by offering as honest an account as possible. He writes that 'you may feel that my response is idiosyncratic – so be it. The important thing is that we be as candid as we can, I in my assertions, you in your disagreements' (Holland 1968, pp. xiv–xv). He proposes, for example, to pay close attention to his use of pronouns: 'I shall . . . adopt a style in writing this book in which I do not assume automatically that I am privy to incontrovertible truths about the text. I shall be frank with "I" or "you" or "we" when the event I am talking about depends on the specific and unique way my mind or yours has constructed it, and I shall use "one" or "people" to generalize about human beings only when I really mean *everybody*' (Holland 1973, p. 4; italics in original).

Holland therefore suggests that '[o]ne might call [his work] metacriticism or even infracriticism' (Holland 1968, p. vii). We cannot escape interpretation, but ought, instead, to be more honest, performing a 'metacriticism' conscious of its own investments and operations and thereby making criticism's (imperfect) state obvious.

A similar conclusion is drawn in a very different context by Patricia Waugh in the opening chapter of her book *Metafiction*. Waugh notes that '[t]he simple notion that language passively reflects a coherent, meaningful and "objective" world is no longer tenable' (Waugh 1984, p. 3). Like Fish, Holland and Iser,

Waugh claims that we can no longer uphold notions of 'objectivity'. She argues, again similarly, that we must turn instead to a meta-discourse: "'[m]eta" terms, therefore, are required in order to explore the relationship between this arbitrary linguistic system and the world to which it apparently refers' (p. 3).

These theorists all suggest that a meta-language or -criticism might more honestly reflect the condition in which we find ourselves when we read, use language or, for Waugh, write fiction. The solution is not, however, that simple. In the paragraphs that follow, I show, by looking more carefully at Waugh's theory of metafiction and at the 'metacriticism' Fish and Holland perform, that neither, in fact, 'works'. The inconsistencies to which they subject us point to a more profound instability, which I will outline in my chapter's second section.

Meta-language, Waugh explains, is a term coined by the linguist L. Hjelmslev, who 'defined it as a language which, instead of referring to non-linguistic events, situations or objects in the world, refers to *another* language: it is a language which takes another language as its object' (Waugh 1984, p. 4; italics in original). The 'meta' prefix means 'behind', 'beyond' or 'after'. A meta-language is, therefore, as in Waugh/Hjelmslev's definition, a language that goes 'beyond' or 'behind' language in order to tell us something about it. Waugh applies this logic to fiction; she claims that '[m]*etafiction* is a term given to fictional writing which self-consciously and systematically draws attention to its status as an artefact' (p. 2; italics in original). In doing so, Waugh argues, it makes a 'statement about the creation of that fiction' (p. 6).

Waugh adds that 'this results in writing which consistently displays its conventionality, which explicitly and overtly lays bare its conditions of artifice' (p. 4). Scholes suggests that metafiction 'attempts, among other things, to assault or transcend the laws of fiction' (Scholes 1995, p. 29). The 'assault' and 'transcend' of Scholes's formulation couches his claim in stronger terms than Waugh's. Nonetheless, both writers express a similar belief that metafiction makes 'conventionality' or the 'laws of fiction' apparent. Byatt's *The Game*, which is 'based on the complex and basically antagonistic relationship between two sisters in their thirties, the unmarried Cassandra, an Oxford don specializing in Medieval romance literature, and Julia, a popular novelist who writes about the problems of contemporary women', provides an example of such a practice (Giobbi 1992, p. 245).[7] (Although I will refer to other novelists elsewhere, I offer Byatt as my example here because many of the themes in her fiction – theory, literature and criticism, as well as academia and the university – are, also, concerns in this opening chapter).

Byatt's work is littered with comments which employ language usually applied to or about, but not found within, the novel. For example, Ivan tells Julia that Cassandra strikes him as '[a] literary convention'. Elsewhere, he tells her that he is '"even laying [himself] open to appearing as the selfish lover in one of [her] books"' (Byatt 1983, pp. 133–4, 146). The novel points to the conventionality of Cassandra's character and to the function performed by Ivan's; the novel proffers, within itself, observations usually made by the literary criticism that takes place outside it. The text performs the interpretative work usually reserved for the literary criticism that follows it; critics of Byatt's work therefore stress her role as writer *and* reader, author *and* critic of her work; Kathleen Coyne Kelly coins the term 'ficticism' to describe the 'hybrid of fiction and criticism that Byatt practices' (Kelly 1996, p. 115).[8]

The novel's most overtly metafictional feature is, however, its use of a 'novel-within-the-novel' (Campbell 1988, p. 160). It occurs to Julia that she might write a book, which she would call 'A Sense of Glory'. She describes it thus:

> Now, I could write this novel about a woman with a dream world that – extends her possibilities. And she introduces a real man into this world, and understands – really understands – *one aspect* of him, this way [. . .] And the dream world, which is beautiful, is quite shattered when she meets him again after a long time (Byatt 1983, p. 136; italics in original).

Giuliana Giobbi explains that 'Julia "translates" her sister's life-lie into a successful novel ("A Sense of Glory")' (Giobbi 1992, p. 247). *The Game*, too, is a 'translation' of Cassandra's life into a novel. Julia's description summarizes perfectly the plot of Byatt's work. Kathleen Coyne Kelly therefore argues that '[h]ere, the writer – Byatt, certainly, but also Julia – invites the reader to *watch* her fashion her fiction' (Kelly 1996, p. 31). Kelly's conflation of Byatt and Julia is telling; through Julia, she implies, we may consider the way in which Byatt has constructed her novel.

Jane Campbell thus argues that '*The Game* . . . takes its place beside other "self-reflexive" pieces of contemporary fiction in which novelists examine the procedures of their art' (Campbell 1988, p. 147). Clare Morgan announces, similarly, that Byatt is 'a "metafictional" novelist in that she employs structural undermining of convention' and that '[p]art of [her] agenda is, then, the politics of narrative' (Morgan 2004, p. 515). Campbell and Hanson's claims that Byatt's novel 'examines' artistic procedure and 'the politics of narrative' reasserts Waugh's belief that metafictional moments 'draw attention to', 'lay bare' and 'display' the novel's conventionality or fictional status. Metafiction, according to these writers, uncovers the 'fictiveness of fiction', to borrow a phrase employed by Byatt (Byatt 1991a, p. 176).

For its theorists metafiction *reveals*, and thereby facilitates a discussion of, the fictionality of the fictional text. However, to suggest that these comments are revelatory is to imply that, prior to their inscription, we believed Byatt's narrative to be 'real'. This claim is obviously absurd. A much earlier example of a meta-moment, the memorable scene in *A Midsummer Night's Dream* in which Bottom et al. prepare their play, highlights this absurdity and thereby hints at what really happens at these metafictional moments. The characters, concerned that 'a lion among ladies, is a/most dreadful thing', decide they must remind their audience that he is not real:

> Snout: Therefore another prologue must tell he is not a lion.
> Bottom: Nay, you must name his name, and half his face must be seen through the lion's neck, and he himself must speak through, saying thus or to the same defect: 'ladies', or 'fair ladies, I would wish you' or 'I would request you' or 'I would entreat you not to fear, not to tremble. My life for yours. If you think I come hither as a lion, it were pity of my life. No, I am no such thing. I am a man, as other men are'–and there, indeed, let him name his name, and tell them plainly he is Snug the joiner (Shakespeare 1989, Act III Sc. i, p. 585).

Snout and Bottom propose to uncover the lion's fictional status, making it clear to the audience from the outset that he is, in fact, Snug the joiner. However, this scene is, of course, funny. Its comedy derives from its misplaced and excessive anxiety; the suggestion that we might think Snug's lion to be real dramatically over-evaluates the power of his performance. The suggestion is ridiculous, especially when considered in relation to the incompetent play these characters finally produce. We, the audience, know that the lion is not real; we do not need to be told.

In the act of telling us, however, Snout and Bottom implicitly propose that their play might transcend its fictional form. They introduce the notion of a 'real' lion, which did not, prior to this moment, exist. Their reference does not clarify the division between fiction and the real, but introduces into fiction a notion of the real it would otherwise have excluded. Thus, their discussion achieves the exact opposite of that which it sets out to do. Instead of delineating the division between fiction and the real, it confuses it.

Kelly's claim that 'the writer – Byatt, certainly, but also Julia – invites the reader to *watch* her fashion her fiction' enacts a similar confusion. Kelly describes Byatt and Julia alike as 'the writer'. Her claim assumes that Byatt and Julia are the same, or at least equivalent. She accords Julia a status as 'real' author. Julia is, however, a fictional character; she cannot be the author of the novel that we read. This impossibility reminds us that the description 'A Sense of Glory' offers of *The Game* takes place *within* Byatt's novel; it occurs within a fictional frame. These comments are not *simply* a description of *The Game* (although they do gesture towards it) but are also a further event in its fictional narrative. The declaration does not stand outside, nor is it simply 'about' the novel, but further contributes to the 'game' that it plays. This complex situation points towards a 'vertiginous illogicality', which is, for Currie, intrinsic to the notion of 'self-consciousness'. He points out that 'something which is defined by its self-consciousness must surely be conscious of its own definitive characteristic. It is not enough that metafiction knows that it is fiction; it must also know that it is metafiction if its self-knowledge is adequate, and so on in an infinite logical regress' (Currie 1995, p. 1).

I will return to the idea of the 'infinite logical regress' later. It suffices here to point out that the 'metafictional' aspects of Byatt's text do not offer us a straightforward or unproblematic revelation. 'A Sense of Glory' and *The Game* are not the same and we do not see the way in which Byatt fashions her fiction. Byatt's novel performs only a '*sort of* turning back', as Derrida writes. The 'pure' self-reflection that Waugh and others claim for metafiction is, he explains, 'a stupid and uninformed rumour' (Derrida 1992e, p. 41; my italics).[9] We discover, in these examples, that we cannot unproblematically point to fiction within a fictional frame; we cannot step outside of it in order to 'reveal' or comment upon it. The moment of revelation eludes us.[10]

The term metafiction in fact contains a contradiction. The meta- prefix seduces us into believing that metafiction speaks beyond fiction and reveals it in other than fictional terms. Its prefix proposes a break; the second half of the term, however, returns metafiction to the very fiction it claims to move beyond. As the examples above have shown, metafictional comment takes place through and within fiction (meta also means 'among' or 'along with'). Inseparable from the ostensible object of its 'critique', it is implicated *a priori* in the very field on which it supposedly comments.

Fish and Holland's metacriticism faces a similar impossibility. It is, equally, unable to step outside of the criticism that 'distorts' reading; it finds itself bound to reproduce the failings of that with which it would break, as I will now show. As I explained earlier, Fish proposes to pursue a mode of criticism which more honestly represents the act of reading and of interpretation. He therefore offers us a model in which 'the getting throughs, the figuring outs, the false starts, the interpretations (as it turns out) prematurely hazarded are not in my analyses regarded as the disposable machinery of extraction; rather, they are the acts of structuring and restructuring, hypothesizing and dehypothesizing, stance taking and stance revising, the succession of which is the structure of the reader's experience' (Fish 1980, p. 144). He claims that '[i]t is as if a slow motion camera with an automatic stop-action effect were recording our linguistic experiences and presenting them to us for viewing' (p. 28). Fish informs us that he will record what Iser describes as the 'time-flow of the reading' (Iser 1978, p. 109).

Fish puts this into practice with a sentence from Thomas Browne's *Religio Medici*, focusing on the first two phrases: '[t]hat Judas perished by hanging himself, there is no certainty in Scripture' (Fish 1980, p. 23). Fish argues that 'the reader', having read the first phrase, 'commits himself to its assertion' but does not, however, know what will come next. There are a number of possibilities; Fish suggests:

> That Judas perished by hanging himself, *is* (an example for us all).
> That Judas perished by hanging himself, *shows* (how conscious he was of the enormity of his sin).
> That Judas perished by hanging himself, *should* (give us pause) (Fish 1980, p. 24; italics in original).

He notes that 'there are, of course' further possibilities but that they '[narrow] considerably as the next three words are read: "there is no". Fish suggests that the reader then expects to find the word 'doubt' and is therefore astounded to encounter instead the phrase 'certainty in Scripture'.

The premise on which Fish bases his analysis is no doubt correct; there *are* a number of moments in our reading when we do not know what will follow and we do, frequently, form and revise our expectations. This is not always true though. Fish's analysis assumes that we read in a strictly linear fashion. It is however equally possible that, skipping across the page, we might in fact see the end of the sentence first; the suspense Fish outlines might never occur.[11] Moreover, Holland satirizes Fish's 'stop-motion method of reading' as one 'which surely came from watching too much football on television' and it is easy to see why (Holland 1980, p. 366). Fish begins (as I do) by citing the sentence as a whole. Thus, his reader already knows the way in which it ends; before he even properly begins his analysis, we successfully read the two phrases. The pause between the first and the second phrase of the sentence is, in this reading, fleeting and momentary. In Fish's analysis, on the other hand, we hesitate at this comma for an almost frustratingly long time. The pace of Fish's analysis paralyses the sentence, rendering his claim to capture our reading of it absurd; it is very different from the 'time-flow' in which we 'actually' read.

Fish admits this failure in relation to his analysis of a different sentence; he writes that '[s]ome of you may want to object that my analysis of the sentence is more tortuous and torturing than the reader's experience of it. And you would be right' (Fish 1980, p. 186). His declamation, although unabashed, intimates frustration. He proposes at the outset to capture the reading experience, but concludes abruptly with a declaration in which 'the reader's experience' and his 'analysis of the sentence' are not the same. Moreover, as Fish analyses it, he repeatedly re-cites fragments of the Judas sentence.[12] Thus, we are forced repeatedly to read them until we are left with the feeling, as noted by Adam Phillips, 'that comes when one endlessly repeats a word only to be left with an enigmatic obstacle as to its sense' (Phillip. 1993, p. 98). The 'reading experience' becomes increasingly distant as Fish places more words between the reader and the sentence s/he reads and has read.

Fish's analysis fails to capture or to take into account the experience of his own reader. His description is thwarted by the fact that it takes place in a text which is itself read. This condition will, of course, pertain to any attempt to represent reading in a written text. Reading does not stop, as Holland realizes. Having gathered responses from a number of interviewees, he admits that 'I "read" what they said, in other words, much as I would read a poem' (Holland 1973, p. 61). The readings Holland wishes to record will, in the act of recording, be subjected to yet another reading and cannot therefore be 'honestly' captured.

We realize this, again, when Fish notes that 'my reader is a construct, an ideal or idealized reader' (Fish 1980, p. 48; italics in original). Fish uses the phrase 'my reader' in order to refer to the generalized reader that he has constructed as the object of his discussion. The phrase also refers, however, to 'my reader' as s/he who reads Fish's text. This double signification highlights the bind in which Fish finds himself caught; the text's attempt to theorize 'the reader' is undermined by the arrival of yet another reader to whom it addresses itself. The 'actual' reader is never the same as the one described. This condition applies, too, to my own analysis. I am, as I write, the reader of Fish's text; as you read the afore-mentioned quotation, however, you are; my 'actual' fails as a description of the reader. It attempts to delineate s/he who reads *now* (as the French *actuel* denotes) only to discover that 'now' is an instant hesitated in the gap between writing and reading. 'When we are reading', for Wood, 'contemporaneity slips away' (Wood 2009b, p. 66).

I am unable to refer to or to articulate the reading that I perform. Any discussion – any writing – of reading finds that it refers elsewhere; even as it attempts to fix one reading, it finds itself read – we cannot capture the experience from which we are nonetheless unable to escape. We are faced, in the examples outlined earlier (and after Derrida) with a 'spiral of infinite regression in representation', which Diane Elam labels *mise en abyme* (Elam 1994, p. 27).[13] Elam illustrates this trope using a Quaker Oats box as an example. She explains that 'the Quaker Oats man appears on the Quaker Oats box holding a small box, which depicts the Quaker Oats man holding a box with the Quaker Oats man . . . and so on *ad infinitum*' (p. 27). The image reproduces itself indefinitely, becoming smaller every time; Elam points out that the abyss 'gets deeper with each additional determination' (p. 30). The sequence is never full or complete; we realize instead that '[r]epresentation can never come to an end, since greater accuracy and detail only allows us to see even more Quaker Oats boxes'. Elam concludes that '[t]his is rather odd, since we are accustomed to think of accuracy and detail as helping us to grasp an image fully, rather than forcing us to recognize the impossibility of grasping it' (pp. 27–8).

This concept recurs in works of contemporary novelists, but is a particular feature of David Mitchell's work. A character in Mitchell's *Cloud Atlas*, Adam Ewing, invokes this infinite structure when he writes that '[o]ccasionally, I glimpse a truer Truth, hiding in imperfect simulacrums of itself, but as I approach it, it bestirs itself & moves deeper into the thorny swamp of dissent' (Mitchell 2004, p. 17). We cannot catch up with 'truth' or reach the heart of the 'thorny swamp'; we attempt to 'grasp' the moment of reading, but it escapes.[14] This impossibility demands that we rethink our approach; reading is clearly not a presence we might capture.[15] To progress our discussion, we must rethink our temporal and ontological categories, engaging with a 'deconstructive' mode of thought to which I will turn in my next section.

The impossible representation of truth and the truth of impossible representation

'What is reading?' proves an awkward question. Miller points out that '[w]e can do it. We can read, but we cannot understand what it is we are doing' (Miller 1987, p. 48). The act of reading is at once obvious and utterly elusive. We cannot formulate or describe what reading is yet we intuit it all too well. The coupling of this utter certainty and complete uncertainty renders our interrogation, when pursued as above, an infuriating pursuit. We should not, however, despair; Royle points out that '[i]ntellectual uncertainty is not necessarily or simply a *negative* experience, a dead-end sense of not knowing or of indeterminacy. It is just as well an experience of something open, generative, exhilarating (the trembling of what remains undecidable)' (Royle 2003, p. 52). In this case, the loop in which we are caught is not a 'dead-end', but a spur to new thinking; it demands that we contemplate an utterly different approach to reading, to time and to experience, as I will show in the following two sections of my chapter.

It is not possible to fully represent reading; any formulation I might make is already and inevitably caught up in the logic and the discourse on which it supposedly comments. I cannot halt reading in order to capture it. This means, however, that reading is still *there*; I am reading even as I fail to grasp what reading is. To access it, in order to get at this still-happening reading, I need to think differently; I need to reject my representational, or philosophical, approach and attempt instead to think in what we might tentatively call a 'non-representational' mode. To consider what this might entail I will, in the paragraphs which follow, move away from reader response (for a moment; it will reappear later) in order to examine two examples: Emmanuel Levinas's theorization of language in *Otherwise than Being* and Derrida's notion of the 'literary'.[16]

Otherwise than Being offers a theorization of language, which summarizes and develops the reflections made thus far. Levinas divides language into a saying (which he equates with 'responsibility' or 'ethics', both terms I will discuss in more detail later) and a said. The said resembles the representational or philosophical mode in which we have proceeded thus far. However, it is not the only option; the saying offers an alternative. Levinas describes saying as

> Not the communication of a said, which would immediately cover over and extinguish or absorb the said, but saying holding open its openness, without excuses, evasions or alibis, delivering itself without saying anything said. Saying saying saying itself, without thematizing it, but exposing it again (Levinas 1981, p. 143).

Levinas refers to a saying which, as language's 'preontological' condition or law, cannot be 'thematized' or figured. Saying, like reading, is 'open' and strange. Saying opposes itself and is other to the closures of the 'representational thought' of the said (Clark 1992, p. 46).

The 'literary' performs a similar function in Derrida's writing. Derrida offers it as an alternative to the philosophical and tells us that '[t]here is no literature without a *suspended* relation to meaning and reference' (Derrida 1992e, p. 48; italics in original). Blanchot writes similarly that 'the work – the work of art, the literary work – is neither finished nor unfinished: it is. What it says is exclusively this: that it is – and nothing more. Beyond that it is nothing' (Blanchot 1982, p. 22). Both writers seem at first sight to suggest that literature, unlike philosophy, loosens its grip on 'meaning' and 'reference'; it simply 'is'. We must, however, read this claim tentatively. Neither the saying nor the literary is a straightforward alternative to representation.

Derrida frequently expresses his claims for the literary in cautious terms. In his interview with Derek Attridge, 'This strange institution called literature', for example, he announces that 'there is no text which is literary *in itself*. Literarity is not a natural essence, an intrinsic property of the text' (Derrida 1992e, p. 44; italics in original). He therefore describes 'this institution of fiction which gives *in principle* the power to say everything' and states '[t]he principle (I stress that it's a *principle*)' (Derrida 1992e, pp. 37, 40; italics in original).[17] Derrida emphasizes the term 'in principle'. In the second of these quotations, Derrida not only prioritizes the term, but also accentuates, in his aside, this very act of prioritization. Derrida's 'in principle' defers definition; he explains that '[e]verything is given over to the future of a "perhaps"' (Derrida 2008, p. 131). The claims Derrida makes for the 'literary' are predicated upon the idea that we do not yet know what it might be.

Jill Robbins, in her book on Levinas, exercises a similar reticence when discussing the saying. She announces, for example, 'I hesitate to call this dimension of the work "Saying" . . ., because I do not think that we should presuppose that we know what the Saying is' and writes later '[a]s I have previously cautioned, however, we should not take for granted that we know what we mean by the Saying' (Robbins 1999, pp. xxiii, 144).

Robbins realizes that to speak as though we 'know' what the saying is is to close it down and therefore to betray its openness. A saying affirmed as such is no longer saying *per se*. Derrida stresses, equally, that if the literary experience were assured, it would no longer be properly literary. A definitive saying or notion of the literary returns us instantly to what Smith terms the 'classically philosophical definition of the classically literary' in which the literary is understood as a 'negative gain, or negative capability', which, by acting as 'the effacement of philosophy's effacement', gains a 'subliminal access' to the '*same* ideal truth' philosophy would present. The literary, in this classical model, offers us, in its 'double effacement', an 'enhancement of the truth' (Smith 1995, pp. 179–80; my italics). In this theorization, the literary is not absolutely other to philosophy's system, but can be comprehended within its logic; this conceptualization brings the literary back to philosophy's same.

The dilemma Levinas and Derrida face gestures towards a difficulty intrinsic in any attempt to think the 'other' of philosophy or representational thought. Derrida explains that, in thinking this other, and '[i]n thinking it *as such*, in recognising it, one misses it. One reappropriates it for oneself, one disposes of it, one misses it, or rather one misses (the) missing (of) it, which, as concerns the other, always amounts to the same' (Derrida 1982, pp. xi–xii; italics in original). We cannot think the other in properly 'other' terms; our every thought brings it back to the same.

We realize, as Clark writes, that the '*concept* of the other, or the notion of a language that correlates with the other' is 'a contradiction in terms' (Clark 1992, p. 16; italics in original). As I suggested earlier, 'pure' saying is impossible and irrecoverable. The first passage I quoted from Levinas's *Otherwise than Being* fails to capture the openness of the saying. In it, saying regresses in a repeated 'saying saying saying' that Robbins describes as a 'primordial stammering of ethical language' (Robbins 1999, p. 19). Levinas is explicit about this dilemma. He sets out to capture the saying, but admits that 'the very discussion which we are pursuing at this moment counts by its said' (Levinas 1981, p. 167). He informs us that *Otherwise than Being* will not succeed in capturing the saying that it invokes; the work is destined to fail. Clark suggests that Levinas 'seems not only to invite but actually to perform a self-refutation, asserting that his own discourse on the other and *le Dire* is necessarily their very occlusion!' (Clark 1992, p. 182) Clark, with faux-incredulity, highlights 'what seems to be a pragmatic contradiction in [*Otherwise than Being*] – simply the fact that Levinas writes books at all' (Clark 1992, p. 181). Simon Critchley suggests in a less playful manner that Levinas presents a 'rather long philosophical suicide note' (Critchley 2007, p. 68).

For Levinas, this moment of 'self-refutation' is less absolute and absurd than Critchley's exclamation would have us believe. He does not lay down his pen, but continues to write, and notes that:

> If the philosophical discourse is broken, withdraws from speech and murmurs, is spoken, it nonetheless speaks of that, and speaks of the discourse which a moment ago it was speaking and to which it returns to say its provisional retreat. Are we not at this very moment in the process of barring the issue that our whole essay attempts, and of encircling our position from all sides? (Levinas 1981, p. 169)

Levinas stresses that even as philosophical discourse 'withdraws from speech', it continues to speak and, as it does so, the 'speaking' it 'a moment ago' performed belatedly appears; a chance arises, as discourse 'returns to say its retreat', for its saying to manifest itself. Levinas does not blithely reject philosophical discourse, but posits the threat of 'occlusion' as fundamental to his project. Levinas does not reject the said (which would be impossible), but speaks philosophy in such a way that its saying may emerge. This is, moreover, the *only* way in which saying might appear; we can locate only 'the approach, the one-for-the-other of saying, *related by* the said' (Levinas 1981, p. 170; my italics). The said betrays (the secret of) the saying.

The saying emerges through the said which compromises it. We may witness the possibility of saying as, and only as, a trace or 'contradiction' within a 'said' to which it is at once foreign and uniquely bound (Levinas 1981, p. 135). Judith Butler writes that '[t]he "preontological" domain to which Levinas refers (of which he says any representation would be a "betrayal") is difficult to conjure, since it would seem to surge up into the ontological, where it leaves its traces. Any finite representation betrays the infinitely represented, but representations do carry the trace of the infinite' (Butler 2005, p. 96). The 'contradiction' Levinas presents is not a dilemma we must overcome but an event in which the 'traces of the infinite' – seldom self-evident and easily overlooked – may be read.

The 'non-representational' cannot be separated from but takes place in and through the 'representational'. These realizations allow us to return to, and to read more carefully, Derrida's claim for the literary and its '*suspended* relation to meaning and reference'. Derrida does not mean here that literature suspends meaning and reference *tout court*. He does not claim that the literary *suspends* meaning; that, he says, would be 'impossible'. We cannot suspend reference altogether; our language continues to refer. Instead, the literary enters into a 'suspended relation to meaning'. Derrida writes that literary works 'suspend not reference (that's impossible) but the thetic relation to meaning or referent' (Derrida 1992e, p. 45). The literary alters its, and our, *relationship* to meaning; Connors suggests that it displays reference 'as though it were bracketed or in inverted commas' (Connors 2010a, p. 121). Although the literary cannot sever its relation to meaning and to reference, it may bracket or suspend it, figuring this relationship otherwise.

Derrida does not claim to step outside of philosophy into the literary, but argues that '[w]e should begin by taking rigorous account of this *being held within* [*prise*] or this *surprise*'. We are held within a language and a logic, which we cannot escape and which, for that reason, we 'cannot dominate absolutely' – our inability to elude this language opens us to 'surprise' (Derrida 1997b, p. 158; italics in original). We cannot escape language but might aim to make its 'limits . . . tremble' (Derrida interviewed in Kearney 1984, p. 112).

The literary is, therefore, for Derrida an '*excessively* philosophical gesture: a gesture that is philosophical and, at the same time, in excess of the philosophical' (Derrida 2001, p. 4; italics in original). The literary is at once excessively philosophical *and* in excess of the philosophical; it takes place at the 'philosophical limit', at the point at which 'philosophy fails to be what it wants to be'. The literary takes place in and through philosophy; it is a 'disputation' we might sense within it, if only we know how to read it – a question to which I will now turn in my final section (Derrida 2001, p. 55).

Reading and responsibility

Having noted in my first section the impossibilities of 'representational thought', I decided that we must instead pursue a 'non-representational' moment. It quickly becomes clear, however, that the 'non-representational' is not a straightforward alternative to representation. To posit is as such as to fall back into representational thinking and thereby to betray that for which we aspire. We must aim instead for an instant which emerges through the hesitation or hyphen of re-presentation itself. By representing reading – and by failing to represent it fully – we may touch upon its non-representational 'happening'.

We cannot successfully represent reading. However, therein lies possibility. I quoted earlier the infuriating moment at which Fish writes '[s]ome of you may want to object that my analysis of the sentence is more tortuous and torturing than the reader's experience of it'. Fish finds himself unable to describe our reading; the experience slips away from his analysis. The reading experience is not, however, as opaque as it might seem at this moment. The shift to 'some of you' accords the reader – Fish's reader – a heretofore unremarked prominence. As Fish's 'reading experience' recedes, therefore, a different reading experience – the experience of reading his text, the text 'you' are reading (which, at this point, of course, you aren't reading) – becomes more evident, more troubling. We cannot describe any reading, yet, in any reading, the quality of reading may be glimpsed. Bennett, citing a question posed by Pierre Bourdieu – 'Can you read a text without wondering what reading is?' – suggests that 'reading seems inevitably to slide into a theorization of reading' (Bennett 1995, p. 14).[18] Even as the experience that we are trying to capture remains 'completely elusive', it happens and we might therefore slide into it (Clark 1992, p. 16).

Fish's text is unable to grasp reading. However, reading might nonetheless be detected in it via an experience that happens *in* reading. Levinas writes that

> In the writing the saying does indeed become a pure said, a simultaneousness of saying and of its conditions. A book is interrupted discourse catching up with its own breaks. But books have their fate; they belong to a world they do not include, but recognize by being written and printed, and by being prefaced and getting themselves preceded with forewords. They are interrupted, and call for other books and in the end are interpreted in a saying distinct from the said (Levinas 1981, pp. 170–1).

Levinas here reiterates a point I outlined earlier: 'the saying' becomes, in writing, 'a pure said'. It cannot therefore be captured by Levinas's (or by any other) book. Levinas notes, however, that books are 'interrupted' and suggests that it is in this interruption of the said said again that its saying might become apparent. Levinas suggests, moreover, that the saying might become apparent *only* in this interruption. Derrida figures this '*structural necessity*' through the notion of the countersignature (Clark 1992, p. 131; italics in original). He explains that

> If something is given to be read that is totally intelligible, that can be totally saturated by sense, it is not given to the other to be read. Giving to the other to be read is also a *leaving to be desired,* or a leaving the other room for an intervention by which she will be able to write her own interpretation: the other will have to be able to sign in my text (Derrida 2001, p. 31; italics in original).

The 'otherness' Derrida and Levinas desire will not become apparent in a text that is 'totally intelligible' and 'saturated by sense'. It becomes evident only when the other is 'able to sign' Derrida's text.

The work is therefore given over to risk. Clark, when writing about Blanchot and Heidegger, suggests that

> a recurrent movement of thought, albeit with some risk, can be traced throughout. Blanchot, no more than Heidegger, does not attempt to write *about* language. Language is rather, as it were, doubled upon itself to let speak, not a discourse *about* anything, but the 'essence' of language itself – though it must be added that 'inessentiality' is the most prominent trait of this 'essence' (Clark 1992, pp. 66–7; italics in original).

It is possible to read, in the work of these philosophers, a strange movement in which language is 'doubled upon itself to let it speak' and in which the 'about' of philosophy is suspended. We are, however, equally able *not* to read their work in this way; I suggested, in my analysis above, that we 'might' and we 'may' glimpse reading or that which exceeds representation. The slippage I just noted is subtle and it is equally possible to read Fish's text (as I did in my chapter's first section) *without* admitting it. For Clark, 'the *heteronomy* at issue' is 'completely elusive' and therefore easy to miss (Clark 1992, p. 16; italics in original). He explains that 'it always remains perfectly possible to read Heidegger, Blanchot and Levinas in terms of the very modes of language that they put into question' (Clark 1992, p. 186). We may still read Heidegger and Blanchot's work in terms of that which it is *about*. It is possible to perform a reading sensitive to the slippage or contradictions that constitute that which exceeds representation in any text. It is, however, equally possible not to. No text can claim or guarantee a reading in which this doubling movement becomes apparent. Clark's observations lead us to realize that the work of these philosophers is not self-assured; the 'literary' quality towards which they aspire is not certain; it can be conferred, or denied, only by reading. It cannot therefore be written or guaranteed.

These texts depend for their future on a reader they do not and cannot fully know; we become aware both of Connors' observation that 'a text can never guarantee its own future conditions of reception' and of the fact that it relies absolutely upon this reception for its future condition (Connors 2007, p. 13). Reading and the literary are closely bound; Derrida goes so far as to conflate the two when he comments on 'literature or reading (you say "reading literature")' (Derrida 1992e, p. 49).[19]

We as readers are responsible for the text and must consider how best to do it justice. These questions of responsibility and justice are not, however, straightforward. Given that we must read in the text that which it is unable to write, we must read what is not there and without any guarantee that we will do so correctly. Derrida asks '[c]an one speak of responsibility or assume a responsibility without difficulty and without anguish? I don't believe so' (Derrida 1989b, p. 846).

Derrida highlights this difficult demand when he announces that the text must leave the other room. What Derrida means by this is far from clear; the terms in which we usually think 'leaving room' – as non-narcissistic, or responsible, or altruistic – are disturbed in Derrida's work. In his essay 'There is no *one* narcissism', Derrida argues that there is 'not narcissism and non-narcissism'. There are, Derrida concedes, 'narcissisms that are more or less comprehensive, generous, open, extended'. However, '[w]hat is called non-narcissism is in general but the economy of a much more welcoming, hospitable narcissism, one that is much more open to the experience of the other as other'. Whatever gesture we might perform would seem to be compromised in advance. Derrida writes that 'I believe that without a movement of narcissistic reappropriation, the relation to the other would be absolutely destroyed, it would be destroyed in advance' (Derrida 1995a, p. 199). Literary criticism and philosophy must, Derrida tells us, perform a 'narcissistic reappropriation' if they are to 'leave the other room' or to respond responsibly.

Derrida tells us that

> [m]y law, the one to which I try to devote myself or to respond, is *the text of the other*, its very singularity, its idiom, its appeal which precedes me. But I can only respond to it in a responsible way (and this goes for the law in general, ethics in particular) if I put in play, and in guarantee [*en gage*], my singularity, by signing, with another signature (Derrida 1992e, p. 66; italics in original).

Derrida must append to the work 'another signature'. To 'respond' to its singularity he must put his own into play. The result is 'as it were a duel of singularities, a duel of writing and reading, in the course of which a countersignature comes both to confirm, repeat and respect the signature of the other, of the 'original' work, and to *lead it off* elsewhere, so running the risk of *betraying* it, having to betray it in a certain way so as to respect it, through the invention of another signature just as singular' (Derrida 1992e, p. 69; italics in original). Derrida informs us, somewhat counter-intuitively, that the most responsible reading is that which 'betrays' and 'leads' its object off elsewhere. Robbins observes similarly that 'the best way for the commentator to respect Levinas's work' is 'to read it deviously, to misunderstand it entirely'. Like Derrida, Robbins argues that the 'best' and most 'respectful' way to read the work of another is to 'misunderstand it' and to betray it. She concludes, '[a]t the limit, then, the discourse of the ethical is *almost* indistinguishable from the discourse of persecution' (Robbins 1999, p. 13; italics in original).

Derrida writes that '[t]his duty of irresponsibility . . . is perhaps the highest form of responsibility'. Derrida likens this 'irresponsibility' to a '[refusal] to reply for one's thought or writing to constituted powers' (Derrida 1992e, p. 38). As I explained at the beginning of my chapter, the 'constituted powers' of the REF demand that we answer and account for the literary. It seems right that we answer and that we defend and justify the work that we do. I explained, however, that the quality of the literary cannot be justified in this way; it becomes apparent, only indirectly, in our refusal or inability to respond to the demands that are made. We best do justice to the literary by failing to account for it. Derrida writes that '[i]t happens that a response may be a nonresponse, and nonresponse is sometimes the best response' (Derrida 1989b, p. 837).

The seemingly irresponsible answer demands further consideration; it remains open to another reader and thereby keeps the question of singularity in play.[20] Such a performance is visible in Derrida's work. I mentioned earlier Derrida's claim that the countersignature sets up 'a duel of singularities, a duel of writing and writing'. A little later in his text, Derrida revises this claim; he states that '[i]n reality, I don't even think it is a matter of a *duel* here, in the way I just said a bit hastily' (Derrida 1992e, p. 69; italics in original). Derrida re-reads and re-writes the phrase 'a duel of singularities'; he countersigns it. This countersignature does not, however, efface the earlier phrase; it is still possible to read it. It does not answer to its revisionary countersignature but still states a duel. The two phrases duel and neither wins; each affirms its singular inscription even as we read its relationship to the other.

Neither of these phrases wins and we cannot adjudicate their duel; should we accept Derrida's first claim, that a 'duel' takes place, or not? The countersignature Derrida's text inscribes points to the 'insurmountable equivocation', which, for Levinas, underlies one's relation to the other (Levinas 1981, p. 170). We must ask, as we read, how we might maintain this 'equivocation' and this 'duel'.

Whatever reading we decide to perform of Derrida's text is, however, haunted by the possibility of another reading. We might read it 'deviously', and therefore generously, but cannot forget, as Derrida points out that 'I am not proprietor of my "I", I am not proprietor of the place open to hospitality. Whoever gives hospitality ought to know that he is not even proprietor of what he would appear to give' (Derrida 2001, p. 85). Even as Derrida's text is subject to my reading, my text is in turn subject to yet another reading. I might perform a 'generous' reading only to find it once again taken away. I explained earlier that Derrida, through the use of the phrase 'in principle', signals towards a literary moment that is not yet decided and that is deferred until the moment of reading. We see now just how radical this deferral is; the future inscribed by Derrida's *yet* is *always* future, a never-to-be-present future of a reading forever open to a further re-reading and reinscription.[21]

Elam therefore explains that 'it is impossible to do justice to justice, to carry out one's responsibility entirely' (Elam 1994, p. 120). We find ourselves engaged in an 'endless work of reparation without the final solace of redemption' (Elam 1994, p. 111). Responsibility, as Clark points out, 'cannot be calculated in advance';

I can never definitely claim it for my text (Clark 1992, p. 186). Elam concludes, however, that 'even though justice is unrepresentable and impossible, one should not stop trying to be just' (Elam 1994, p. 120). Perhaps – everything here is 'given over to the future of a "perhaps"' – then, between my writing and your reading, such an event might occur.

Theoretical conclusions and practical beginnings

Introductory stricture demands, at this point, that I end my 'theorization' of responsibility and propose the 'practical' project that will employ this framework in the chapters to come. We are encouraged to read an introduction as that which legitimizes and justifies that which follows. My tentative use of quotation marks around the terms 'theorization' and 'practical' imply, however, a distrust of these very distinctions; they return us unthinkingly to the thinking I have contested. To frame the preceding chapter as a theorization of responsibility, ethics and reading is to place its value in the said and to prize it in terms of what it might *tell* us about these things. I have, however, *already* performed a series of readings from which questions of ethics and responsibility cannot be abstracted; the questions about the 'propriety' or otherwise of any interpretation with which I conclude have been at play from the outset.

We find that we have already begun. Derrida therefore writes that '[w]e must begin *wherever we are* and the thought of the trace, which cannot take the scent into account, has already taught us that it was impossible to justify a point of departure absolutely. *Wherever we are*: in a text where we already believe ourselves to be' (Derrida 1997b, p. 162; italics in original). We cannot 'justify a point of departure absolutely' because, in our justification, we find that we have departed already; my introductory chapter does not, and cannot, *simply* legitimize that which follows. I *have*, obviously, adopted a strategy and an approach; I do occupy a position. We find, however, that it is impossible to justify these stances absolutely; '[j]ustifications there are', Connors explains, 'but not absolute ones' (Connors 2010a, p. 12). Our choices are, as Derrida writes, '*exorbitant*' 'in spite of the theoretical precautions that [we] formulate' (Derrida 1997b, p. 161; italics in original).

My introductory chapter is not conclusive; it refuses to serve as a theoretical basis for what follows. Simply by coming to an end, however, it appears to settle on a certain point or concept; each chapter of my book inevitably draws a conclusion. However, these conclusions must be interrogated. My book occupies a province in which question-and-answer does not pertain; it relies instead on failure and re-beginning. It is thrown repeatedly back on interruption and repetition. Blanchot writes that '[w]henever thought is caught in a circle, this is because it has touched upon something original, its point of departure beyond which it cannot move except to return' (Blanchot 1982, p. 93).

Each chapter of my book examines in its own right the concept which presents itself as conclusion in the chapter which precedes it. We have seen, from my introduction, that reading cannot be considered without an awareness of the writing that would represent or record it. My first chapter therefore turns to and is intrigued by composition – its chaos, its revisions, its trial and error – but realizes, losing its composure somewhat, that it is able only to access it in the composed form of a finished text. Writing is never fully present; it can only be traced. My second chapter therefore examines the trace only to find, again, that by presenting the trace it betrays the inessentiality by which we are initially fascinated. My third chapter interrupts the others in order to question the reliance of my book on Derrida and Levinas. It might seem, given that I refer to their work the most, that the thought of these writers offers the conclusion *par excellence*. As my chapter shows, however, both philosophers caution against taking their thought as theory. My book has, by this point, repeatedly realized that the work depends on you and that I can beg, but cannot guarantee, your kindness. My fourth chapter will contemplate tact, which, establishing itself as a distant touch or a touching distance, situates its quality in the 'between'. The con-tact my chapter proposes is impossible; we can only touch upon tact at a tangent. My final chapter appeals directly to you, but also asks, can this appeal be made? Can this reliance be wholly thematized?

Although each taking a different concept, all my chapters rehearse, with a local colour and specificity, an argument more or less the same as the one set out here in my introduction. Each chapter will find, as this chapter did for reading, that its chosen notions elude or escape it but that, in and through this impossibility, it 'happens' or may be glimpsed. This is the structure of desire itself, as I will point out in my coda. The repetition of this structure is both inevitable and necessary. We must begin again each time; each concept must be considered on its own terms.

I will examine the above concepts in and through texts by Maurice Blanchot, A. S. Byatt, J. M. Coetzee, Jacques Derrida, Emmanuel Levinas, David Mitchell, Toni Morrison, Philip Roth, Eve Kosofsky Sedgwick, Ali Smith and Tim Winton. All the texts on which I will focus thematize questions of reading; they are particularly interested in the notions of failure and ethics I have discussed thus far.

The texts on which I have chosen to focus in each chapter are, of course, those that strike me as the most apt, the most suited to the concept I discuss. At the same time, however, I must admit that they seem somehow resistant to the project I wish to perform. A. S. Byatt's *Possession*, for example, appears to me to be the perfect novel with which to explore questions of tact, and yet its protestations against theory leave me with an uncomfortable sense that it does not want to sit alongside the texts by Derrida with which it has so much in common. This feeling is, of course, to be expected, given the realizations I have made thus far. I have noted the 'impossibility of knowing what [the text] might be up to'; for de Man this results in a 'pathos' of 'anxiety (or bliss, depending on one's momentary mood or individual temperament) of ignorance' (de Man 1979, p. 19). I have tried not to disguise or ignore this anxiety; it might, I suspect, be better to read with it. As I pointed out earlier, for Derrida ethics and responsibility ought to be difficult, and anguished.

The literary texts I will discuss are often referred to collectively as contemporary fiction – a phrase my title employs. However, my aim is not to make a statement about contemporary fiction in general. The analyses I will perform of my chosen texts are not generalizable; they do not make a statement about *all* contemporary fiction. There are many other works that fall into this category, which are not as explicitly engaged with questions of reading, ethics or failure. The label 'contemporary fiction' is a convenient term with which to group the texts I will discuss; however, what I have to say is specific to the texts about which I will say it.

Moreover, although I have limited my choice of texts to those belonging to the spheres of 'deconstruction' and contemporary fiction, these boundaries are somewhat arbitrary. I could just as easily have pursued my investigation across a much broader historical span. As I pointed out at the very beginning of my chapter, the dilemma the REF highlights is not historically specific but a general condition by which literary study is marked; the logic I will discuss may be discerned in the literature and criticism of any period. The fictions and theories upon which my book chooses to focus are not the only texts in which the instabilities I wish to explore become evident.

However, my time is limited. I have therefore restricted myself to that which we can classify as contemporary fiction and deconstruction partly because both 'contemporary' and 'deconstruction' are terms particularly attuned to their arbitrary nature. I have chosen them *because* their legitimacy is so far from 'absolute'. Deconstruction is a term we might wish to employ tentatively, as I will explain in a later chapter, while 'contemporary' worries those who theorize it, as Terry Smith's 'Contemporary art and contemporaneity' shows. Smith's essay asks 'what is contemporary art?' Part way through, he admits that 'the answer has seemed obvious to the point of banality. Look around you. Contemporary art is most – why not all? – of the art that is being made now' (Smith 2006, p. 683). This admission undermines Smith's very project; the suggestion that the answer to his question is obvious and banal sits uneasily with the proposed aim of his essay to offer an exploration and a definition of the contemporary. Smith dismisses this thought. However, it returns again later in his text when he writes '[w]hat is *contemporaneity* other than a pointer (empty as a signifier, overfull as a signified) to whatever it is that is occurring in all of the world right now? How could such a term match, let alone supplant, *modernity* and *postmodernity* as a descriptor of the state of things?' (Smith 2006, p. 696; italics in original) Again, he dismisses this concern. Nonetheless, these repeated admissions frame 'contemporary' as a fragile term; Smith's essay is haunted by the potential emptiness of the signifier on which it focuses.

'Contemporary' might, Smith admits, be a vague and unhelpful term, a 'soft signifier of current plurality' (Smith 2006, p. 701; italics in original). Admitting everything taking place now, it performs no distinction. However, even this notion of the contemporary as 'now' is unstable, as Steven Connor points out. '[C]ontemporary time' is, he argues, a 'strange phrase, flickering between oxymoron and tautology' (Connor 1999, p. 21). As we realized when attempting to capture the time flow of reading, the present is not easily captured. Derrida writes of '[a] time said to be contemporary that would be anything but contemporary – anything, except proper to its own time. It would resemble nothing, nor would it gather itself up in anything, lending itself to any possible reflection. It would no longer relate to itself' (Derrida 2005b, p. 76). As I will show in more detail in my following chapter, the moment 'said to be contemporary' or present misses the present or contemporary it is 'said to be'. Luckhurst and Marks explain that '[t]he instant of the "now" always eludes the grasp, can never be self-identical: it is either no longer or not yet present' (Luckhurst and Marks 1999, p. 3). We find, in the act of announcing the present, that we move into a new present; the one which we set out to capture turns out to be past. Thus, the very term 'contemporary' fails to capture that which it sets out to grasp.

The thought of the literary and the philosophical will also continue to trace my analyses; I will, in the following chapters, read the two side by side. You may have noticed that, in the list I offered above of the writers on which I will focus, I refused to differentiate the 'literary' from the 'theoretical'. Given that it is possible to perform a philosophical – and, by implication, a literary – 'reading of any text whatever', I am reluctant to assign my texts the label of one or the other.[22] However, even as I do not necessarily wish to reassert these assumptions, I cannot pretend ignorance of them. We read some of these texts primarily as philosophical and others in a predominantly literary fashion. That said, the distinction is not absolute. My 'philosophical' texts avow, as I have shown, an aspiration towards or interest in the literary; the literary texts I will read, on the other hand, attempt to philosophize their workings. I read these two not because literature *per se* 'hold outs the possibility of a repeated encounter with alterity' nor because philosophy will articulate 'truth' (Attridge 2004b, p. 28). Instead, the dialogue and interplay of these two discourses will question the status of my own writing, allowing it to aspire, perhaps, towards a wish Derrida articulates for a mode for which he admits 'autobiography' as 'the least inadequate' because 'most open' name (Derrida 1992e, p. 34): '[s]till now, and more desperately than ever, I dream of a writing that would neither be philosophy nor literature, nor even contaminated by one or the other, while still keeping – I have no desire to abandon this – the memory of literature and philosophy' (p. 73).

1

Composition

Reading cannot be captured or grasped, but might, in this failure, happen. Literary criticism, by loosening its pretensions to represent, must attend to this impossibility. In order to consider how it might do this, we must pay attention to criticism's composition, to the way in which it is written.

Derrida writes that we must accept 'the impossibility of [the work] ever being *present*, of its ever being summarized by some absolute simultaneity or instantaneousness. This is why, as we will verify, there is no *space* of the work, if by space we mean *presence* and *synopsis*' (Derrida 1978a, p. 14; italics in original). Derrida points out that the work is never yet determined. And yet the literary criticism that would treat of this work has, for Derrida, '*already been determined*, knowingly or not, voluntarily or not, as the philosophy of literature' (Derrida 1978a, p. 28; my italics). As a 'philosophy', literary criticism speaks 'objectively' – detached and definitive – adopting an authoritative tone. It claims to know the text about which it writes, proceeding as though both its rules and its object of study were laid out in advance.

As I showed in my introductory chapter, however, such calm authority and detached commentary is not in fact possible; this tone masks the actual impossibilities of representation. Criticism institutes itself at a *false* distance from the reading and writing upon which it would comment; it disavows its role in the constitution of the textual object, which is, in fact, as I have shown, determined (and necessarily compromised) only at the point at which it is read. Critical writing is not *in fact* detached and definitive. To appear 'distant and penetrative', it 'pushes' its 'writing-strokes away' (Wood 2007, p. 143). Sarah Wood, whose creative-critical work questions the need for this pushing-away, points out in 'All the way to writing' that '[i]t is a frequent pretension of critical writing to imply that its significance depends on hypostasising the movements of writing that get critical activity started in the first place' (Wood 2007, p. 143). It is a 'pretension' of critical writing to hypostasize its movements and to disaffirm its status as writing; Wood points out, however, that these movements are the very thing that gets it started. Critical writing will always, inevitably, be composed of 'writing-strokes', no matter how hard it attempts to deny this fact.

Wood thus challenges us to reconsider critical writing's relation to the philosophical. Wood invokes Derrida, who 'writes that one day criticism will not have to wait for philosophy . . . He writes about going all the way to writing: *"Jusqu'à l'écriture"*' (Wood 2007, p. 137).[1] Wood pursues a critical (or, as she often calls it, a 'poetic') writing conscious of its always-implicated investments. Wood, arguing that '[c]ritical writing that goes all the way to writing invites readers to forget, to un-know how to read literature and in so doing to pay attention to the movements of writing' (p. 137), performs a criticism which endeavours to keep literature and reading open, denying her readers the ability to 'know' what either might be. As I will show in more detail in my chapter's first section, Wood's critical *writing* draws us towards a more 'literary' and uncertain, less 'philosophical', form of critical pursuit.[2]

She is not the only one to promote this shift in focus. Maurice Blanchot claims in *The Infinite Conversation* that 'the work counts less than the experience of the search for it . . . an artist is always ready to sacrifice the work's accomplishment to the truth of the movement that leads to it' (Blanchot 1993, p. 397). Blanchot aligns the 'movement that leads to' the work, rather than the work itself, with 'truth'; the work or effort which produces the finished text is, for him, more important than the product itself. Roland Barthes, too, asserts that the 'writerly' or '*ourselves writing*' is 'our value' (Barthes 1974, pp. 4–5; italics in original). And Hélène Cixous announces that for writers 'what's important is the process. The tempest, the rough draft' (Cixous 1998, p. 44). Cixous, like Blanchot and Barthes, attributes composition a greater importance than the composed; she declares 'I love the creation as much as the created, no, more' (Cixous 1998, p. 20). Derrida, Wood, Cixous and Blanchot all encourage us to think a mode of critical writing conscious of its status as writing and attentive to its movements.[3]

This interest in the nature of composition is not new; it is shared, for example, by two much earlier writers: Henry James and Edgar Allan Poe. In 'The philosophy of composition', Poe announces 'I have often thought how interesting a magazine paper might be written by any writer who would – that is to say, who could – detail, step by step, the processes by which any one of his compositions attained its ultimate point of completion' (Poe 2009, p. 61). James echoes this sentiment; in *The Art of the Novel* he declares that 'it would be really interesting' to map 'the how and the whence and the why' of a novel's gestation (James 1962, p. 339). Poe and James do not, of course, simply speculate; in the works from which I just quoted, they also perform the proposed project. James '[trusts]' that the 'numerous pages' of his prefaces 'record with clearness' what he 'saw' when writing his fictions (p. 341).

However, the project Poe and James pursue differs from the one suggested by Derrida, Wood, Cixous and Blanchot. Poe and James reflect, in essays detached from the work itself, upon a writing which has already taken place, upon a composition which is now completed. Derrida, Wood, Cixous and Blanchot, in contrast, long for a writing that displays its *own* composition. But what would such a writing look like? How might we capture this tempestuous 'process'? A number of Wood and Cixous' works explicitly undertake the proposed project: Wood's 'All the way to writing' and 'Edit' and Cixous' 'Without end, no, State of drawingness, no, rather: The Executioner's taking off' in *Stigmata* and 'Post word' in the collection *Post Theory*. Both Wood and Cixous take the process of composition as their theme; they allude to the production of the work, '[t]he to-be-in-the-process of writing' (Cixous 1998, p. 20). Cixous is fascinated by 'creation' and keen to 'confide' to her readers 'the mysteries of passage' (p. 143). She attempts in her writing to grasp '"the beforehand of a book"' (p. 20) and the '[t]empest before the immobilisation, the capture, the concept' (Cixous 1999, p. 211). Wood, too, promises in her essays to '[investigate] writing as it is born, before it aligns itself with anything, before it amounts to much, before judgement. Even before a priori. Freshly picked or still growing' (Wood 2007, p. 140). Both writers claim to represent the moment before completion, before writing is fully formed and fixed.

However, my reading of these essays is, perhaps, already too philosophical. Cixous' claim that 'I love the creation as much as the created, no, more' is not as definitive as my analysis suggests. Cixous' original French announces '*j'aime la création autant que la créé, non, plus*' (Cixous 1991, p. 55). Both the French and the English play on the phrase *non plus*/no more. Without the comma, Cixous' sentence implies that she loves the creation more than the created 'no more'. That is to say, not any longer. When read attentively, the language of this passage hints at a less emphatic, more dissatisfied, relation to writing's 'creation'.

I noted James's claim that his prefaces 'record with clearness' the genesis of his fictions. He follows this claim, however, by noting that 'one element of fascination tended all the while to rule the business – a fascination, at each stage of my journey, on the noted score of so shifting and uneven character of my original passage' (James 1962, p. 341). Here, James concedes that his 'original passage' was 'shifting and uneven' – less clear than he at first intimates. Indeed, James admits that it would not only be 'really interesting' but also 'admirably difficult' to map composition. Poe makes a similar admission; he punctuates his search for a 'writer who would . . . detail, step by step, the processes by which any one of his compositions attained its ultimate point of completion' with the phrase 'that is to say, who could'. Poe's aside suggests that the project might be more difficult than he first implies.[4] Again, when read attentively, these essays appear less positive about their ability to record the act of composition.

I will return to consider the necessity of such an attentive reading in my chapter's third section. First, though, I will outline the reasons behind these equivocations by reading Cixous and Wood's work alongside a number of fictional texts, which also take composition as their theme. As I will demonstrate in my chapter's second section, these fictional texts make especially clear the *impossibilities* we encounter when trying to represent the act of writing and thereby highlight a dilemma we must bear in mind when approaching Wood and Cixous' work.

Many texts attempt to capture the act or event of writing. The example *par excellence*, Sterne's *Tristram Shandy*, 'makes the process of composition part of [its] narration', as Everett Zimmerman points out (Zimmerman 1987, p. 127). This chapter focuses on a number of more recent works that display a similar fascination with their own production: J. M. Coetzee's *Diary of a Bad Year*, Philip Roth's *Zuckerman Bound* trilogy, A. S. Byatt's *The Biographer's Tale* and David Mitchell's *Black Swan Green*. In all four of these novels, the protagonist is a writer. Jason in *Black Swan Green* is a young poet whose work is published in the parish newsletter under the pseudonym Eliot Bolivar. In the opening paragraph of the first novel in Roth's *Zuckerman Bound* trilogy, *The Ghost Writer*, the novel's first person narrator, whose name we later learn is Nathan Zuckerman, introduces himself as a man of 'twenty-three, writing and publishing my first short stories' (Roth 1998, p. 3). Zuckerman thus establishes himself as 'the writer-hero of Roth's own version of an artist's life', as Thomas Pughe points out (Pughe 1994, p. 83). Elizabeth Lowry notes that 'the hero' of Coetzee's *Diary of a Bad Year* 'is an ageing writer who bears a striking resemblance to Coetzee' (Lowry 2007, p. 3). When he first meets Anya, a woman who lives in his apartment complex and whom he eventually employs as his typist, he tells her 'I happen to be a writer by profession' (Coetzee 2008, p. 17). Finally, in Byatt's *The Biographer's Tale*, the protagonist, Phineas G. Nanson, abandons his academic life and the language of literary theory in order to become a writer; he '[becomes] addicted to forbidden words, words critical theorists can't use and writers can' (Byatt 2001, p. 250).[5] He tells us that 'in terms of writing, this looks like a *writer's story*. PGN was a mere Critick, steps centre-stage, assumes his life, Finds his Voice, is a Writer' (Byatt 2001, p. 251).[6] Louisa Hadley thus suggests that we label Byatt's novel a 'Künstlerroman, a novel that traces the development of the artist' (Hadley 2008, p. 89). We could, equally, describe the other three novels I will discuss in the same way.

Wallhead suggests that 'Byatt . . . is developing one of her favourite subjects, the analysis of artistic creativity, its sources and procedures' (Wallhead 2003, p. 294). Similarly, Stephen Wade claims that Roth's *Zuckerman Bound* offers us 'cumulative discourses and dialogues on art, on the relationship between life and writing, the idea of what is "real" and the pains of authorship' (Wade 1996, p. 90). Critics of these novels point out that they pose questions concerning artistry, creativity and creation. They suggest, moreover, that these questions are asked and answered thematically, at the level of representation and deliberate reflection. However, the situation is yet more complex. The protagonists of my chosen novels are presented to us not only as writers but, moreover, as the authors of the very texts we read. John Bayley points out that 'Byatt's biographer introduces himself to us in a manner not exactly auspicious: indeed he has hardly opened his mouth before we know him to be the author . . . of the book' (Bayley 2001, p. 16).

Phineas tells us 'I don't think my mother's death had anything to do with my decision, though as I set it down, I see it might be construed that way', that '[t]he pleasure, for me, I suppose, as I write, is that this time I was thinking of Foucault, and even more of Linnaeus, amongst *things*' and that '[a]ll writing about photographs, including this writing I am at present engaged in, has something decayed (decadent) and disgusting about it' (Byatt 2001, pp. 1, 115, 140; italics in original). The phrases 'as I set it down', 'as I write' and 'this writing I am at present engaged in' all refer, in the first person and the present tense, to the process by which Phineas constructs his text. Thus, these comments generate a second narrative alongside the main story Phineas purports to tell us; they invite us to picture Phineas seated at a desk putting together these words. They invite us to picture him in the act of writing the text that we read.

Diary of a Bad Year, Zuckerman Bound and *Black Swan Green* also suggest – although more subtly – that their protagonists have authored the work we encounter. In Coetzee's *Diary of a Bad Year*, Señor C tells Anya

> What I am in the process of putting together is strictly speaking not a book, I said, but a contribution to a book.
>
> The book itself is the brainchild of a publisher in Germany. Its title will be *Strong Opinions* (Coetzee 2008, pp. 20–1).

'Strong Opinions', we notice, is also the title of the novel's first section; it is implied that the text Señor C supposedly composes and that which we read are one and the same. Similarly, at the end of Roth's *The Ghost Writer*, Lonoff tells Zuckerman:

> 'And you must have things to write down. There's paper on my desk.'
> 'Paper for what?'
> 'Your feverish notes.' (Roth 1998, p. 128)

I will discuss the complexities of Lonoff's suggestion in more detail in my chapter's second section. It suffices to point out here, however, that Lonoff tells Zuckerman to begin making notes for his next novel or short story. He tells him "'I'll be curious to see how we all come out someday. It could be an interesting story. You're not so nice and polite in your fiction . . . You're a different person'" (p. 129). Lonoff authorizes Zuckerman to place him and Hope into fiction. The novel we have just read is, of course, such a story. It is implied that the words we have read are those that Zuckerman has written.[7] Similarly, in *Black Swan Green*, in a scene I will again examine more closely in my second section, Jason sits down to write and the words he composes are those we have already read in the novel. Mitchell's work is, for Thomas Jones, the 'story of a stammering poet finding his true voice as a writer of fluent prose' (Jones 2006, p. 34). Jones implies that Jason is the author of the 'fluent prose' that we read as *Black Swan Green*.

Thus, these texts purport to unfold writing as it happens, depicting its moment or present and claiming to subject us to composition in their very texture. These novels write about their writing and refer to their gestation. This self-reflexivity is frequently celebrated as a sophisticated gesture; Patricia Waugh suggests that novels such as those I will examine (to which she applies the label 'metafiction') signal a 'mature recognition' of their 'existence as *writing*' (Waugh 1984, p. 19; italics in original). Similarly, Hal Jensen claims that in *The Biographer's Tale* we encounter an 'exposure of the tricks of literary composition' (Jensen 2000, p. 23). Waugh frames the self-consciousness of these novels as their coming-of-age; she implies that the novel finally recognizes its written form, attaining a self-awareness it previously lacked. Jensen, too, aligns the trope with 'exposure' or revelation.

The situation with which these novels present us is, however, more complex than these critics suggest. These writerly moments do not simply convey information and do not function as an unproblematically 'mature' self-knowing; writing and composition cannot be straightforwardly exposed or simply thematized. This dilemma becomes apparent when we examine in more detail the claims made by Barthes and Blanchot, which I cited earlier. I explained that Barthes asserts in *S/Z* that the 'writerly' or 'ourselves writing' is 'our value' (Barthes

1974, pp. 4–5). *S/Z* describes the 'writerly' as the 'perpetual present' of '*ourselves writing*'; Barthes explains that '[t]he writerly is the novelistic without the novel, poetry without the poem, the essay without the dissertation, writing without style, production without product, structuration without structure' (p. 5; italics in original). The writerly is aligned with process and a notion of writing as event. Reading this list, however, we realize that it will remain unattainable: How could we ever isolate production from the product it produces? How could we locate a production that produced nothing?

If we are to represent 'ourselves writing' we must – impossibly – write the 'becoming' or 'perpetual present' of a 'production without product' (p. 5). Blanchot suggests that, in order to render its 'movement' the work must 'sacrifice' itself. To attain or capture its composition, the 'work' would have to forfeit its status as a work. This, of course, cannot be done; the notion of a production which produces nothing is inherently paradoxical; broaching many age-old philosophical paradoxes about time, the act of 'ourselves writing' remains elusive. Composition remains a troubling moment, which cannot be simply grasped. Nonetheless, writing continues to hold promise; we do not need to abandon the concept altogether. Our failure to capture it places the moment of reading into relief; as I will show in my chapter's third and final section, our inability to capture writing forces us to consider the possibility of reading.

Representing writing's trial and error

Although I have explained already that composition's representation will prove impossible, the first section of my chapter will consider the way in which my chosen texts depict writing. This will, of course, entail a deliberate misreading or naivety; I must begin as though it were possible to represent composition's moment. This blindness is, however, necessary; we must begin somewhere. It will become clear, I hope, that it is only by (tentatively and contingently) establishing a frame in which writing appears possible that we might become conscious of its actual, and potentially productive, impossibility.

The protagonist of Mitchell's *Black Swan Green* is a young poet called Jason, who writes under the pseudonym Eliot Bolivar. Moreover, as Thomas Jones points out, 'Eliot Bolivar's poems turn out to have the same titles as the chapters of [the novel]' (Jones 2006, p. 34). We realize this fact gradually; when Jason meets Madame Crommelynck he tells us that '[w]hile she smoked, she murmured my poem "Rocks" from May's magazine' and, later, she tells him '"[y]our best poem in here," she rifled through the parish magazines, "your 'Hangman'. It has pieces of truth of your speech impediment, I am right?'" (Mitchell 2006, pp. 183, 196). 'Rocks' and 'Hangman' are the titles of chapters two and five of the novel. Even later Jason tells us that '[a] poem called "Maggot" about why kids who get picked on get picked on began buzzing round my head' (p. 283). 'Maggot', we discover, is the novel's eighth chapter. Jones points out that 'we never get to read the poems'. However, we are invited to view the events narrated in each chapter of the novel as the inspiration for a poem Jason writes; we are, according to Jones, offered 'a full account of the events that provide [the poems] with their shadowy subject-matter' (Jones 2006, p. 34).

Although Jason's poems are not present in the novel, it offers itself to us as an account of that which precedes them and prompts their creation. The novel offers us glimpses of the process by which Jason composes his work. When standing next to the lake, for example, he muses somewhat poetically '[m]aybe I heard a poem, seeping from its cracks' (Mitchell 2006, p. 88). Elsewhere, he tells us 'I got sucked in by a poem about a skater on a frozen lake who wants to know what it's like to be dead so much, he's persuaded himself that a drowned kid's talking to him. I typed it out on my Silver Reed Elan 20 Manual Typewriter' and, later, 'I doodled for a bit (if you pretend not to look for words they come out of the thickets) but my Biro died' (pp. 41, 283). Jason's references to poems seeping from the cracks of a frozen lake and words coming from the thickets are mysterious and evocative; they invoke a Romantic model of artistic creation and inspiration. His overly specific references to his 'Silver Reed Elan 20 Manual Typewriter' and his mention of a tool as mundane as a 'Biro', in contrast, return us to the banal, the material and the everyday. Both sentences generate a comic anti-climax as the literary and the mundane converge.[8]

In spite of their humour, these moments remind us that the literary text is not spontaneously formed; no matter how ingenious the finished product may seem, the processes which contribute to its creation may be as boring as typing and finding a biro that works. The circumstances surrounding the composition of the text may in fact – in spite of the myths we cherish concerning artistic creation – be somewhat unexciting.[9]

Anya, in *Diary of a Bad Year*, informs us that Señor C 'doesn't like typing (has an "insuperable distaste," as he puts it)' (Coetzee 2008, p. 30). Anya therefore types his manuscripts for him; she explains that '[h]e dictates great thoughts into his machine, then hands over the tapes over to me, plus a sheaf of papers in his half-blind scrawl, with the difficult words written out in careful block letters. I take away the tapes and listen to them on my earphones and solemnly type them out' (p. 29). Anya points out that, although we finally read a single text, it is not created in a single act; instead, composition is a series of different processes: the text is first dictated and written by hand, then typed and then returned once more to its author.

Moreover, the text does not remain the same at every stage. Anya tells us that she '[f]ix[es] [Señor C's texts] up too here and there where I can, where they lack a certain something, a certain oomph, though he is supposed to be the big writer and I just the little Filipina' (p. 29). Anya draws our attention to a process in which correction and, by implication, error play a central role. Señor C also highlights this fact; he tells us that '[a]s a typist pure and simple, Anya from upstairs is a bit of a disappointment. She meets her daily quota, no problem about that, but the rapport I had hoped for, the feel for the sort of things I write, is hardly there. There are times when I stare in dismay at the texts she turns in. According to Daniel Defoe, I read, the true-born Englishman hates "papers and papery". Brezhnev's generals sit "somewhere in the urinals"' (p. 25). Anya, too, makes mistakes which need to be corrected. Señor C admits, somewhat wearily, that 'we proceed in this error-strewn way' (p. 32). *Diary of a Bad Year* sets out for us a process of composition governed by trial and error, by correction and re-correction, by drafts and revisions.

Roth's *The Ghost Writer* also alerts us to this fact. The protagonist of Roth's novel, Nathan Zuckerman, visits E. I. Lonoff, a writer whom he greatly admires. Zuckerman, looking around Lonoff's study, spots a quotation from Henry James's 'The Middle Years': '"[w]e work in the dark – we do what we can – we give what we have. Our doubt is our passion and our passion is our task. The rest is the madness of art"' (Roth 1998, p. 56). Zuckerman straight away sits down to read the story, which he does not know, and discovers that its hero, Dencombe, is a writer and, moreover, '"a passionate corrector" never able to arrive at a final form' (p. 82). This addiction to correction is mirrored in a number of the *The Ghost Writer's* characters. In one strand of the novel's narrative, Zuckerman discovers (or fantasizes) that Amy Bellette is, in fact, the famous Anne Frank. The narrative tells of the process by which Amy/Anne learns of the publication of her teenage diary. When she finally gets hold of it she reads it through; we are then told that 'she read the whole thing from the start again, making a small marginal notation – and a small grimace – whenever she came upon anything she was sure [Lonoff] would consider "decorative" or "imprecise" or "unclear"' (p. 97).

Lonoff displays a similar perfectionism; he explains that "'I turn sentences around. That's my life. I write a sentence and then I turn it around. Then I look at it and I turn it around again'" (p. 13). Each of these characters suffers from an almost-absurd desire to correct his/her work. They thus inform us that writing is neither glamorous nor spontaneous but is labour-intensive and error-strewn; the repetition of Lonoff's ponderously simple sentences, in particular, suggests that turning around sentences is a particularly dull and infuriating affair. Lonoff thus invokes the lengthy and potentially painstaking process behind the creation of the literary work.

This sentiment is shared by the author the book quotes: Henry James. In *The Art of Fiction*, James refers to the 'difficult, dire process of selection and comparison, of surrender and sacrifice' that constitutes composition and writes that 'the profession of delight has always struck me as the last to consort, for the artist, with any candid account of his troubled effort – ever the sum, for the most part, of so many lapses and compromises, simplifications and surrenders' (James 1962, pp. 6, 126).

The work's gestation may be complex and lengthy. Neither Lonoff nor Zuckerman is entirely happy to discover this. Lonoff's dissatisfaction becomes especially apparent when, at one point in the novel, Amy addresses Zuckerman:

> 'I've just found twenty-seven drafts of a single short story,' she told me.
> 'Which story?' I asked eagerly.
> '"Life Is Embarrassing."'
> 'To get it wrong,' said Lonoff, 'so many times.'
> 'They ought to construct a monument to your patience,' she told him (p. 19).

Lonoff laments so much getting it 'wrong'; he cringes at writing's 'trial and error'. His dissatisfaction is echoed later, in *Zuckerman Unbound*, by Zuckerman himself. Zuckerman tells us that he 'thought he'd chosen the intensification of everything and he'd chosen monasticism and retreat instead. Inherent in this choice was a paradox that he had never foreseen. When, some years later, he went to see a production of *Waiting for Godot*, he said afterwards to the woman who was then his lonely wife, "'What's so harrowing? It's any writer's ordinary day. Except you don't get Pozzo and Lucky'" (p. 425). Writing promises to be the 'intensification of everything'. It does not, however, fulfil this pledge, but is instead comparable to the painful inaction and repetitiveness of *Waiting for Godot*.[10] (Equally, there is perhaps something 'inactive' and 'repetitive' about these novels themselves; I must admit that, at times, I find myself bored when reading them. Yet, as Barthes writes, '[i]t can't be helped: boredom is not simple. We do not escape boredom (with a word, a text) with a gesture of impatience or rejection' (Barthes 1990b, p. 25). I will consider what my boredom might mean later).

Zuckerman's complaint in the second of my examples echoes that made in the first; Lonoff eschews the disorder of the 'process', the 'tempest' and the 'rough draft'. Both characters '[seek] the finished', privileging the fixed and the polished and, as such, downplay composition, relegating it to a disposable and inconsequential moment on the way to the composed. However, the reactions of Amy and the Zuckerman of the first quotation suggest a much different attitude. Amy and the young Zuckerman express awe and excitement; for them, composition holds a certain fascination. Amy is, in fact, at Lonoff's house in order to collate the drafts of his work so that they might be deposited in an archive. She – like many academics – is intrigued by Lonoff's many drafts and by the errors he commits on his way to the final product.

For Cixous and Wood, too, it is writing's very error-strewn nature that holds promise. Wood, unlike Lonoff, does not cringe at writing's unsteadying nature but privileges it. Cixous celebrates '[n]ecessary error, school mistress, faltering essential companion' (Cixous 1998, p. 22). Somewhat counter-intuitively, Cixous asks us to favour 'error'. In 'Post word', she praises 'all those, poets, who are *the prophets of the instant* and who, at lightning speed, want to write, write, write, *before,* in the still-boiling time before the cooled fall-out of the narrative when we feel and it is not yet called such-and-such, this, him or her. Tempest before the immobilisation, the capture, the concept. Where there is already the murmur of words but not yet proper-name-words' (Cixous 1999, p. 211; italics in original). Cixous encourages us to favour the 'tempest' and the 'murmur' and to relax our fixation on the 'capture', the 'concept' and the 'proper-name-words'. Her sentence, with its many short phrases and commas, performs the 'unsteady' and the 'faltering' movement of which it speaks and which it asks us to value. Cixous asks us to pursue a more 'literary' or 'deconstructive' course; Wood and Cixous echo Derrida's claim, which I quoted in my introduction, that we ought to look not for the fixed, but for the 'trembling', of language.

But how to capture this trial and error? What might this before or instant look like? How might a not-yet-finished writing appear? I pointed out in my introduction that, according to Zimmerman, *Tristram Shandy* 'makes the process of composition part of its narration'. What does it mean to do this? Zimmerman suggests that '[Tristram] does not cover up the seams of his narration – the leaps in time, the alterations of voice, the digressiveness – but exposes them to scrutiny and comments on their weaknesses. As we are close to his consciousness, the book emphasizes presence and presentness' (Zimmerman 1987,

p. 127). Byatt's *The Biographer's Tale* – as the one of my chosen texts in which the protagonist's authorship is most explicit – could be said to engage in a similar process. Phineas frequently draws our attention to his choice of words:

> Adumbrate is a good word, in this context; it sprang to the pen (Byatt 2001, p. 141).

> A man . . . who records and respects his subject's desire to be buried (I avoid, as he did, the anthropomorphism, 'to rest') (p. 166).

He alerts us to what he ought to include, and what might be best left out:

> They showed pictures – both still and moving – of. I don't have to write down what they were of (p. 170).

He foregrounds the style of his narration:

> I am not writing an autobiography. I am writing in the first person for the sake of precision, because this procedure allows me to say certain things I am reasonably sure of (p. 100).

And he highlights decisions he must make concerning the order of his narrative:

> I am not quite sure in what order to recount the next few parts of my tale, as I find that my memory for exact sequences is faultier than I would wish. I feel a desire in myself – an aesthetic desire – to punctuate my assimilation of Destry-Scholes's shoeboxes . . . with my encounters with the Strange Customer (p. 152).

All in all, the narrative appears to grant us access to the thought and logic behind its construction; we seem to witness its very unfolding. In the first three of my afore-mentioned groups, Phineas asserts positively the reasons for the choices he has made, making it clear that the words and style of his text are not unthinking or accidental, but are the result of intentional decisions. In the final quotation, however, Phineas admits that he is 'not sure' in what order to tell us about the events that have occurred.

For the most part, Phineas is uncertain more often than he is certain; the majority of his comments betray an extreme indecisiveness:

> I would penetrate his surface compartments and lay bare his true motives. I then thought, how very nasty all these metaphors were, and one at least of them contained another word ('penetrate') I had vowed for ever to eschew (p. 23).

> The image doesn't really work . . . I should never have made a real writer; I can't think my images through (p. 99).

> I start too many hares. (What *does* that mean? I have never seen a hare run. I am an urban animal. Ah, but in the mind's eye . . . And whose voice is *that*, with its plangent Ah, but. . .?) (p. 168; italics in original)

(A mixed metaphor. Let it lie.) (p. 171)

The 'flavour of the moment'. (Can I perpetrate a phrase like that? Let it stand. Try anything once.) (p. 250)

That is an over-the-top sentence (p. 260).

As Hal Jensen points out, 'Byatt's narrator is forever reconsidering his own choice of words' and is engaged in a 'perpetual ruthless analysis of word and phrase' (Jensen 2000, p. 23).[11] Phineas inscribes a word, reconsiders it and contemplates whether or not to erase it. He offers us what Barthes describes as a 'foam of language which forms by the effect of a simple need of writing'. This 'foam' or 'prattle' is, for Barthes, closely tied to the tedium of boredom; he writes that 'I am offered a text. This text bores me. It might be said to *prattle*' (Barthes 1990b, pp. 4–5).

Cixous (or, rather, the 'I' that 'narrates' 'Without End') represents a process similar to the one in which Phineas engages when she writes '[i]t's like this: I grope. I try the word "hesitation." I taste it. No pleasure. No taste. I cross out. I try: "correction." I taste. No. I taste ten words. Finally I fall on the word: "essay". Before even trying I already sense a pretaste . . . I taste. And, that's it!' (Cixous 1998, p. 22). Cixous, although less anxious than Phineas, also narrates the thought process underlying revision, presenting to us the 'trial and error' of composition. The many parentheses and ellipses of Phineas's texts and the short sentences of Cixous' represent a syntax whose flow is impeded suggesting that these texts, instead of being finished, remain disjointed by this ongoing and 'ruthless analysis'.[12]

Cixous' text acquires a hesitant tone even as she tells us that it is her wish to represent in her work the 'desire, trial, and error. Trial, that is to say, error. Error: progression' by which writing proceeds (Cixous 1998, p. 21).[13] Cixous' halting syntax and revisionary 'that is to say' maps a wary progression. She replicates this pattern in her essay's title – 'Without end, no, State of drawingness, no, rather: The Executioner's taking off' – and again in her final postscript:

N.B And now, what to call this essay?
– 'Without End' – No. – 'The Executioner's Taking Off' – No. Rather: Oh no, enough already, it's time! No more repenting! Not another word! (p. 31)

Within her essay, too, she tells us 'I wanted to call this text: "For the Instant," or "At the Instant," but I changed my mind' (p. 29). The essay offers us a variety of possible titles; as they proliferate, it becomes clear that settling on one and rejecting the others is a difficult process, in which one might repeatedly change one's mind. Cixous' increasing desperation is captured by her multiple exclamatory sentences: 'enough already, it's time!' 'no more repenting!' and 'not another word!' Moreover, the essay's very syntax captures this process of continual revision. In both the title and the postscript, Cixous offers us a number of possible titles – 'Without end', 'State of drawingness' and 'The Executioner's taking off' – punctuated and separated by three 'no's. Thus, we witness a process in which one might think of a title, then think 'no' and choose another. The repeated 'no's interrupt the flow of the sentence; it is fragmented and disjointed by Cixous' 'endless repenting'.

Both the essay's supposedly rejected titles and the process by which it decides between them remain within the text. It is as though we have come across a draft of Cixous' not-yet-completed essay. In *The Biographer's Tale*, Phineas also writes '[n]o, I am doing *too much writing* now. Cross that out? Leave it for the moment)' and '(beware cliché, PGN)' (Byatt 2001, pp. 153, 167; italics in original). Phineas addresses these comments to himself; they appear as authorial notes, intended to assist him when he comes later to revise his text. We do not expect to read such comments in a composed and finished piece; again, we are left with a sense that we have encountered the text mid-way through its composition.

Wood, too, announces in 'Edit' that she is 'mid-riffing in mid-air, writing not out of the middle of the picture, nor out of some authentic heart of writing, but merely mediocrely and eccentrically and derivatively from my solar plexus, anatomically the complex of nerves situated at the pit of one's stomach' (Wood 2006, p. 54). The bodily words 'midriff', 'solar-plexus' and 'stomach' evoke a writing originating from the gut; 'Edit' presents us with an intuitive writing that proceeds without plan and improvises as it goes. As such, Wood's text offers us a 'spaced-out or spacey writing' marked by a 'tendency to play with sound', a 'shared or divided writing' (Wood 2006, p. 54). The texts we read by Wood, Cixous and in *The Biographer's Tale* all give the impression that they are unfinished, that they are in the process of being composed and that the trial and error of this activity is still inscribed within them; they all purport to represent the composition which precedes the composed.

But can we truly call that which Cixous' text voluntarily publishes 'error'? Can we really call a published text 'unfinished'? These texts claim to represent writing as it takes place. Their declarations are, however, clearly untrue; the text is published and whole. We know that their assertions that the process of writing is ongoing are feigned. This is most apparent in *The Biographer's Tale*. The suggestions I have made imply that Phineas authors the work that we read. However, this cannot be true; a fictional protagonist cannot author the work. Thomas

Jones, in his review of *Black Swan Green*, is especially conscious of this fact. He complains that 'all too often, [Jason's] creator's hand is visible', explaining that '[t]he idea that a novel like this would stream out of a 13-year-old's pen isn't convincing . . .: Mitchell may work fast – he's had four novels published in seven years – but that doesn't mean that the prose splurges out. The supposed naturalism of Jason's voice is highly artificial, and making romantic claims for its authenticity puts it under more strain that it is able to bear' (Jones 2006, pp. 34–5). I am reluctant to dismiss this dilemma as Jones does; I am not sure that the novel *does* make 'romantic claims' for the 'authenticity' of Jason's voice and think perhaps that its 'highly artificial' nature might be one of its more interesting effects. I cite Jones's criticism, however, because it makes clear the disjunction by which these texts are troubled. Writing does not actually 'happen' as they claim; the actual writing by which they are composed takes place elsewhere. Jason is not the author of *Black Swan Green*; we remain conscious that the 'creator's hand' is David Mitchell's. Equally, *The Biographer's Tale* is composed not by Phineas but by A. S. Byatt. The declarations these texts make are undone by the writing in which they occur and by the reading to which they are subjected. By representing writing within novels which are themselves composed by a similar process of writing, these texts deny it a single or stable appearance.

The references made by Phineas and Jason are made problematic by our awareness of another writing that lies behind them. The doubling of Phineas/Byatt, Jason/Mitchell forces us to read Phineas and Jason's claims provisionally. I will show, in the next section, that this effect, although more prominent in fiction than in the creative–critical genre in which Wood and Cixous write, in fact points to a disjunction or non-coincidence which applies to *all* attempts to capture writing. These novels 'teach' us a sceptical reading, which we must also employ in relation to Wood and Cixous' work if it is to continue truly to work. The moment of composition remains elusive, as I will show in the next section of this chapter before returning in my final section to the question of reading.

A 'fumbled prophecy'

The texts I consider here propose to display the entirety of their composition, the truth of their very beginnings and the trial and error by which they are pieced together. These claims are, however, troubling, as the third novel in Roth's *Zuckerman Bound* trilogy, *The Anatomy Lesson*, suggests. Thomas Pughe explains that '*The Anatomy Lesson* is set more than three years after the publication of *Carnovsky*, and Nathan has not written a longer piece of fiction since' (Pughe 1994, p. 105). The novel is framed as Zuckerman's battle with writer's block. The inability to write is painful, as the opening of Cixous' 'Post word' makes clear. Cixous writes '[t]hen I started thinking about how to inscribe "myself" . . . Then I sat early in the morning at my desk and I started trying to begin starting to write a something not unworthy of you' (Cixous 1999, p. 209). Cixous is unable to begin; the more she thinks about beginning the more impossible it seems, as the repetition of the word 'started' in the phrases 'started thinking about' and 'started trying to begin starting' suggests. Cixous captures the maddening stasis one feels when unable to write.

In *The Anatomy Lesson*, too, both Zuckerman and the novel's other characters become increasingly frustrated at his inability to begin another novel. Diana tells him '"[t]here's only one thing for you to do and that's *to get on with it*. WRITE ANOTHER BOOK. *Carnovsky* is not the end of the world . . . It cannot stop you in your tracks like this"' (Roth 1998, p. 370; italics in original). Zuckerman seeks desperately for the inspiration which would allow him to 'get on with it'. When he meets Jaga, for example, he interrogates her 'thinking that if only she told him enough, he might find in what she said something to start him writing' (pp. 390–1). Fascinated by her plight, he proposes '*The Sorrows of Jaga*' as his next book. However, he is unable to transform his conversation with Jaga into a novel: 'after Jaga he'd been unable to write even three words' (p. 411). He admits that 'he couldn't get anywhere' even with this idea (p. 394). *The Anatomy Lesson* tells us that *The Sorrows of Jaga* has not been written.

The reader of *The Anatomy Lesson,* however, encounters 'three words' and more on 'The Sorrows of Jaga'; her tale forms an episode within the novel. Her narrative is not as absent, or as unwritten, as Zuckerman professes. The novel undercuts its own complaint; it produces the writing whose absence it laments. Moreover, *Zuckerman Unbound* itself acknowledges the paradoxical nature of Zuckerman's predicament. At the end of one of Zuckerman's lengthy diatribes, for example, '[t]he doctor laughed' and asked '"You writing a book or what?"' (p. 490). The doctor's comment reminds us that a book has indeed been written; writing has evidently taken place. Cixous' 'I started thinking about how to inscribe myself' opening to 'Post word' is similarly complicated. The essay informs us that Cixous has not yet started to write; she is still contemplating how to begin. However, the sentences that tell us of this fact produce – with increasing prolixity – this very (supposedly un-begun) writing.

I explained in my last section that *The Biographer's Tale* contemplates the decisions surrounding its composition; Phineas deliberates upon what he ought to include in his text. He also, frequently, informs us of that which he has decided to exclude:

> I thought of saying, two complete revolutions of a roller, and then thought, I had got the roller from cricket, and needed the reference (Byatt 2001, p. 132).

> I was – I was about to write, ashamed, but that isn't true. I was embarrassed (p. 122).

> I was about to write, I knelt reverently because the adverb tripped off the pen. But that wasn't true (p. 134).

> I was going to write, we *fell* into the bed, but we didn't. And I am not going to describe what happened, though I am going to record that it *did* happen, because I am not that sort of writer. I think. It's becoming more difficult to know what sort of writer I *am* (pp. 186–7; italics in original).

The phrases 'I was going to write', 'I thought of saying' and 'I was about to write' all gesture towards words or phrases that Phineas has considered using but has decided, ultimately, to leave out. Phineas alerts us to the words he has elected to exclude from his text. There is, however, an evident irony in this claim. The comments made by Phineas grant these supposedly absent words and phrases a presence in the text. Phineas cannot announce 'I was going to write, we *fell* into the bed' without writing 'we *fell* into the bed'. His denial accords the phrase a place in his text; his comments insert into the novel that which it claims to leave out.

Phineas announces 'I have once or twice started a sentence in this last paragraph with a more or less automatic address to an imaginary reader. "Have you noticed those billboards . . ." I wrote, and crossed it out. Worse, I ascribed opinions to this person. "You might think everyone has to be interested in himself" I wrote, and scratched it out. Who is this "you"? No one. Or me, and I know what I think, I think' (p. 100).[14] Phineas again alerts us to a process of revision whereby he wrote, in the preceding paragraph, the phrases 'you might think everyone has to be interested in himself' and 'have you noticed those billboards' and then crossed them out. However, we do not read these phrases in the paragraph in question; we do not even see a phrase scratched out or the space in which they would have been inscribed. Their erasure is absolute. In the lengthy explanation Phineas offers, however, the phrases are inscribed in full and are not crossed out at all; Phineas's narrative un-erases the comments whose erasure it discusses.

These examples from *The Biographer's Tale* point towards an illogic; the claims Phineas makes concerning the composition of his text undo the very act or process to which he refers. Although they state that he has excluded or erased aspects of his text, these announcements perform the very opposite, including and presenting these moments to us. We witness a similar disjunction in Cixous' Beckettian 'Without end, no, State of drawingness, no, rather: The Executioner's taking off'.[15] As I explained earlier, the title of Cixous' text narrates the act of choosing among three different titles; it represents a process in which one thinks of a title, discards it and then chooses another. Paradoxically, however, the process of consideration and rejection to which Cixous' 'no's refer does not in fact occur. The supposedly discarded titles 'State of Drawingness', 'The Executioner's taking off' as well as the 'For the Instant' and 'At the Instant' mentioned within the body of the essay are published within and by Cixous' text. All five phrases are granted a presence by the work; moreover, all three of the phrases 'Without end', 'State of drawingness' and 'The Executioner's taking off' function as the title of Cixous' essay. The 'no's do not revise the essay's title, but comprise it. The choice to which Cixous alludes does not take place; the essay fails to discard its supposedly rejected titles.

The words or phrases with which these examples present us are at odds with, and counteract, the processes – of erasure, exclusion and revision – to which they refer; we realize that we cannot announce the absence of a word or phrase without according it a presence. Cixous' 'Post word' enacts this tension on a grander scale, subjecting the text as a whole to the dilemma. 'Post word', which appears in the collection *Post Theory*, is preceded by an editors' note, which explains that '[t]he text presented here is a letter sent by Hélène Cixous in response to a request by the editors for a short epilogue to this collection' (Cixous 1999, p. 209). The letter itself is an apology; Cixous explains that, hard as she has tried, she has been unable to compose the piece the editors have asked her to write as conclusion to their book; she announces that 'I have done the work and I have judged it incompatible with the collection of dedicated and passionate essays you have gathered' (p. 212). Cixous justifies her failure, and lists, in the past conditional, a number of points her ultimately rejected essay would have made; she writes 'I would have called my "contribution" *Avantposte*', '[i]t would have had four sections' and '[t]he fourth would have been a prosopopoeia of Theoria (I have not written it)' (pp. 210, 212). Cixous' letter accounts for the absence of the essay 'Post word'.

Somewhat counter-intuitively, the letter tells us that 'Post word' does not exist; it asserts that the piece commissioned by the editors of *Post Theory* has not been written. Moreover, it frames itself as a piece not intended for publication. Of course, neither of these claims is true; the letter we read as the conclusion to

Post Theory has clearly been published and is, moreover, entitled 'Post word'. The 'editor's note' that precedes the letter registers this substitution from the outset; it declares that Cixous' letter 'responds' to – and thereby fulfils – the request made by the editors. As such, we suspect (although we could of course never be certain) that this letter *is*, and always was, the piece Cixous intended to write. Cixous hints at this possibility; at the end of her letter she writes '[m]y dear friend, if you feel it would help you disentangle the situation with the press, you can show them (whoever they are) my letter' (p. 213). Cixous' offer indicates that this letter, by justifying and excusing the absence of the expected piece, takes the place of the proposed work.

Moreover, the letter tells us that the essay 'would have had four sections'. The phrases 'would have called' and 'would have been', as well as Cixous' final 'I have not written it' inform us that these intended sections are not present. Cixous then writes, however, that '[t]he first section runs like this' and proceeds to detail its content (p. 210). The first section would not only have proceeded in this manner, but also does, as the shift into the present tense indicates; the first section is inscribed and published here. Cixous' letter not only *would have had*, but also *has* these four sections. The letter repeatedly attempts to assert the absence of the work, but fails; the work Cixous negates remains legible.

We thus become conscious of a non-coincidence between that which these statements enact and that which they constatively state; they do not refer unproblematically to an act or an event that has taken place in these texts' composition. As such, they gesture towards a deferral or errancy inherent in any attempt to represent writing and to which Wood's 'Edit' also alerts us. Wood declares 'I want to try and think about the spacing of this' and invokes its action time and again (Wood 2006, p. 51):

> he writes, having just hit the space bar (p. 48)
> Time to press the space bar again (p. 49).
> I just hit the space bar. Should I have kept that to myself? (p. 51)
> I press tab, for a change. And return (p. 52).
> Fifty-two spaces. I hit the space bar. I go, I write. I hit return (p. 53).
> I punch the space bar (p. 53).
> Learn what? I press the space bar (p. 54).
> Space bar again (p. 55).

The act of hitting the space bar is entirely banal; it is, quite obviously, an activity one practises repeatedly when typing any text. Wood evokes one of writing's most obvious facets. She discovers, however, that it is not possible to refer unproblematically to it. In her final declaration, Wood admits that 'I hit the spacebar. I keep doing that – far more often than I've admitted' (p. 56). We can see, in the blank spaces throughout her essay, the product of Wood's spacebar-hitting. It is evident that she has been hitting the spacebar from the outset, even at the moments at which she does not admit it. Wood's confession is somewhat redundant; we know, before she has told us, that she 'just hit the space bar'. Wood asks, with decided irony, 'should I have kept that to myself?' She could not possibly keep this act a secret; her writing betrays it. The confession Wood makes reveals nothing we did not already know.

Wood's admission is absurd because unnecessary and belated. By the time she writes 'I just hit the space bar', the space her key-hitting has produced is already visible in her text. Moreover, she cannot declare 'I just hit the space bar' without repeating the action further; in the singular 'space bar again' declaration Wood hits the spacebar twice more. It would, therefore, never be possible for her to account for every spacebar-hit she makes; her admissions proliferate the action to which they refer.

Byatt's *The Biographer's Tale* replicates this endless failure. Phineas writes, 'I notice that my writing is becoming perhaps too impassioned. But then, what sort of a piece of writing is it, for what purpose, for which reader? I may be passionate or dispassionate as I choose, since this document has no importance anyway' and '([n]o, I am doing *too much* writing now. Cross that out? Leave it for the moment)' (Byatt 2001, pp. 141, 153; italics in original). Phineas comments on his text's excess. However, his reflections occupy more space than the phrases on which they comment. His concerns that he is writing 'too much' themselves produce 'too much writing'; they generate the very problem to which they refer. Phineas cannot express his anxiety for the text without exacerbating it.

We are caught in the dilemma represented most notably in a much earlier novel, Sterne's *Tristram Shandy*. Tristram promises to narrate the entirety of his life but as he writes his account he engages in a further activity – writing – which he is bound, also, to narrate. Unable to catch up with himself, he realizes that 'at this rate I should just live 364 times faster than I should write' (Sterne 1976, p. 286). By writing about his writing, he generates yet more writing about which he must also write. The project is endless and impossible; Tristram cannot escape or halt his life in order to narrate it. Cixous admits that '[w]e live more quickly than ourselves, the pen doesn't follow' (Cixous 1998, p. 30).

In each of these examples, the novel's attempt to capture the moment of composition engages it in an inevitable proliferation.[16] Behind each writing lies yet another act of composition for which, in turn, the novel must account. Composition's admission, always bound to take place again *in writing*, is not free from the logic it declares. The composition we would represent does not exist independently from the composed we would dismiss; an act of composition lies behind all writing, even the writing that attempts to reveal composition. Thus, we cannot refer to composition without composing yet more writing; the two cannot be separated and the moment of writing moves ever-further away.

Both *Black Swan Green* and *The Ghost Writer* demonstrate this inevitable regression. At the end of *The Ghost Writer,* Lonoff, leaving the house in pursuit of his wife, Hope, tells Zuckerman:

> 'you must have things to write down. There's paper on my desk.'
> 'Paper for what?'
> 'Your feverish notes.' (Roth 1998, p. 128)

Murray Baumgarten thus explains that 'Lonoff tells [Zuckerman] . . . to start writing about what he has witnessed' and that this moment 'returns to the problems with which the novel began' concerning life and art, and their 'inextricably intertwined' nature (Baumgarten and Gottfried 1990, p. 171). Alexis Kate Wilson points out that 'Philip Roth ends the novel [*The Ghost Writer*] by playing with the idea of life becoming art' (Wilson 2005, p. 103). Both of these writers suggest that Lonoff authorizes Zuckerman to place him and Hope into a story or a novel; he permits Zuckerman to transpose this 'real life' scene into writing and fiction.[17]

However, neither Baumgarten nor Wilson acknowledges the irony of Lonoff's offer. Lonoff tells Zuckerman he ought to begin taking notes about what he has seen so as to write about it later. In making this suggestion, Lonoff implies that the novel depicting these events has not yet begun or been written. However, the 'events' which Lonoff permits Zuckerman to convert into fiction are, of course, those of which we have just read. The novel depicting them *has* been written and it is called *The Ghost Writer*. The fiction Zuckerman is meant to produce is the novel we are just completing.

We surmise that *The Ghost Writer* is the not-yet-written novel that Lonoff evokes; producing a kind of ghost-effect, he proposes that Zuckerman write the book we have just read. To read what Zuckerman writes, we conclude, we must return to the novel's beginning. However, this would once again bring us back to Lonoff's comment and its implicit claim that the novel has not yet been written; it commands us once again to return to the novel's beginning, and so on, *ad infinitum.* We are caught in an endless loop. Similarly, in *Black Swan Green*, Jason sits down at his desk intending to write a poem although the result, he admits, is more of a 'confession' (Mitchell 2006, p. 331). A facsimile of a handwritten page then follows. This document opens: '[t]hat *ace* song Olive's Salami by Elvis Costello and the Attractions'. We have read these words before. Jason's confession duplicates the opening of an earlier chapter entitled 'Goose Fair' (p. 307). Jones notes that we find 'reproduced in facsimile, the "manuscript", in 13-year-old handwriting, of the opening sentences of the previous chapter, verbatim' (Jones 2006, p. 34). The document continues for a few lines before Jason concludes 'and on it went. When the bell went for morning break I found I'd filled three sides' (Mitchell 2006, p. 331). Jason's 'and on it went' implies that his confession continues. If we want to read its entirety, we should reread the earlier chapter. But when does Jason's writing stop? Nothing marks its end. If we continue to read we return once again to the point at which Jason begins his 'confession'. Jason writes his confession and, as he writes, he recalls the moment at which he began to write and thus begins once again to write his confession. And so on. We are caught in the infinite regression of the *mise en abîme* I outlined in my introduction.

Derrida, in 'The law of genre', notes that Blanchot's *La Folie du Jour* employs a similar framing mechanism; it ends with an interrogation in which the narrator is asked to provide the *récit* we have just read. The effect is identical to the one that I noted in relation to *Black Swan Green*. Derrida explains that 'if "I" or "he" continued to tell what he has told, he would end up endlessly returning to this point and once more beginning to begin, that is to say, to begin with an end that precedes the beginning. And from the viewpoint of objective space and time, the point at which he stops is absolutely unascertainable'. Derrida's 'beginning to begin' reproduces the 'unarrestable, inenarrable and insatiably recurring' regress about which he writes (Derrida 1992b, p. 237). This '*double chiasmatic invagination of edges*' means, for Derrida, that it is '[i]mpossible to settle upon the simple borderlines of this corpus, of this ellipsis unremittingly cancelling itself within its own expansion' (pp. 238–9; italics in original). These texts attempt to isolate the moment at which their narrators begin to write, but cannot. They belatedly offer an account of their origins, but cannot grasp the instance to which they refer.[18]

These novels behave like the 'glass worm' Wood evokes in 'Edit'. Wood explains that 'this shy, defenceless creature's tail breaks off easily, thus allowing it to escape from predators' and that '[s]ome words and texts also behave like this. We read them hungrily, as if to death, but they break and a portion, an envoi or concluding part, gets away' (Wood 2006, p. 50). We attempt to grasp writing, but it breaks away, escaping and leaving us no 'concluding part'. Wood therefore explains that writing is at once 'directly familiar and teasingly unlocatable' (Wood 2007, p. 139). To state even the plainest of facts about writing – such as 'I hit the spacebar' – is to involve oneself in a regression which loses what it states. We thus discover that '[t]o be plain about writing is to become elliptical, to escape or withdraw' (Wood 2007, pp. 145–6).

We therefore find that Wood's 'All the way to writing', rather than going 'all the way' as its title proposes, seems mostly not to have gone very far towards writing at all. The essay repeatedly invokes this failed happening:

> Only something hasn't happened. Let me tell you (p. 138).
> I don't seem to have started. I'm still outside (p. 138).
> something has not happened (p. 141).

In 'Edit', too, Wood writes 'I digress, where were we, what are we in the middle of here?' (Wood 2006, p. 54). These essays repeatedly invoke their lack and failure; they start off thinking about writing only to confess that 'something has not happened'. Halting repeatedly before that which do not know, they appear dangerously close to paralysis. 'Edit' evinces a final, despairing, 'I give it up, this thinking of the absolute mystery' (p. 55). The 'something' they seek gets away from Wood's essays; that which was meant to take place has not occurred. Cixous also admits that 'I have the feeling that I always write from the perspective of what passes away' (Cixous 1998, p. 44). Cixous fails to possess writing; she finds, instead, that it is forever passing away. We realize that 'there is no moment of writing, no simple present or presence' (Wood 2007, p. 146).

Cixous, in *Three Steps on the Ladder of Writing*, tells us that '[w]riting is the delicate, difficult, and dangerous means of succeeding in avowing the unavowable. Are we capable of it? This is my desire . . . though this doesn't mean I have succeeded. I make the effort. So far I haven't succeeded' (Cixous 1993, p. 53). Cixous makes it clear that there is something 'unavowable' about writing. Thus, in order to capture it, we must succeed 'in avowing the unavowable'. Cixous admits 'I haven't yet succeeded'. We realize, however, that she will never succeed, no matter how much 'effort' she expends. The unavowable can never be avowed. Once avowed, the supposedly unavowable would be no more; the very act of avowal is incompatible, in this case, with that which it would present. The project Cixous proposes is doomed to fail; writing cannot be captured.

Cixous still claims, however, that it is her 'desire' to grasp the moment of writing; she continues to crave and to chase after it. Derrida asks,

> [d]issemination question: what is 'going on', according to what time, what space, what structure, what becomes of the 'event' when 'I write', 'I place beside me an open inkstand and a few sheets of unspitballed paper', or 'I am going to write', 'I have written': about writing, against writing, in writing [. . .]? (Derrida 1981, p. 41)

As Derrida's quotation marks imply, 'I write' never conveys writing's pure 'event' or happening. There is, however, still something 'going on', even if it is not the 'something' we had hoped for. Derrida therefore continues to wonder '[w]hat's the story with the autography of pure loss and without a signature? And how is it that this performance displaces such force in going without truth?' For him '[t]he structure of the feint describes here, as always, an extra turn' (p. 41).

In Cixous' essays, '[w]riting is not arriving; most of the time it's *not arriving*' (Cixous 1993, p. 65; italics in original). Writing does not arrive; we cannot recount it clearly. Similarly, Wood announces that writing is 'something aporetic, unparaphraseable by those who believe in paraphrase' (Wood 2007, p. 142) and that 'it defies commentary and translation' (Wood 2009b, p. 67). Neither Wood nor Cixous can 'paraphrase' writing. This is not to say, however, that nothing happens when we attempt to capture it. The aporia with which these essays' failures present us forces us to rethink our belief in paraphrase. Thus, we realize that although the comments these texts make do not refer directly and unproblematically to the moment or act of composition, something does occur in them. Cixous' emphatic repetition draws our attention towards an alternative possibility: even though writing does not arrive, it is not fully absent; its 'not arriving' becomes apparent. Writing cannot be made fully present; nonetheless, as Wood tells us, it is '*about*. Outside. Around. In the offing' (Wood 2007, p. 146; italics in original). She also points out that 'it's a delight, one feels it' (Wood 2009b, p. 67). We remain, as Wood writes, '[h]eld by a word, by something in a word that's beyond it, and beyond me' (Wood 2006, p. 53). Writing, although 'beyond' us, nevertheless evokes its 'beyond'; it refers us to the reading which occurs 'beyond' or after it, as I will show in my chapter's final section.

Prophetic fumblings

In the repeated failures of these works we realize, as Wood writes, that '[p]oetic writing is fumbled prophecy at best' (Wood 2007, p. 145). Composition cannot be captured; we fumble its prophecy. However, it is this very failure that renders writing prophetic; our fumblings refer us to writing's future – to reading – and thereby alert us to its very condition. The infinite regress or *mise en abîme* into which our attempts to capture writing places us render us conscious of our position as readers. *Black Swan Green* hints towards this situation when Jason asks '[d]o spirals end? Or just get so tiny your eyes can't follow any more?' (Mitchell 2006, p. 231). The uncanny quality of the spiral lies in this uncertainty; we cannot witness its increasing distance without questioning our own position. In this case, equally, our dilemma highlights our stance as readers. We cannot grasp writing, but in our failure reading becomes apparent. The impossible moment of writing refers us to our moment of reading.[19]

Cixous, in 'Without end, no, State of drawingness, no, rather: The Executioner's taking off', writes both that there '[t]here is not one single sentence in this text which I didn't write twenty times' and 'I just wrote this sentence, but before this sentence, I wrote a hundred others, which I've suppressed, because the moment for cutting short had arrived' (Cixous 1998, pp. 31, 20). Cixous points to a process of revision; behind any sentence lies twenty or a hundred rejected variations. However, we do not find twenty or a hundred versions of the afore-mentioned sentences in Cixous' essay; the process of revision towards which Cixous gestures is not apparent to us. The revisions that occurred as Cixous composed her text are no longer legible.

The failure inscribed in this example opens questions of legibility and of reading; in particular, it alerts us to a discrepancy between the time of writing and the time of reading that *Diary of a Bad Year* also highlights. I mentioned earlier that the novel's protagonist, Señor C, complains that '[a]s a typist pure and simple, Anya from upstairs is a bit of a disappointment . . . There are times when I stare in dismay at the text she turns in'. He lists her laughable mistakes: '[a]ccording to Daniel Defoe, I read, the true-born Englishman hates "papers and papery". Brezhnev's generals sit "somewhere in the urinals"' (Coetzee 2008, p. 25). Señor C concedes that he and Anya proceed in an 'error-strewn way' (p. 32). He alerts us to the fact that 'Strong Opinions' – the text we read in the top section of the page and that Anya has supposedly typed – contains imperfections. However, we have already encountered the passages to which Señor C refers. We have read that '[o]ne recalls Daniel Defoe's comment on religious strife in England: that adherents of the national church would swear to their detestation of Papists and Popery not knowing whether the Pope was a man or a horse' (p. 13). And, later, that 'somewhere in the Urals an enemy watched and waited with a finger on a button' (p. 19). In the text that we have read, the 'errors' to which Señor C refers no longer exist; they have been erased or corrected. Señor C's comment does not refer to 'errors' we find in the text, but creates them for us after the fact. The 'errors' that would have *preceded* the final text, taking place in the process of its composition, are not referenced until *after* we have read it.

At the end of 'Without end, no, State of drawingness, no, rather: The Executioner's taking off' Cixous asks 'now, what to call this essay?'[20] The question, posed at the end of the text, accounts for the order in which Cixous' work is composed; she finishes the essay and then titles it. This is perfectly logical: although the title begins the text, it is not necessarily composed first. As we read, however, we do not share Cixous' dilemma. She poses it too late; we have already read the text's title, on its opening page. For us as readers the question carries no force. In reading, the time of writing is lost and what Cixous writes as present, we read as past.

We are 'born for lateness' (Cixous 1998, p. 30). We read the 'perpetual present' of writing always as past. We do not read a present writing, but always that which has been written. By the time we read, writing is complete; the act of reading announces that writing is past. Our attempt to capture writing is thus thwarted by what Derrida terms the 'passageway of deferred reciprocity between reading and writing' (Derrida 1978a, p. 11). We realize that reading and writing do not occur at the same time and that, therefore, neither is fully present to the other; each occurs in the absence of the other and they do not and cannot take place at the same instant. The moment of writing is always and inevitably resituated at and by the moment of reading. Yet without this compromising deferral, neither would be possible.

Wood therefore points out that '[w]riting-intelligence' is 'both dyadic and promiscuous' (Wood 2007, p. 139). Writing, or 'writing-intelligence', is activated only in relation to the reading that comes after it and that therefore deprives it of any pure presence. Thus, any reference to writing poses a dilemma to and for reading, as *Diary of a Bad Year* demonstrates. When we open Coetzee's novel we discover that the page is, unusually, divided into two sections. Its upper section contains Señor C's 'strong opinions' while the lower section narrates his encounters with Anya and his attempts to hire her as his typist. Later, a third section is added, which narrates the same series of events from Anya's point of view. Thus, the novel presents at once, but separately, the finished text of 'Strong Opinions' and two narratives of the events surrounding its composition.

The three sections of the page are clearly related; the lower two refer both to each other and to the text we read above. 'Strong Opinions' is supposedly composed in the time to which the lower two narratives refer. However, we cannot read them simultaneously. The novel's graphology poses a dilemma: in what order ought we best to read its sections? A number of possibilities present themselves. We might begin, for example, by approaching *Diary of a Bad Year* as we traditionally would a novel, reading the whole of the work's first page and ignoring the line across the middle. We realize, however, that the top of the next page follows on from the text interrupted in the middle of the last. As we resume Señor C's 'Strong Opinions' at the top of each page, we struggle to remember where we left it before the break on the previous page. This method fragments our impression of the two narratives and soon becomes irritating, especially when the third section is introduced and even more so when the novel begins to break mid-sentence on page sixty. It is easier to read one section continuously until it reaches a natural pause and then return to do the same with the section beneath. And so on. Alternatively, we realize, we could read each narrative separately, perusing the novel from its first to last page three times over.

None of these methods is entirely satisfactory, however. As I explained already, a 'normal' approach to the novel soon becomes awkward; equally, reading the top section continuously until it pauses and then returning to read the one below requires one to move backwards and forwards repeatedly and always to remember where one has stopped and started. To pursue the easiest course and read each section separately, however, leads one to miss many of the connections between them. Whichever course we choose, we suspect another may be better; at the most basic level, this novel-about-writing forces us continually to consider the way in which we read.[21]

(An aside, before I begin the analysis of Wood's writing with which I wish to conclude my chapter. The attitude of Wood's text towards citation is, one might say, unorthodox. In 'Edit', for example:

> If it were to be something like that, the Complete Works of Jacques Derrida would not exclude everything else – let's call it 'the desire for everything + n' ('Strange' 35) or 'this catastrophe' ('Che' 235) or 'my chances' ('Chances' 2) or whatever it is that goes unnamed in *Of Grammatology*, curled up in a sentence about the 'recognition' and 'respect' that 'has always only protected, . . . never opened a reading' (158) (Wood 2006, pp. 47–8).

This sentence patches together phrases from four different essays by Derrida. Abstracting them from their original sentences, it gives us no sense of their original meaning. Short phrases are excerpted so as to form a quotation-mosaic, which makes no attempt to properly 'read' 'This strange institution called literature', 'Che cos'è la poesia', 'My chances' or *Of Grammatology*. It is frankly irresponsible. But perhaps performs, for that very reason, as I suggested in my introduction, the highest form of responsibility. Wood's text mishandles Derrida's work. But in doing so leads us (if we are inclined to read it generously) to wonder: Does not all citation do this? does Wood's work merely exaggerate a tendency inherent in all quotation? Wood's essay, unlike others, does not pretend to tell us about Derrida's work; the deformations her citations perform are at least blatant. They make us conscious that the *only* way we can be sure whether or not the citation is 'true' to Derrida's text is to return to it. Wood's essay refers us back to the original; it leaves it to be read. The reading that follows will attempt to re-produce this movement. It cites extensively from 'Edit' and 'All the way to writing', weaving together phrases from both essays, in order to construct its conclusion.

This is, of course, a risky undertaking. Derrida writes that '[i]n certain cases, quotation, the rhythmic return of the same wears down the mark; it is boring, provokes disgust, pushes towards oblivion'. My final paragraphs might repulse and bore you. This may well have something to do with the demand that they level. Barthes suggests that 'there is no *sincere* boredom: if the prattle-text bores me personally, it is because in reality I do not like the demand' (Barthes 1990b, p. 25). Patricia Ann Meyer Spacks echoes this sentiment when she writes that '[a]s an interpretive category, it [boredom] implies an embracing sense of irritation and unease' (Spacks 1995, p. 13). How true my quotation-web 'conclusion' is to Wood's writing is a question which remains and which only you can answer. You perhaps do not want this responsibility. Or, then again, you might embrace it. 'In other cases', Derrida continues, '[quotation] is the contrary' (Derrida 1989b, p. 865). The experience may be sublime; for Barthes, '[b]oredom is not far from bliss' (Barthes 1990b, p. 26)).

'All the way to writing' also challenges us. As I mentioned earlier, Wood's essay frames for us its many failures, announcing 'I don't seem to have started', 'something hasn't happened' and 'something has not happened' (Wood 2007, pp. 138, 141). The difficulty Wood declares is patterned, too, in its very structure. After introducing Derrida's *jusqu'à l'écriture*, Wood's essay announces 'Donald Rumsfeld won an award'. Specifically, it turns out, Rumsfeld has won the Plain English Campaign's 'Foot in Mouth' trophy. Wood quotes Rumsfeld's 'winning' comment but begs '[p]lease don't think that I am about to interpret this' before pointing out 'I don't seem to have started . . . While you wait for me to arrive, here's Jean-Luc Nancy' (p. 138). Wood's essay appears equally disinclined to interpret Nancy; instead, it declares 'I have just quoted Jean Luc-Nancy. Quotation is itself a way of saying something hasn't happened' (p. 138).

Wood's text repeatedly re-starts itself (for reasons that I hope will become clear, my chapter will, in its following paragraphs, enact a similar pattern). It represents this fact visually, dividing itself into sections separated by • • •. One of the sections of the essay contains only one sentence; it states, in its entirety, '[t]he distance the words must cross begins by not existing' (p. 140). The essay proceeds impatiently; it introduces an idea but soon abandons it, moving onto a new suggestion, as if lacking faith in its own project and disconcerted by its repeated failures.

It might look as though it is 'merely lashing about' (Wood 2006, p. 52). The repeated 'cutting short' of 'All the way to writing' leaves us with the impression that it is thoroughly thwarted and close to despair. Wood tells us, however, that her essay is 'content to hear what's understood, what's wanted, what matters most, get away. You don't write looking up to see what you have done' (Wood 2007, p. 139). The essay celebrates its cutting short and does not mind that it has failed to go 'all the way to writing'. It realizes that writing is neither a '[form] of production' nor 'reducible to knowledge'. Wood therefore informs us that '[i]f you want to get to writing, you have to go about things a bit differently. You have to work with the openings, hollows and punctures that writing offers' (p. 138). The 'openings, hollows and punctures' of writing refuse to let it be known; we may, however, use these very impossibilities. By allowing writing to get away, Wood suggests that her text opens new and different possibilities. Wood announces that '[s]yncope, cutting short, contraction, condensation, editing, even the elision of a syllable from a word, can always be read as the promise that restarts what it thwarts' (Wood 2006, p. 52).

Reading Wood's essay is a disorienting experience, as my summary in the preceding paragraph aims to suggest. 'All the way to writing' forces us repeatedly to re-situate ourselves; we are not allowed to settle. Wood's essays disconcert their readers in other ways too. They change register suddenly from, for example, a lengthy and dense quotation of Freud to a breezy and colloquial 'I couldn't say' (Wood 2006, p. 48). They are, moreover, littered with 'shards of words and splinter letters' and the 'heaping and heaving of silent sounds' (Wood 2007, pp. 140–1). Wood announces 'Ango. Meditango. It's spoken to me, this harmless worm or wordbit, as if ça me dit, as if "it speaks" as if the id were writing, speaking and speaking to me here, in me, a French-speaking id or il or elle or eel me dit' (Wood 2006, p. 51). Displaying a 'tendency to play with sound', Wood's essays are, as the incongruous eel at the end of the sentence suggests, never far from a 'collapse into syllarubble' ('syllarubble', making rubble of the word syllable, performs that which it conjures) (Wood 2007, p. 141).

Wood's work thus 'counteracts certain inevitable contractual obligations' (Wood 2006, p. 54). The essay behaves like the 'glass worm' I mentioned earlier. No matter how 'hungrily' we read it, we are denied its 'concluding part'; it presents us with '[t]hought-excrement, fractured suffix, God knows what, remains' (p. 50). The text breaks, and gets away from us. It leaves us holding only the 'snapped-off syllable' of a thought. We could easily become frustrated and despondent. Wood, however, wonders if 'perhaps' these remains are 'a gift'; we might read them as a present kindly given (p. 52).

The essay breaks away, seeming to free itself from its 'contractual obligations'. We might therefore think that we, too, are freed. However, we do not necessarily find that this is the case. We might discover instead that we are 'caught up, tangled up, complicated, precisely by what cuts us loose' (p. 52). We, as readers, find ourselves working to broach the essay's gaps; we assume that there is, in fact, a logic behind them, if only we could work out what it is. Wood's essay halts writing in order to get reading going. The gaps invite us to read all the more thoroughly; we realize that we must piece together the essay's writing.

Wood's essay fails to capture the movements of writing so that they might be restarted elsewhere. This scheme, in which 'you stop it to set it going', is, however, risky. It would be easy enough to miss what happens here. The text itself keeps going 'as if nothing had happened, as one always continues, right up to the end, as if nothing had happened, that's what continuing is . . .' (p. 56). Writing must continue, leaving its reader to notice what has or has not happened. S/he might, of course, simply follow, blindly, 'to the end'. His/her attention cannot be guaranteed. Writing depends upon a certain readerly patience and cooperation, a 'kind of critical attention [which] will never simply be likely or possible' (Wood 2007, p. 137).

I began my chapter by invoking dissatisfaction with the philosophical and the way in which criticism traditionally privileges it. Derrida also challenges us to rethink criticism's language; he declares that

> [e]mancipation from this language must be attempted. But not as an *attempt* at emancipation from it, for this is impossible unless we forget *our* history. Rather, as the dream of emancipation. Nor as emancipation from it, which would be meaningless and deprive us from the light of meaning. Rather, as resistance to it, as far as is possible (Derrida 1978a, p. 28; italics in original).

We cannot reject the language of criticism for another; such a gesture is neither possible nor desirable. Instead, we must pursue the 'dream' of an inevitably failed attempt at 'emancipation'. Derrida and Wood invoke 'writing' as this already-failed attempt. As I have shown, writing is by no means self-evident; it cannot be simply captured. By exhorting us to go 'all the way to writing' they propose a more writing-centred mode of criticism knowing that the movements of writing do not present a simple or attainable alternative. We must engage ourselves in a writing always already conscious of its impossibility. It is fundamental to keep the movement of writing open; the writing Derrida and Wood laud must remain a productive dilemma with which we are never yet finished.

The texts I have examined here attempt to isolate a moment of writing, referring to acts of composition and claiming to tell the truth of the process from which they originate. However, this origin cannot be grasped; it cannot be separated from the product it composes. We repeatedly read writing's presence as past. Equally, however, no product can deny its production. Even if we do not grasp composition, we 'glimpse' it. And as we do so, our position is thrown into relief; the moment of reading becomes apparent. Our inability to read the moment of writing is not a failure, but a telling inevitability which reveals the very condition of a writing whose movements remain always to be read.

Or, to put it differently: my chapter began, fascinated by what it might mean to be in the process of writing. At its inception, it glimpsed composition's trial and error as a writing whose movements remained. It thus set out in pursuit of writing, but never caught up with it; we repeatedly read writing's presence as past. However, the passage we cannot capture 'luckily, leaves traces' (Cixous 1998, p. 144). Wood declares that '[p]oetic writing brings the most surprising news: what we can't see and what can't be told' (Wood 2007, p. 139). These writings do not simply fail to 'tell' us about writing but 'bring the news' of what we can't be told: writing's movements always remain to be read.

Or: we began with the promise of a literary criticism, glimpsed in Wood and Cixous' essays, which, offering itself as an alternative to the composed and finished pretences of philosophical texts, would not 'hypostatize' the movements of writing. But we must not be too hasty to laud Wood and Cixous' success. To read their essays as texts that definitively move writing would be to 'hypostatize' them once more. We might do best to voice our claims for their writing in tentative terms. We must continue to read them as 'compromise-formation[s]', which, unable to achieve their aim, await further (readerly) negotiations (Wood 2006, p. 53). There is no 'concluding part' – '[o]ne could tell this over and over' (Wood 2007, p. 146).

Traces

Writing, or composition, leaves only traces; I may trace, but cannot capture it. But what is the trace? What does it mean to trace? This chapter considers the trace in its own right; it is provoked by a novelistic trend Philip Hensher identifies in an article entitled 'Short and curlies' in which he groups Tim Winton's *The Turning*, David Mitchell's *Ghostwritten* and *Cloud Atlas* and Ali Smith's *Hotel World*. My chapter will add to the above list Toni Morrison's *Paradise*, Smith's *The Accidental* and J. M. Coetzee's *Foe*.[1] All of these books appear initially to be collections of short stories; they are formed by apparently discrete sections. Smith's *Hotel World,* Mitchell's *Cloud Atlas* and *Ghostwritten*, for example, contain six, six and nine sections, respectively, each narrated by a different character.

Soon, however, we begin to notice that the individual narratives are subtly interconnected. One of the stories in *The Turning*, 'Abbreviation', narrates Vic's encounter with Melanie, a girl with 'a finger missing' whom he meets – and by whom he is subsequently kissed – when thirteen and on holiday (Winton 2005, p. 25). The episode recurs in a later story, 'Damaged goods':

> Vic's first love was also older – in fact, quite a lot older – a farm girl whose ring finger ended at the first joint, the result of an accident with a hay baler. The finger that her wedding ring would have to slide on to ended in a stump. At thirteen he was enchanted. By the finger as much as by the girl herself. His first kiss. She let him touch her breasts. It only happened the once – the whole thing lasted less than a day, a holiday encounter – but the strange excitement lingered (p. 58).

The story is re-told by Vic's wife who situates the tale against that of 'Strawberry Alison', another 'damaged specimen' who '[caught] his imagination' and who, in turn, reappears in 'Long, clear view': '[f]or the school social you gargle with Listerine, spray your hair with VO-5 and try to work up the guts to speak to the girl with the spoiled face, the one you haven't stopped thinking about for weeks' (pp. 58, 194). The stories intersect; the book gradually, through a series of brief instances, builds up a substantial narrative of Vic's life. Hensher explains that 'the stories coalesce into a single main narrative and numerous subordinate ones' (Hensher 2005).[2]

Equally, the first section of Morrison's *Paradise* recalls a massacre at a Convent just outside a town called Ruby. The account that follows, entitled 'Mavis', offers a seemingly unrelated narrative in which a woman flees her violent husband. Eventually, however, '[w]hen the road ran out of trees, she saw ahead to the left a house' (Morrison 1999, p. 37). Mavis arrives at the convent of the novel's first pages. This pattern is repeated; in each section the novel introduces a new character who finally ends up at the house outside Ruby. Some, like Grace, arrive brazenly – '"Hi." She cracked her gum like a professional. "Is this Ruby? Bus driver said this was it"' – and others more mysteriously: '[t]hey moved this way for more than a mile. The walker going somewhere; the hitcher going anywhere. The wraith and her shadow . . . By the time they saw the Convent Sweetie was cozy' (pp. 55, 126–9). The Convent – and its never entirely forgotten tragedy – forms a centre to which each account is drawn: 'Mavis Albright left the Convent off and on, but she always returned, so she was there in 1976' (p. 49). The novel's 'variety of subplots' come together in a process Kubitschek finds 'dizzying' (Kubitschek 1998, p. 164).

Hensher is similarly disoriented; he describes *The Turning* as 'a fairly disconcerting experience' and 'an unfamiliar new animal'. He suggests that it 'starts to look like a new form altogether'. He argues, specifically, that 'the distinction between novels and short stories is becoming blurred' (Hensher 2005).[3] The critics of these novels concur; they are uncertain as to how best to classify these works: Are they novels? Or short stories? Anderson points out that when Mitchell's 'first book, *Ghostwritten*, was published, critics were undecided whether it was a novel or a collection of short stories' (Anderson 2004). Poole claims, similarly, that *Ghostwritten* 'left some wondering how much of a novel it was' (Poole 2001).

Sophie Ratcliffe suggests that *The Accidental* is 'a work that explores the very idea of a novel as a contained form'. For Ratcliffe, Smith's work displays a discomfort with its novelistic status: 'Smith's parodic, patterned deliberacy reveals her suspicion of the ways in which the novel, in its attempt to comprehend or express the problem of particularity, might, accidentally, swamp the instances that it is trying to preserve' (Ratcliffe 2005, pp. 19–20). For Ratcliffe, *The Accidental* incorporates short-story-like qualities in order to overcome the imperfections of the novel. Skidelsky, writing about Winton's work, identifies a similar discontent. In this instance, however, it lies in the opposite direction; for Winton, he claims, the short story is inadequate: '[i]n his novels, Winton has long been concerned to connect people and events in subtle and complicated ways, and short stories present an obvious difficulty for him, which he perhaps tries to solve here by establishing links between the tales' (Skidelksy 2005, p. 21). All of these comments display a similar realization that, ultimately, these texts are properly neither novels nor short stories; they do not fit neatly into the categories available to us.[4]

These works resist easy categorization; they are not easily understood. *Paradise* offers us a series of 'partial testimonies', which, as Stephane Robolin explains, 'trace out deeply disturbing contours of an atrocity' (Robolin 2006, p. 313). The novel's main 'atrocity' is not instantly accessible; it is 'traced out' for us to piece together. Critics of these works stress their fragmentary nature; the 'main narrative' of *The Turning* is, for Hensher 'told in fragments, often inconclusively, through distinct short stories out of chronological order' (Hensher 2005). Eleanor Birne suggests that Smith's novels are 'made up of incomplete fragments; different points of view' and that in *The Accidental* 'things do not progress neatly; they circle and return' (Birne 2005, p. 31).[5] Ratcliffe describes *The Accidental* as an 'allusive, ambitious and formally acrobatic work' (Ratcliffe 2005, p. 19). These critics all draw attention to the fact that these texts are constructed via echo, repetition and changes in perspective; they play with and subject us to the trace.

As they do so, two inflections of the trace emerge. As my chapter will show, the trace functions, on the one hand, and as I will demonstrate in my first section, as a marker of absence, as the uncanny remainder left over by any echo or repetition. Alternatively, as I will explore in my second section, it prompts a desire, which Derrida might call 'archive fever', to gather and to collect (Derrida 1996). In this case, it is adopted as a mark of presence. The trace thus sets us in pursuit of two contradictory spectres. It prompts us to read in two very different ways; on the one hand, it prompts us to give ourselves over to dizziness; on the other, it spurs us to hoard and to control. This is not to say, as de Man stresses, that 'the [text] simply has two meanings which exist side by side'. Rather, '[t]he two readings have to engage each other in direct confrontation, for the one reading is precisely the error denounced by the other and has to be undone by it' (de Man 1979, p. 12). Each inflection threatens to undo the other; we find that neither of these possibilities can quite exclude its opposite. At the end of my first section, presence intrudes; the project prompted by the absent-trace fails. Similarly, in my second section, absence haunts the impulse engendered by the trace-as-presence. The presence and the absence the trace conjures alike remain elusive. My third section therefore proposes that we must work with the inseparability of the trace's two senses and wonders how we might better inscribe it – and our encounters with it in these texts – in light of their dependency.

Uncanny echoes

The 'Hong Kong' section of Mitchell's *Ghostwritten* narrates the disastrous day of a British businessman who is recently estranged from his wife, has sex with his cleaner and lives with a ghost. At the end of the section, he dies:

> Now I understand what this insane fucking day has been about!
> Hilarious!
> I am fucking dying (Mitchell 1999, p. 108).

This narrative is not, however, wholly confined to the work's 'Hong Kong' section; elements of it recur in the text's other accounts. The cleaner reappears in 'Holy Mountain' as the protagonist's daughter; she writes to say "'[m]y employer died. A foreigner, a lawyer with a big company, he was extremely wealthy. He was very generous to me in his will'" (p. 151). The businessman's wife also shows up elsewhere. She is, it transpires, the Katy Forbes next to whom Marco wakes up in 'London'; asked about her husband, Katy remarks "'[w]e separated, then he went and died'" (p. 268). Mo in 'Clear Island' witnesses and re-narrates his death; she comments that "'[t]he peculiar thing was, he seemed to be laughing'" (p. 364). And, finally (I think – there's always a chance there's yet another link that I've missed), Tim Cavendish in 'London' receives a phone call telling him that the company formerly belonging to his brother (whom we assume to be the same Hong Kong businessman) has gone bust (p. 303). The businessman is not the only character to reappear in this way; repeatedly, as Hensher writes, 'a central drama' in *Ghostwritten* 'turns, in the next episode, into a casual mention' (Hensher 2005).

In Smith's *Hotel World*, too, protagonists from one section appear again as minor characters in another. The main character in 'Present historic', a homeless woman called Else, is offered a room in a hotel by one of its employees. The employee who performs this act of benevolence features at the centre of the novel's next account, 'Future conditional'. Both characters notice her name badge:

> Else sees that she's wearing a badge with four letters on it. L.I.S.E. She wonders what it's short for (Smith 2002, p. 70).

> She looks down at her Name Badge, LISE backwards upside down (p. 101).

Else also reappears; she returns yet again in the 'Perfect' section of the novel when she is met by its protagonist, Penny, who describes her as 'one of the most interesting people she'd met in a long time' despite mistaking her for 'some kind of druggy eccentric guest or maybe even a minor ex-rock star' (p. 139). The protagonist from one account returns unexpectedly in others.

The plot of *The Accidental* builds in a similar manner; a casual remark made in one section returns as a more substantial episode later. Magnus, for example, notes that 'Amber is doing something to his mother's knee', but it is not until Eve's section that the novel elucidates: '[Amber] had come across the room and knelt down in front of Eve. Now she was holding Eve's knee with both her hands and pressing the muscles round it with her thumbs' (Smith 2005, pp. 149–50, 192). Again, the novel returns to the event we glimpsed – and perhaps barely registered – earlier in order to explain it more fully.

In all three of these novels we encounter in one section an echo of a previous instant or event from another. However, not all of the echoes we encounter in these works are major or integral to the main plot; there are inconsequential and subtle ones, too. Although I will consider the inconsequential echo more thoroughly later, it suffices to point out here that a comet-shaped birthmark appears in each of *Cloud Atlas*'s sections without any real explanation (Mitchell 2004, pp. 85, 122, 124, 204–5, 319, 324, 361). Similarly, in *The Turning* the narrator of 'Aquifer' tells us 'I was there when two-year-old Charlie lurched up between his father's legs and lost some toes in a bright pink blur' (Winton 2005, p. 42). The incident echoes Melanie's amputated finger but in fact bears no substantial relation to the narrative in which it appears. Equally, in both the 'Hong Kong' and 'London' sections of *Ghostwritten*, a coffee machine overflows because 'I'd used two filters instead of one' (Mitchell 1999, pp. 70, 288).

There is no obvious reason or explanation for these repetitions; Hensher therefore claims that Mitchell's work is marked by 'unsuspected connections' and 'remote, powerful influences' (Hensher 2005). Mo informs us in 'Clear Island' that '[p]henomena are interconnected regardless of distance, in a holistic ocean more voodoo than Newton' (Mitchell 1999, p. 375). Mo's invocation of 'voodoo' and a 'holistic ocean' presents the work's interconnections as a mysterious and unaccountable phenomenon. This description is echoed in the critical responses to these fictions. Akoma claims that Morrison 'directs her artistic vision to the unknown quality in African American experience' and towards 'the "trick" of life that defies any unitary narrative' (Akoma 2000, p. 23). For Akoma, *Paradise* refuses unity in order to capture the 'unknown' and that which defies explanation. Ruth Scurr celebrates *Hotel World* as 'fragmented, tenuous, allusive, sparse' and the lives it depicts as 'shadowy' (Scurr 2001, p. 7). Poole views Mitchell's novels as 'spectral patterns interleaved, ripples interpenetrating in a pond' (Poole 2001). The 'fragile chains of narrative connections between distinct stories' are, for Hensher, a 'haunting idea' (Hensher 2005). These 'spectral patterns' and 'ghostings' are identified once again, and explained more fully, by Griffiths; he notes the 'residual flickering of events as traces in the narrative system' of *Ghostwritten* and explains that 'although the one narrative is not wholly present in the other, it is on the fringe of becoming, for the structure of the narrative implies what has been narrated before (or after)' (Griffiths 2004, p. 84).

All of these responses are marked by a vocabulary of spectrality and partial presence. Griffiths' 'fringe of becoming', in particular, conjures a troubling sense of semi-absence, a never-quite-grasped echo by which novel and reader are haunted; these texts offer us what *The Biographer's Tale* calls 'a kind of ghostwriting, a ghost of writing' (Byatt 2001, p. 257). The very title of Smith's *The Accidental* explicitly signals this relation to the non-essential and non-substantial, especially if we consider it in its Aristotelian sense. Aristotle opposes the 'accidental' to the 'substantial'; he uses the term in order to designate the qualities of an object which do not affect its essence.

The interconnections of these works invoke, for their critics, absence, the spooky and the uncertain; they dizzy and disorient us. They conjure a 'non-sense or insignificance', which, as Derrida points out in 'My chances', 'we frequently associate with chance' (Derrida 2007b, p. 348). Derrida points out that chance is inseparable from the idea of anticipation. Chance is 'exactly what thwarts or undoes our *anticipation*' (Derrida 2007b, p. 348; italics in original). He therefore explains that '[t]o attempt to think chance would be in the first place to interest oneself in the *experience* (I emphasize this word) of what happens unforeseeably' (p. 349; italics in original).

The traces of these novels invoke notions of coincidence and contingency. Ratcliffe describes *The Accidental* as a 'novel about contingency and accidents' (Ratcliffe 2005, p. 19). Anderson claims of *Cloud Atlas* that 'serendipities and coincidences ghost Mitchell's sextet' as well as 'more tangible, equally thrilling connections' (Anderson 2004). Derrida frames his essay in this way; he does not only speak of chance, but also informs us that the analyses he performs, and the texts of which he writes, are the result of a series of 'lucky finds' (Derrida 2007b, p. 358). He claims that his essay is itself the product of chance.

Mitchell's novels are, however, quick to remind us that these 'coincidences' are not in fact coincidental. Marco invokes the dilemma of fate and chance and asks, with a great deal of irony,

> does chance or fate control our lives? Well, the answer is as relative as time. If you're in your life, chance. Viewed from the outside, like a book you're reading, it's fate all the way.
>
> Now I don't know about you, but my life is a well and I'm right down there in it (Mitchell 1999, p. 292).

Marco attributes the problem to a question of perspective and chance triumphs; it's obvious that his 'life is a well' and that he is 'right down there in it'. His conspiratorial 'I don't know about you' implies that we will agree. However, Marco's allusion to 'a book you're reading' undoes the statement it precedes. His privileging of chance is, within the context of the novel, somewhat disingenuous; Marco's chance is 'viewed', by the reader and by the book's author, 'from the outside'.

The reappearances and traces of the novel are very much 'fated'. The novel, and its chance encounters, is the product of a design laid out in advance. The novel accedes to this fact when Marco announces '[t]his all seemed choreographed' (p. 315). Equally, when Timothy Cavendish reads the manuscript of 'Half-Lives' he tells us that '[o]ne or two things will have to go: the insinuation that Luisa Rey is this Robert Frobisher chap reincarnated, for example. Far too hippie-druggie-new age. (I, too, have a birthmark, below my left armpit, but no lover ever compared it to a comet. Georgette nicknamed it Timbo's Turd)' (Mitchell 2004, p. 373). Cavendish disparages 'backflashes, foreshadowings and tricksy devices' as tropes which 'belong in the 1980s with MAs in Postmodernism and Chaos Theory' (p. 152).[6] These comments are clearly pertinent to the novel as a whole; Cavendish invites us to view its interconnections critically and to dismiss them as cheap novelistic tricks. The very fact that, for Cavendish, these things can 'go' reminds us that they are the result of authorial, or editorial, decision.

That which is privileged by critics as fleeting and inessential is, paradoxically, the result of a highly structured and carefully constructed mode of writing. Anderson admits realistically that, in *Cloud Atlas,* 'no detail seems accidental, no turn of phrase incidental' (Anderson 2004). The moments we privilege as odd and uncanny are in fact the result of a fastidious authorial design. Thought in this way, *Cloud Atlas* is not so much a novel which conjures the world's mysterious interrelation as a book in which all accident and coincidence has been effaced.

Derrida makes a similar point in relation to 'My chances'. Although he informs us early on that his essay is constructed by a series of 'lucky finds', he later admits that '[i]t would be possible to demonstrate that there is nothing random in the links formed by my lucky finds. An implacable program is imposed by the contextual necessity that requires one to isolate [*découper*] solid sequences (stereonomy), cross and adjust subsets, mingle voices and proper names and accelerate a rhythm, which merely gives the *feeling* of randomness to whoever does not know the prescription' (Derrida 2007b, p. 358; italics in original). There is, Derrida concedes, an 'implacable programme' and 'prescription' at work; his essay has the '*feeling*' of randomness but is not truly random.

Although these novels appear to capture chance, the coincidental and the inessential, their attempt is undermined. The structure of the novel, and the decided inclusion of supposedly 'chancey' traces, compromises the very coincidental quality it wishes to attain. The trace's determined inscription undermines its quality. The traces in these novels carry the force of chance, but are clearly not chance or the inessential *tout court*. Blanchot, in *The Infinite Conversation*, admits that those who wish to theorize the trace are faced with an insurmountable dilemma. *The Infinite Conversation* chases notions such as the impossible and the inessential. It discovers repeatedly, however, that, in their inscription, these strange terms become 'petrified in a watchword' (Blanchot 1993, p. 23). In his book *Equals*, Adam Phillips explains that 'we may wonder now what hope there is for the strange, the weird or the uncanny if we think we know what these words are referring to . . . Strange, weird and uncanny, that is to say, are words peculiarly undone by definition. If they say what they mean, what could they possibly mean?' (Phillip. 2002, p. 116)

Phillips makes it clear that we use these words – strange, weird, uncanny and trace – to conjure that which resists name or explanation. Yet every word fails; there could be none that did not name or explain. Cavendish, in *Cloud Atlas*, points to a similar disjunction between the uncanny and language; he writes that '[s]ometimes the fluffy bunny of incredulity zooms round the bend so rapidly that the greyhound of language is left, agog, in the starting cage' (Mitchell 2004, p. 170). Cavendish's metaphor is bizarre; the notion of a 'greyhound of language' itself provokes incredulity. However, this comic statement also conveys a more serious point; for Cavendish, incredulity (at the uncanny) leaves language behind. It would thus, we infer, be disingenuous to re-appropriate it linguistically.[7] Blanchot writes that 'instead of leaving the empty part empty, one can name it and, in a word, fill it by obscuring it with the strongest, the most august and most opaque name that can be found' (Blanchot 1993, p. 119). By presenting the trace, by returning our incredulity to language, we betray the very inessentiality which intrigues. In the very act of labelling and fixing moments such as those we encounter in these novels as traces (or with any other classification, for that matter) we risk their uncanny quality.

Phillips concludes that our 'usage' of these words 'can never be unknowing enough. As words they may be more like gasps or exclamations. It is as though these are the words that have to be taken on their own terms, or as their own terms. Words to refer to things that words can't refer to; words that refer to other words, but only disingenuously' (Phillip. 2002, p. 116). Blanchot explains similarly that 'if the thought of the impossible were entertained, it would be a kind of reserve in thought itself, a thought not allowing itself to be thought in the mode of appropriative comprehension. This is a dangerous direction, and a strange thought' (Blanchot 1993, p. 43). To properly think the trace, we must, for Blanchot, manage not to think it; we must avoid 'appropriative comprehension'. The trace, if it is to retain its status *as* trace, bears only tracing; we must offer it without asserting it. We would need an entirely un-word-like word, a name about whose naming abilities we remained uncertain.[8]

Phillips encourages us to think 'strange', 'weird' and 'uncanny' in this less name-like manner when he suggests that we read them as 'gasps or exclamations'. Such a shift is legible, too, in Hensher's article. At its end, Hensher, having grouped these novels by their common structure, announces '[n]ow, all we need is a name for it' (Hensher 2005). We can, however, also read in his article a reluctance to name the strange trope it has identified. It declares, twice, that we need a new name; in addition to the conclusion I have cited already, it decides, earlier, '[w]e almost need a new word' (Hensher 2005). Yet it does not provide one. The *need* for a name is thus unresolved and becomes itself a disconcerting trace within the article.

However, this reading leaves us with yet another 'strange thought'. I believe I have identified a trace in Hensher's article, but perhaps, in naming it, I have 'petrified' this movement too. I believe I have identified a trace but perhaps, by labelling it, I have once again compromised its moment. How might we guarantee that its strangeness remains open? We cannot. The demand is impossible, failure inevitable. Blanchot suggests that '[f]orgetting this non-thought might be the most appropriate measure' and proposes '[l]et us forget it, then, so as to remember it only through forgetting' (Blanchot 1993, p. 119). And so we shall, moving instead in the next section to a very different sense of the trace. But the question of memory will never be far away – I will return to it more explicitly in my final section – and the sense of strangeness will no doubt return.

Gathering and synchrony

Derrida, in *Of Grammatology,* outlines a concept, borrowed from Rousseau, which he labels the 'supplement' and which is, in many respects, identical to the notion my chapter calls the trace. Derrida formalizes the sense we get in the above section of the trace as uncanny when he writes that 'the supplement supplements. It adds only to replace. It intervenes or insinuates itself *in-the-place-of;* if it fills, it is as if one fills a void . . . As substitute, it is not simply added to the positivity of a presence, it produces no relief, its place is assigned in the structure by the mark of an emptiness' (Derrida 1997b, p. 145; italics in original). He admits, however, that the supplement 'harbours within itself two significations whose cohabitation is as strange as it is necessary' (p. 144). We have already, in the final paragraphs of the preceding section, begun to glimpse such a contradiction. Derrida glosses the second sense thus: '[t]he supplement adds itself, it is a surplus, a plenitude enriching another plenitude, the *fullest measure* of presence. It cumulates and accumulates presence' (p. 144; italics in original). In addition and in contrast to the impulse already outlined, the trace impels us towards a project preoccupied with presence – a project of gathering and archiving, which I will consider more fully in my next section. It will soon return us, however, to a sense of trace-as-absence; the project fails, bringing us back to the trace's other inflection. The trace is notable in both cases because of what it claims to, but cannot, do. Neither signification can be separated from the other, as Derrida points out; the trace is marked by a double movement. My chapter's third section will attempt to think these two significations together in order to more accurately trace the uncanny moments with which these novels present us.

For academics in particular but, I suspect, for other readers too, the impulse when reading these novels is to make a list of all the connections, to collect them together.[9] They provoke a project of 'gathering and synchrony' you may have noticed in my previous analyses, whose imperative, as Levinas writes, is to '[l]eave nothing lying around! Let nothing be lost!' (Levinas 1991, p. 4) We are gripped by what Derrida calls 'archive fever'. We begin, when we first read works such as Mitchell's *Ghostwritten,* to notice the novels' many connections. We note them (either mentally or on paper); a list starts to form. The list becomes a challenge; we read wishing to record *all* of the novel's correspondences. Our reading is driven by a 'highly compelling tracing and exposure project', which Sedgwick aligns with a paranoid stance (Sedgwick 2003, p. 124). Clare Birchall, in her analysis of conspiracy theory, quotes Jodi Dean in order to point out that conspiracy-thinking – like the fervent search these fictions provoke – is characterized by a belief that "'things are not what they seem and everything is connected'" (Birchall 2006, p. 34).

We begin to note the connections in Mitchell's work, but soon realize, however, that we do not (and could not) account for all of them in a single reading. These are what Calinescu calls 'rereadable' texts; he declares that 'texts containing regularities (regularities worth discovering) and strategic possibilities invisible to the eye of the naïve reader are rereadable texts' (Calinescu 1993, p. 153). Calinescu continues, 'rereading and the characteristic absorption that accompanies it strive for an interpretation of the text in terms of a complete hermeneutic system in which the significance of each part is seen in the light of the whole and that of the whole in the light of each part' (p. 168).[10] Griffiths points out, for example, that *Ghostwritten*'s 'circular structure constitutes the text's invitation to the reader to reread the novel and to revise the virtual text now in place' (Griffiths 2004, p. 97).

Desperate to piece together their 'complete hermeneutic system', we are prompted to re-read these books. Mitchell's *Cloud Atlas* thematizes such a process. The first section of the novel, 'The Pacific journal' ends mid-sentence and the next section, 'Letters from Zedelghem', begins. This narrative appears entirely unrelated to the first until in one letter, Robert Frobisher writes:

> Poking through an alcove of books in my room I came across a curious dismembered volume, and I want you to track down a complete copy for me. It begins on the 99th page, its covers are gone, its binding unstitched. From what little I can glean, it's the edited journal of a voyage from Sydney to California by a notary of San Francisco named Adam Ewing [. . .] The journal seems to be published posthumously, by Ewing's son (?) (Mitchell 2004, p. 64)

'The Pacific journal' resurfaces in the apparently unrelated account by which it is interrupted. As it does so, Frobisher offers an alternative perspective on the novel's previous account; he revises what we have already read. The pattern continues; each of the novel's texts is read or viewed in the section by which it is followed. In 'An orison of Somni~451', for example, the novel's previous section, 'The ghastly ordeal of Timothy Cavendish' reappears as a film 'made before the foundation of Nea So Copros in a long-deadlanded province of the abortive European democracy' (p. 243).

In Coetzee's *Foe*, too, the text we read in one section of the novel reappears in that which follows; Dominic Head describes the novel as a 'densely allusive work which insists on the primacy of textuality' (Head 1997, p. 115). We find, in the novel's first section, a narrative in which a man, Cruso, is stranded on an island with his servant, Friday, and a woman, Susan Barton. In the second section, the narrative shifts to London. Soon, however, Susan refers to the narrative we read previously; she writes to Foe in order to tell him "'I have set down the history of our time on the island as well as I can, and enclose it herewith. It is a sorry, limping affair (the history, not the time itself) – 'the next day', its refrain goes, 'the next day . . . the next day' – but you will know how to set it right'" (Coetzee 1987, p. 47). The novel's first section is reframed as Susan's unsuccessful attempt to record 'the history of our time on the island'. We are invited to reread it as 'sorry' and 'limping'. In the third section the perspective shifts once more. Again, however, the text we read in the second section resurfaces: "'(I wrote you letters on the Bristol road, I have them with me, I will give them to you)'" (p. 114). The text of the previous section becomes an object to be read in the subsequent one.

The patterns established by both *Cloud Atlas* and *Foe* could, we realize, continue indefinitely; given that each of the novel's sections provokes another, the novel might potentially never end. However, they do of course contain a finite number of sections; 'Sloosha's crossin'' – the 'last', most central section of *Cloud Atlas* – is allowed to conclude, provoking the return, and subsequent completion, of each of the novel's previous texts. The novel itself alludes to the complex structure which results when, in 'Letters from Zedelghem', Frobisher describes the sextet he has composed: '[i]n the 1st set, each solo is interrupted by its successor: in the 2nd, each interruption is recontinued, in order' (Mitchell 2004, p. 463).

Even at the end of 'Sloosha's crossin'', however, a voice interrupts Zachry's narrative to announce that 'Zachry my old pa was a wyrd buggah, I won't naysay it now he's died' (p. 324). Zachry's son intrudes in order to 'read' the section's narrator and to offer an interpretation of the narrative we have just read. Although the novel refrains from dedicating a further section to his reading, 'Sloosha's crossin'' alludes to the reader 'behind' the text. The novel indicates the arbitrary imposition of its conclusion; it signals its infinite regression even at its limit.

Cloud Atlas thus flags re-reading's potentially infinite nature.[11] I quoted earlier Griffith's claim that *Ghostwritten* invites re-reading. Griffiths adds that the 'conglomerate of virtual chapters' in *Ghostwritten* '[creates] a potential virtual text. This virtual text is dynamic in the sense that it is never completed but always open to revision as new input is continually injected to enrich the virtual dimension' (Griffiths 2004, p. 97). The re-reading to which our 'archive fever' sets us is 'never completed'; it does not end. We re-read the text; this second reading provokes, however, more echoes and repetitions; it thus demands yet another reading, which will again discover more traces. It is always possible to read the text again and therefore to notice further connections. There might always be one more reading and one more previously unrecorded correspondence. The text cannot be wholly determined. We realize that the archive will never be complete. Derrida points out that '[o]ne will never be able to objectivize [the archive] with no remainder. The archivist produces more archive, and that is why the archive is never closed. It opens out of the future' (Derrida 1996, p. 68). The present archive is inadequate and looks to a completion, which is always deferred. Derrida therefore admits that 'if we want to know what' the archive 'will have meant, we will only know in times to come. Perhaps' (p. 36). The archive is never present.

Our conspiracy-driven 'archive fever' provokes an excessive and potentially endless reading; 'over interpretation' and 'conspiracy theory' are, Birchall points out, closely bound (Birchall 2006, p. 75). The inevitably infinite nature of the project is recognized, too, in the analysis Sedgwick offers of paranoia. Sedgwick notes that '*you can never be paranoid enough*' (Sedgwick 2003, p. 142; italics in original). There is no end to paranoid thought. Both Sedgwick and Birchall signal this aspect of paranoia through their choice of titles. Sedgwick subtitles her essay 'you're so paranoid, you probably think this essay is about you' (alluding to a Carly Simon song) while Birchall heads one of her chapters 'just because you're not paranoid, doesn't mean they're not out to get you'. The thought of conspiracy informs us that we do not know what we think we know or that what we think we know is wrong. Conspiracy theories attempt to tell us this; they offer an alternative knowledge. However, their very premise threatens to thwart this corrective move. The knowledge they offer is vulnerable, too, to a paranoid reading, as Sedgwick and Birchall's titles show. Birchall explains that 'conspiracy *theory* can suggest that all knowledge is only ever "theory"' (Birchall 2006, p. 73; italics in original). Paranoia is all-encompassing. The thought that inspires conspiracy reading does not go away, but undermines the 'corrective' interpretation offered.

The archive is subject to a similar disturbance. Susan, in Coetzee's *Foe,* is rendered anxious by the realization that '"surely, with every day that passes, our memories grow less certain, as even a statue in marble is worn away by rain, till at last we can no longer tell what shape the sculptor's hand gave it"'. She therefore presses Cruso to compose a written record of his time on the island: '"Is it not possible to manufacture paper and ink and set down what traces remain of these memories, so that they will outlive you; or, failing paper and ink, to burn the story upon wood, or engrave it upon rock?"' Despite Susan's plea, Cruso, however, '"was unmoved. 'Nothing is forgotten,' said he; and then: 'Nothing I have forgotten is worth the remembering"". Cruso's dismissal renders Susan desperate: ""'You are mistaken!' I cried. 'I do not wish to dispute, but you have forgotten much, and with every day that passes you forget more!'"" (Coetzee 1987, p. 17)

Although Cruso at first declares that 'nothing is forgotten' he quickly revises his statement in order to announce more moderately that nothing he has forgotten is 'worth the remembering'. The alteration implies, somewhat aptly, that he has initially forgotten even that forgetfulness is possible. Ultimately, both Susan and Cruso acknowledge that forgetfulness is inevitable. For Susan it is therefore necessary that Cruso preserve his story in some way. We must find a way to store or to record our memories if they are to last. We are, as Derrida writes, *'en mal d'archive*: in need of archives' *because* forgetfulness – and absence – are possible (Derrida 1996, p. 91; italics in original).

Derrida points out that '[t]here would indeed be no archive desire without the radical finitude, without the possibility of a forgetfulness which does not limit itself to repression' (p. 19). A perceived absence causes us to search fervently for the completed archive, for presence. The archive is conditioned by the forgetfulness it would deny. It therefore finds that it cannot get away from forgetfulness; every archive reminds us of the absence by which it is informed. Thus, to be *en mal d'archive* 'is never to rest, interminably, from searching for the archive right where it slips away. It is to run after the archive, even if there's too much of it, right where something in it anarchives itself' (p. 91). Every archive is haunted by absence; the desire for presence for which the archive stands is betrayed by the very act of archiving.

The trace cannot be wholly gathered or made fully present; we thus realize, as Derrida explains, that '[t]races . . . produce the space of their inscription only by acceding to the period of their erasure. From the beginning, in the "present" of their first inscription, they are constituted by the double force of repetition and erasure, legibility and illegibility' (Derrida 1978c, p. 226). The trace cannot be made present without admitting its 'erasure' and 'illegibility'. Birne, for example, notes that all three of Smith's novels take place at holiday sites and explains that '[t]hese are comprehensible repetitions and correspondences. But there are odder ones. Smith is interested in clocks and stopped watches' (Birne 2005, p. 30). Birne's 'odder ones' is apologetic; it promotes the link she has identified anxiously. Would anyone else have noticed? Is the correlation perhaps 'odd' because it emerges from her preoccupations, not the novel's? I am left with a similar feeling in *Ghostwritten* when, for example, the noncorpum announces '[h]ad I transmigrated at that time, everything would have been different' (Mitchell 1999,

p. 198). The noncorpum alludes to an earlier announcement made by Satoru in 'Hong Kong': 'if I hadn't taken the decision to go back and answer it, then everything that happened afterwards wouldn't have happened' (p. 54). Or does he? Is this really a deliberate allusion, worthy of note? Attridge, reading *Foe*, records single word echoes of *The Tempest* and the Book of Common Prayer's Version of Psalm 45, but admits 'the allusiveness remains uncertain because these *are* single words. How can a single word be a quotation?' (Attridge 2004a, p. 66).[12] In all three of these examples the writer expresses uncertainty; the trace does not appear definitely for him/her but is, even at the moment it is identified, marked by the possibility of its disappearance. They all fear that their claims may be dismissed and that others might assert that the trace they identify is not *really* an allusion. Sarah Wood, describing *Of Grammatology*, but with equal pertinence here, writes of 'the experience of a trace whose movement is hidden from us and which only becomes describable as a kind of drifting-off' (Wood 2009a, p. 107). The trace appears haunted by its possible illegibility.

Just as the absent-trace was thwarted by presence, the model of trace-as-presence is marked by a notion of absence. The very different responses these texts provoke – conspiracy and contingency – are problematic in the same way. We've been patterning this point for a while in ever-decreasing turns. I will now expound the dilemma one final time, in an even tighter circle, before moving, in my chapter's final section, into a discussion of memory, which, ultimately, allows us to think the trace's two inflections together.

The two impulses I have outlined are not necessarily confined to one analysis of these texts or another; in fact, they often appear side by side in the same essay or review. Many critics *both* praise the inessentiality of the work *and* attempt to archive its traces (although none explicitly indicate the contradiction they thereby present). Akoma, for example, celebrates *Paradise* for its 'unknown quality', as I mentioned earlier. In the same essay, however, he offers in an unproblematic and straightforward manner the instances that gradually coalesce as we read the narrative; he provides a linear summary of its plot (Akoma 2000, p. 8). Similarly, Birne writes that '[a]fter the various false starts of *The Accidental*, it gradually becomes possible to establish what's going on' and proceeds to elucidate exactly what is 'going on' in the novel (Birne 2005, p. 30).

In Birne's summary, we lose the 'false starts' and gradual realization for which she lauds the text. The formulations Birne and Akoma provide of the books' content iron out their 'contingent' and 'perplexing' natures. The narrative is no longer strange. Hensher admits in relation to *Ghostwritten* that '[i]t would not do to bring the whole cast . . . within spitting distance of each other; it would do a lot to destroy the thesis of the book' (Hensher 2005). By collating the connections within the novel – by archiving them – we risk effacing the spectral quality that initially fascinates us.

In such conspiracy readings, 'contingency is dismissed', as Birchall explains (Birchall 2006, p. 46). Conspiracy-thought, in its quest to find an interpretation and an explanation, effaces whatever is odd and uncanny about the trace. Derrida admits this in the second section of 'My chances'. As I explained earlier, Derrida aligns chance with 'non-sense or insignificance'. Later in his essay, however, he contemplates the notion of superstition through a reading of Freud's 'The forgetting of names and sets of proper words'. Superstition (another form of conspiracy-thought) attempts to locate in an instance of chance a significance; it thus returns chance to the sense with which it claims to be incompatible.

Derrida explains that the archive 'keeps, it puts in reserve, it saves, but in an unnatural fashion' (Derrida 1996, p. 7). In Smith's *Hotel World* Lise attempts to recall Sara Wilby, the girl who died in the hotel in which she works and whose ghost narrates the novel's first section:

> But though she's tried, she can't even remember what Sara Wilby looked like that night, two nights before she died. It is much easier to picture her from the photographs in the papers and on TV than to try to remember. The photographs in the papers and on TV seem to have wiped Lise's memory of the real Sara Wilby even cleaner (Smith 2002, p. 110).

Lise is able to picture Sara from the 'photographs in the papers and on TV' but senses that these records are not the same as the 'real' Sara or a 'real' memory (although, as the only record Lise is now able to conjure, they are not without worth). These printed archives are insufficient. The archive 'will never be either memory or anamnesis as spontaneous, alive and eternal experience. On the contrary: the archive takes place at the place of originary and structural breakdown of the said memory' (Derrida 1996, p. 11). Both Derrida and Lise note a disjunction between the experience of memory (or reading) and those practices, such as the archive (or criticism), which claim to enshrine these experiences.

Derrida, following Freud, is therefore determined

> to exhume a more archaic *impression* . . . to exhibit a more archaic *imprint* than the one the other archaeologists of all kinds bustle around, those of literature and those of classical objective science, an imprint that is singular each time, an impression that is almost no longer an archive but almost confuses itself with the

pressure of the footstep that leaves its still-living mark on a substrate, a surface, a place of origin (Derrida 1996, p. 97; italics in original).

Derrida invokes an archive which would inscribe the moment or act of remembering. Rejecting the solidified and finished product which betrays, he desires the instant of archiving itself. We realize, however, that this moment is not easily attained. It exists, of course, only if we continue to archive. We may experience it only fleetingly on our way to composing the problematic finished product. We may glimpse the absent trace *through* the presencing-project that the archive proposes.

We cannot choose between our two inflections of the trace; we cannot decide between our desire to gather and the necessity to leave these traces be. Each project returns us to the other. *Cloud Atlas's* Timothy Cavendish invokes this double bind when he muses

What wouldn't I give now for a never-changing map of the ever-constant ineffable?
To possess, as it were, an atlas of the clouds (Mitchell 2004, p. 389).

Cavendish's desire to map the ineffable is, of course, paradoxical. A map, unlike the ineffable, is 'never-changing'; it is not possible to compose a fixed and stable atlas of the ever-changing clouds. Equally, however, Cavendish realizes how easily the ineffable gets away; he desperately desires a map in order to preserve it. The desires these novels provoke are, ultimately, contradictory and irreconcilable; the trace subjects us to a 'strange cohabitation', as I will now show in my chapter's final section.

Spectral memories

Memory and forgetting underscore both approaches to the trace. The archive, as we have seen, relies on memory as a tool lending itself to a process of positive and infinite accumulation. It depends upon a model of memory, identified by Ann Whitehead, in which 'forgetting is merely incidental'. Whitehead explains that, according to this conceptualization (which she allies with classical and early-modern thought), 'memory is a system used for storage and retrieval, and the object to be located is precisely that which was initially laid down. Forgetting, in this system, results either from a fault in the storage system or from a decay in or misrecognition of the memory traces' (Whitehead 2009, p. 48). The absent trace, in contrast, demands forgetfulness and assumes it to be absolute. The works I am considering show us, however, as I will demonstrate in this final section, that neither of these assumptions is correct. They offer us a more sophisticated thinking about remembering, which moves us closer to an analysis which takes into account the 'strange cohabitation' of contingency *and* conspiracy in our response towards these texts; it shows the way in which the trace 'occupies the middle point between total absence and total presence' in our reading (Derrida 1997b, p. 157).

Forgetting, in our model of the trace-as-absence, 'easily assumes the appearance of a simple lacuna, a lack, uncertainty'. Derrida explains that '[i]t is habitual to consider that to forget, to be forgetful, is exclusively "to omit"' (Derrida 1979b, p. 141). The characters in Mitchell's novels reveal, however, that the process is not quite so simple. In *Cloud Atlas*, Zachry thinks, '[b]ut I cudn't forget that ghost-girl neither, nay, she haunted my dreams wakin'n'sleepin'' (Mitchell 2004, p. 278), while the narrator of *Ghostwritten*'s Petersburg section announces, 'I shoved whatever it was that I mustn't think about upstream, but it kept floating down' (Mitchell 1999, p. 256). Both characters experience an inability to forget; memory returns. *number9dream* offers a more sustained exploration of this dilemma as Eiji tries to forget the death of his sister, Anju. He announces triumphantly '[a] whole evening without thinking about Anju, until now' (Mitchell 2001, p. 108). Eiji's achievement is undone by its recognition; he cannot successfully forget but points out that 'once you try to forget something you already remember it' (p. 69). Astrid in Smith's *The Accidental* also realizes that 'sometimes things like faces or memories come into your head on their own and you can see things so clearly that you couldn't not see them if you tried. It is insane' (Smith 2005, pp. 227–8). Sedgwick – in a passage I find peculiarly memorable – captures this infuriating logic especially well; she writes that '[t]he injunction to forget, of course, to forget something-in-particular after its jolting anamnesis, as you know if you've ever tried to do it – four in the morning, haplessly alert, knowing you'll never get back to sleep if you can't stop thinking about a certain X – opens an interminably self-defeating involution' (Sedgwick 1994, p. 58). To *attempt* to forget is to engage oneself in an act of memory; to decide to forget, we must first remember that which we intend to erase. Our forgetting is undone at the outset. There is, Eiji and Sedgwick realize, no forgetfulness that excludes memory absolutely.

The model of forgetting as absolute and as a lack is inadequate; a presence continues to haunt the omissions forgetfulness would perform. The notion of memory as positive is similarly suspect. In Smith's *Hotel World,* for example, the characters struggle to remember; their attempts echo persistently across their accounts. Sara Wilby's ghost thinks

I climbed into the, the. The lift for dishes, very small room suspended over a shaft of nothing, I forget the word, it has its own name (Smith 2002, p. 6).

Their beady. The things they see with. The things we see with, two of them, stuck in a face above a nose. The word's gone. I had it a moment ago (p. 8).

a slight squint in the, the. The things she saw with (p. 12).

the season after winter, I forget the word for it, the season when the flowers will push their heads regardless out again (p. 14).

(That's the name, the name for it; *that's* it; dumb waiter dumb waiter dumb waiter.) (p. 17; italics in original).

I want to ask her the name again for the things we see with. I want to ask her the name for heated-up bread.
I have already forgotten it again, the name for the lift for dishes (p. 26).

I will miss mist. I will miss leaf. I will miss the, the. What's the word? Lost, I've, the word. The word for. You know. I don't mean a house. I don't mean a room. I mean the way of the   . Dead to the   . Out of this   . Word.
I am hanging falling breaking between this word and the next (pp. 30–1).[13]

While Lise recalls

There was something she had to write down. She was waiting to remember it (p. 83).

So there was a story after all, somewhere, insistent, strung between this place and the last and the next, and she was trying to remember it (p. 84).

There was something Lise had to write down, again. What was it? (p. 85)

What if she remembered and then had to write it down before Deidre came in case she forgot it? (p. 85)

Each of these accounts displays certain vagueness; Lise refers to 'something' and 'it' while Sara's ghost leaves a series of blanks.[14] Sara's ghost presents us with a series of false starts, pauses and trailings-off through her incomplete ('I climbed into the, the') and fragmented syntax ('lost, I've, the word'). Language drifts-off, forgets itself. At the same time, however, there is a persistent sense of something almost grasped. The repetition of 'again', here and 'the', in the earlier account, maintains an 'insistent' tone.[15]

The 'something' functions at once as an absence and as that which the section promises to reveal. In Lise's account, a long sentence builds towards the 'something' she must remember: 'so there was a story after all, somewhere, insistent, strung between this place and the last and the next and she was trying to remember it'. The repeated 'and's of this sentence progress towards the 'story' promised by Lise's 'after all' only to end on the downbeat 'she was trying to remember it' – the story once again recedes. This pattern is repeated again when the question 'what was it?' suddenly and anti-climactically interrupts 'there was something Lise had to write down, again'. Similarly, in the novel's first account, the repeated 'the's take us at once closer to and further from the word which ought to come next.[16]

The difficulty which *Hotel World*'s characters experience, and to which the novel subjects us as readers, shows that memory is not perfect; its efficacy is not guaranteed, as the work of Freud most famously admits. Freud points out in 'Childhood memories and screen memories', for example, that if we were to 'subjected to analytic enquiry' 'the memories that a person has retained' from childhood 'it is easy to establish that there is no guarantee of their accuracy. Some of the mnemic images are certainly falsified, incomplete or displaced in time and place' (Freud 1975a, p. 87). Freud admits the obvious – yet nonetheless unsettling – fact that our memories may be false, incomplete or displaced. There are, frequently, occasions in which 'what the memory reproduces is not what it should correctly have reproduced, but something else as a substitute' (Freud 1975a, p. 85).

Mitchell's novels frequently reiterate this point. We are told in *Ghostwritten* that '[m]emories are their own descendants masquerading as the ancestors of the present', that 'access to memories does not guarantee access to truth. Many minds redirect memories along revised maps' and that '"[t]he act of memory is an act of ghostwriting"' (Mitchell 1999, pp. 175, 295, 326). Mitchell's characters emphasize, through a series of aphorisms, that memory effects a number of transformations. It does not preserve the past perfectly, but ghostwrites, redirects and transforms it; our remembrances are not truly, but merely masquerade as, the 'ancestors of the present'. The aphoristic form of these assertions is a particularly apt way in which to present this point. Aphorisms offer themselves as succinct phrases we might wish to commit to memory. All too often, though, they are soon forgotten.

Astrid, in Smith's *The Accidental,* suggests that '[i]t is amazing how quick you forget, even something you think you know, even something you really want to remember. It is amazing how memory works and won't work. A face can be just a blank' (Smith 2005, p. 227). Freud therefore admits that I have 'every reason' to 'distrust my memory' (Freud 1984, p. 429). Timothy Cavendish in Mitchell's *Cloud Atlas* thinks wryly, 'if memory serves ("Memory Serves." Duplicitous couplet)' (Mitchell 2004, p. 165). Memory refuses to cooperate, seeming instead to work against those who attempt to employ it. Astrid in Smith's *The Accidental* also frames memory as an independent entity with a volition of its own: '[w]hen Astrid thinks of the village the weirdest details come into her head like the lamp-post next to the field on the road from the house into the village and all the high grasses growing round its base. Why would anyone's memory want to remember just seeing a lamppost like that?' (Smith 2005, p. 233) In Astrid's final sentence, memory is the subject of the verb; it, not she, remembers.

Astrid is, moreover, incredulous that her memory would want to remember 'just seeing a lamppost' and that when she thinks about the village she recalls only the 'weirdest details'. Astrid does not explicitly say, but implies, that there might be better details and more useful images she could have retained. To store the image of a lamppost, we realize, Astrid's memory has had to exclude other things. It would not be possible to remember everything; some things must be forgotten. Whitehead explains that forgetting does not 'only [form] the shadowy underside of memory but, more precisely, shapes and defines the very contours of what is recalled and preserved' (Whitehead 2009, p. 14). Forgetfulness inscribes memory from the outset; every memory is haunted by the thought of that which it has had to leave out. The 'error' of forgetting is not coincidental but internal to memory.

No memory can wholly shake mis-remembrance or forgetfulness. This becomes especially apparent in the series of essays Freud writes on forgetting. At one point, for example, Freud recalls the time he forgot the name Singorelli. He realizes, after some contemplation, that this forgetfulness is not without cause. He admits that, at the time, he was trying to forget the death of a patient, Trafoi. He thus explains that 'I forgot *the one thing against my will,* while I wanted to *forget the other thing intentionally*' (Freud 1975b, p. 40; italics in original). For-getting, Freud argues, is 'motivated by repression' (p. 43). Elsewhere, he traces the '*substitute names*' which 'force themselves upon us with great persistence' in order to identify similar repressions in his patients (p. 38; italics in original). The act of forgetting points to a memory which has been concealed or hidden; it therefore offers the clue to a memory which might, through the investigative work employed by Freud, now be uncovered.

The omissions that forgetfulness performs return us once again to memory. However, the process does not end there. The repressed memories Freud reveals cannot elude the spectre of another forgetting or mis-remembrance. There is, of course, no proof that the memories Freud extracts are indeed true or the repressed memories responsible for the forgetting in question. In all of Freud's accounts, memories are revealed with an ease at odds with his claim that they are repressed. He could in fact be creating a series of 'false memories' of the type he identifies in 'Childhood memories and screen memories'. The truly repressed memory might still be forgotten. We occasionally glimpse this possibility when reading Freud's work. He writes, for example, that 'I shall however certainly not venture to affirm that all cases of name-forgetting are to be classed in the same group. There is no question that instances of it exist which are much simpler. We shall, I think, have stated the facts of the case with caution if we affirm: *By the side of simple cases where proper names are forgotten there is a type of forgetting which is motivated by repression*' (Freud 1975b, p. 44; italics in original). Cautious formulations such as this one recur throughout Freud's essays. They betray an anxiety; Is there something that Freud's analysis misses? Are there instances in which Freud's determined claim that forgetting is 'motivated by repression' might mislead? Might his interpretation, in these cases, cover up that which truly motivates forgetting? What, in other words, might Freud's work have forgotten?

Forgetting and memory are interrelated; one refers us to the other. The two are closely bound and one is always haunted by the other. At one point in Mitchell's *Cloud Atlas* Somni is involved in a car crash, which 'shook free an earlier memory of blackness, inertia, gravity, of being trapped in another ford; I could not find its source in my own memories' (Mitchell 2004, p. 330). Somni's reference to 'an earlier memory' encourages us to read this moment as another of the novel's connections. The invocation of 'blackness, inertia, gravity' and 'being trapped' remind us (remind me, anyway (there will, in this final section, be a certain emphasis on the first person, for reasons which will become clear)) of the end of 'Half lives', when Luisa, in her car, is forced off a bridge into a river. However, Somni has not read 'Half lives'; she is related to it only indirectly, via Timothy Cavendish's narrative. The incident has no obvious 'source' in her memory. Perhaps, I think as I read these sentences, I will be offered an explanation later in the novel. I finally discover, of course, that this hope is misplaced. No explanation is offered; I am never told whether Somni has read Luisa's text.

Am I therefore correct to read this as an echo? Does Somni's car crash truly recall Luisa's? These texts subject our reading to a number of anxieties, which *The Turning*, in particular, refuses to assuage. In 'Abbreviation' Vic is asked

> From the city?
> He shook his head. Not anymore, he said. We just moved down south. Angelus.
> It's pretty crap (Winton 2005, p. 25).

In the book's previous story, 'Big world', the protagonist announces '[m]e, I love the city, I'm from there originally' (p. 5). At another point he reminisces, telling us, 'I get to thinking about the last night of school and the bonfire at Massacre point' (p. 12). The bonfire, too, is echoed in 'Abbreviation': '[u]p the beach a little way, out in front of the big old army truck and the striped circus tent, there was a fire burning twenty feet high. It was a real monster' (pp. 29–30). It occurs to me, momentarily, that the characters may be the same. But nothing else lines up. It is not the same bonfire and the protagonist of 'Big world' is not Vic, although I make the mistake again reading 'Damaged goods' when I learn that '[i]n his last year of school Vic did what all the country boys did. He rode around in cars and saved for one of his own' (p. 63). I am reminded of the road-trip narrated in 'Big world' before I remember that Vic features there only marginally – he is not either of the main characters who save up to buy a car.

The text is littered with such false echoes. The opening paragraphs of 'Aquifer' announce

> Very late one evening not long ago I stirred from a television stupor at the sound of a familiar street name and saw a police forensic team in waders carry bones from the edge of a lake. Four femurs and a skull, to be precise. The view widened and I saw a shabby clump of melaleucas and knew exactly where it was that this macabre discovery had taken place (p. 37).

Angelus reappears repeatedly as the location of the stories in this novel; it thus becomes 'familiar' to its reader. When the narrator notes a 'familiar street name' I expect to share the recognition he inscribes; I suspect we are about to return to Angelus once more. But I am wrong: '[b]efore dawn and without waking my wife or even leaving her a note, I rose, made myself coffee and began the five-hour drive back from Angelus to the suburbs where I grew up' (p. 38). Angelus appears only to disappear – it is not, in this case, the place to which the narrative is drawn, but the town it leaves behind.

Again, in 'Cockleshell' '[h]e wonders if the Larwood kids still wet the bed' and I wonder if he is referring to the kids who wet the bed in 'Aquifer' (p. 117). But when I go back to check I discover those children were the Boxes (p. 41). I begin to feel a bit like Vic in 'Long, clear view':

> The things you hear solve nothing; they're just nasty bits of information you could have done without, specks and splashes of dirt that puddle and pool in your head, things about the parents of kids you know, news of teachers, things you aren't meant to hear, stuff you shouldn't be listening to (pp. 195–6).

The description Vic offers of his life in Angelus serves also to summarize my experience of reading the book. I, too, find 'bits of information [I] could have done without' – false allusions which only confuse. I am, I realize, hearing 'things [I'm not] meant to hear'.

In Mitchell's *Cloud Atlas*, Hae-Joo completes a code with the words '"[t]ravel far enough, you meet yourself"' (Mitchell 2004, p. 336). The phrase sounds as though it is a reference from another novel, a case of Mitchell citing his own words. This is not in fact the case. It looks like a quotation, but is not one. I have perhaps begun to notice echoes where there are none.

Or, then again, perhaps the sentence from *Cloud Atlas is* a quotation. In which case I admit defeat – I cannot find its source. But perhaps someone else can. I read conscious of the possibility of another, more knowledgeable, reading, which would reveal my failures. My reading is haunted by the possibility of another.

Mitchell's work is dense with the repetition of tiny details: Luisa Rey's mother in *Cloud Atlas* lives in a town – Ewingsville – whose name echoes the Adam Ewing of the novel's first section (Mitchell 2004, p. 431). The quotation at the beginning of *Ghostwritten*, from 'The bridge of San Luis Rey', recalls the name Luisa Rey in *Cloud Atlas*. Luisa Rey 'the writer' calls into the radio show of 'Night train' later in the novel (Mitchell 1999, p. 385). *Ghostwritten*'s Katy Forbes, like each of *Cloud Atlas*'s protagonists, has 'a birthmark shaped like a comet' (p. 305). Tim Cavendish of 'The ghastly ordeal' appears as Marco's editor in *Ghostwritten*'s 'London' section. *Ghostwritten* repeatedly echoes *Cloud Atlas*. These allusions are, however, frail. Even as I notice them, I know that not every reader of *Ghostwritten* will; s/he may not have read *Cloud Atlas,* and might never do so.

We notice many of the more subtle references in these texts with a sense of how easily they might be missed. Hensher admits that 'only a very alert reader will make the connection' he notes between the first and second stories in *The Turning* (Hensher 2005). The verbal allusions we find within *Foe,* for example, are sparse, limited to a word or a phrase:

> 'At last I could row no further. My hands were blistered, my back was burned, my body ached. With a sigh, making barely a splash, I slipped overboard' (Coetzee 1987, p. 5).

> '"Then at last I could row no further. My hands were raw, my back was burned, my body ached. With a sigh, making barely a splash, I slipped overboard and began to swim towards your island"' (p. 11).

'I am not a story, Mr Foe. I may impress you as a story because I began my account of myself without preamble, slipping overboard into the water and striking out for the shore' (p. 131).

'I presented myself to you in words I knew to be my own – I slipped overboard, I began to swim, my hair floated about me, and so forth, you will remember the words – and for a long time afterwards, when I was writing those letters that were never read by you, and were later not sent, and at the last not even written down, I continued to trust in my own authorship' (p. 133).

Bringing the candle nearer, I read the first words of the tall, looping script: 'Dear Mr Foe, At last I could row no further.'
    With a sigh, making barely a splash, I slip overboard (p. 155).

And forming a different strand:

The staircase was dark and mean. My knock echoed as if on emptiness (p. 113).

The staircase is dark and mean. On the landing I stumble over a body (p. 153).

The repetitions of this novel, contained in the brief phrases 'I slipped overboard' and 'dark and mean', are eminently miss-able (or, at least, they would be had I not listed them so comprehensively).

We might, moreover, read the novel as a whole in an intertextual mode. Attridge explains that 'it was in *Foe* that Coetzee made canonic intertextuality a fundamental principle: its manner of proceeding is to rewrite, and fuse together, the biography of Daniel Defoe and those of several of Defoe's fictional characters' (Attridge 2004a, p. 69). We could level *Foe* against our knowledge of Daniel Defoe's *Robinson Crusoe*.[17] It is, however, equally possible to read *Foe* without this knowledge. The novel signifies differently in this case. Nonetheless, it remains legible. It is not necessary, we realize, to notice the echoes in order to comprehend these fictions. We read the trace of *Robinson Crusoe* conscious of a reading in which it does not figure. Our reading is traced by another.

The multiple sections and shifts in perspective that these novels employ show us that '[p]oint of view is always more than one' (Royle 2004, p. 158). However, this fact is not simple. It means, for Royle, that point of view 'is always other than, more or less than, itself. Which is to say that it is spectral and blind' (p. 158). These works attune us to the possibility that a further shift may always take place and that there always remains a revelation we have not yet witnessed. We realize that '[t]here is no epiphany, no moment of revelation that is not at the same time a moment of blinding or blindness, a blindness that has to do not only with privation of vision but also with speech or voice' (p. 157). Every point of view entails an exclusion; there is no perspective which closes down all others, no perspective which is not haunted by unknowing. This awareness haunts my reading; my interpretation – my perspective on these works – is not, and never will be, complete. But neither will any other. I offer my reading anxiously, but not hopelessly.

The traces we encounter in the texts I have examined divide our response. We want, on the one hand, to celebrate them as a sign of uncanny interrelation or interconnectedness, of contingency and of an absence in excess of any two marks. At the same time, however, we are driven to archive them – to collect, list and gather. This gathering effaces the inessentiality we wished to privilege, returning it to essence. Then again, the inessence still haunts; the archive is never complete, the void opened by the trace is never filled. Thus, neither of these two contradictory projects can fully exclude the other. Turning to the concept of memory that underpins both notions my chapter pursued, in its final section, a reading – both paranoid and forgetful – that kept both notions of the trace in play.

Deconstruction and Ethics

'(but one ought to say *but* for every word)' (Derrida 2007a, p. 149; italics in original).

This suggestion (of Derrida's) will provide the motif, or guiding principle, of this chapter as it explores the thought of alterity. The theme is not new – each of my chapters pursues it under a different name: reading, writing, trace, tact, you. And there are other labels, too – *différance*, force, the other, queer – many of which derive from the work of Derrida and Levinas, to whom my book returns time and again as alterity's 'best' thinkers. We may surmise, from this reliance, that Derrida and Levinas provide *the* theory (it is often called deconstruction, or ethics) from which the work is drawn.

It might seem that Derrida's 'deconstruction' or Levinas's 'ethics' provides the 'answer' – alterity's thought *par excellence*. But, they tell us, alterity – if it is to be thought properly – allows no final thought. Both Derrida and Levinas remain wary of any term which appears to name their work and that would designate it a definition and a method.[1] This chapter interrupts the others (its opening quotation is abrupt, not the gentle introduction one might expect to a chapter) in order to echo this suspicion, wondering explicitly whether alterity's thought could ever become a theory.

And in style, too, it is more a series of interruptions than a coherent and uni-fied whole, hence the opening quotation from Derrida (which both proposes interruption and marks itself as (bracketed) rupture).

There is a problem with my introductory chapter: Derrida and Levinas are too close. I blithely introduce the 'saying' of Levinas as a notion that equates with Derrida's concept of the 'literary'. Their similarities serve my argument. But can such radically different thinkers really be so simply equated? As 'Violence and metaphysics' shows (or, properly, as its *reputation as* a critique of Levinas sug-gests), Derrida is not even sure that he agrees with Levinas.

And elsewhere, too, he cautions, '[i]t is thinkers such as [Levinas, Heidegger and Blanchot] to whom, strangely enough, one may consider oneself closest; and yet they are, more than others, other. And they too are alone' (Derrida 2004c, p. 120). Given Derrida's effort to assert his separation from Levinas, I probably should not lump them together (or at least not without justifying myself). I need to pull them apart.[2]

But doing so will take time. It is not as simple as adding a couple of sentences to my introduction; 'Violence and metaphysics' is a formidable and complex essay. It will take a whole chapter, this chapter, to elucidate the many differences between Levinas and Derrida.

Yet, to be honest, I am still not convinced that these differences are as fundamental or as important as many have argued. Derrida cautiously permits us to elide them: 'faced with a body of thought like that of Levinas, I never hold any objection. I am prepared to subscribe to everything that he says. That is not to say that I think the same thing in the same way; but that the differences at issue are very difficult to determine' (Derrida and Labarrière 1986, p. 74; translated in Smith 1995, p. 109). This chapter might, again, be about the ways in which Derrida and Levinas are, in many respects, the same.

This oscillation between sameness and difference is not as equivocal as it sounds; we often realize both at once. When writing about Heidegger and Levinas, Derrida outlines a 'schema' that 'accentuates their opposition but, as is often the case', he admits, 'also permits one to conjecture about their proximity' (Derrida 1978b, p. 149).

Robert Smith establishes the Levinas/Derrida 'debate' along these lines in *Derrida and Autobiography*; he announces that his aim is '*both* to make *and* dispense with distinctions' (Smith 1995, p. 109; my italics). As such, he writes,

> Derrida shares with Levinas an emphasis on the relation with the other that comes about before existence, and, consequently, an interest in re-elaborating concepts of time. But where Derrida situates repetition, Levinas situates ethics – although this should not be taken as a significant divergence between the two, and the said 'situating' barely belongs to a taxonomy (p. 109).

Smith first delineates a broad split between Levinas and Derrida, noting their radical difference in 'situation': one works with and within ethics, the other in terms of repetition. But what is the fundamental difference between the way in which Derrida thinks repetition and the way in which Levinas thinks ethics? We would be hard pressed to formulate a 'taxonomy' (moreover, Levinas and Derrida propose ethics and repetition alike as concepts resistant to such taxonomic projects). With this thought, Smith brings the two closer together again. This double move characterizes, too, both Derrida's response to Levinas and Levinas's response to Derrida.

Breaking with philosophy, and bringing us back again

Derrida discusses Levinas's work in two essays: 'Violence and metaphysics' and 'At this very moment in this text here I am', as well as in his book, *Adieu: to Emmanuel Levinas.* Levinas, too, is author of an essay about Derrida. It is called 'Tout autrement', translated as 'Wholly otherwise' (there are two versions: one appears in *Proper Names,* the other in *Re-reading Levinas.* I will be using the translation in *Re-reading Levinas*, which is, in my opinion, closer in tone to Levinas's French).[3] I want first, and mainly, to think about it alongside Derrida's 'Violence and metaphysics'.

I will argue that 'Violence and metaphysics' offers a 'critique' of Levinas, which is, in many ways, *the same* critique we find in 'Wholly otherwise'. Derrida identifies the same 'fault' in Levinas's work as Levinas finds in Derrida's. And, as my graphological caution implies, these similarities will force us to re-think what 'critique' and 'fault' might be.

Both essays begin by hailing the end of philosophy. Derrida portentously invokes a 'philosophy' that 'died yesterday' (Derrida 1978b, p. 79) while Levinas wonders whether we might be 'at the end of a naïveté' (Levinas 1991, p. 3). For Derrida/Levinas, the thought of Levinas/Derrida signals a new beginning within philosophy's history.

According to Levinas/Derrida, Derrida/Levinas proposes a philosophy that would break away from the Western tradition of a metaphysics of presence. Levinas writes that '[a] new style of thinking is dawning on us in reading these exceptionally precise texts which are yet so strange'. Derrida's *Voice and Phenomenon,* he suggests, 'overthrows logocentric discourse' (Levinas 1991, p. 3). With exclamatory drama, he declares '[h]enceforth [i.e. after Derrida], significations do not converge on the truth – truth's no great matter!' (p. 5) 'Suspension of truths! Strange epoch!' (p. 3)

Derrida, too (but more calmly), introduces a notion of rupture, identifying in Levinas '[a] thought which . . . seeks to liberate itself' (Derrida 1978b, pp. 82–3). He claims,

> It is at this level that the thought of Emmanuel Levinas can make us tremble.
>
> At the heart of the desert, in the growing wasteland, this thought, which fundamentally no longer seeks to be a thought of Being and phenomenality, makes us dream of an inconceivable process of dismantling and dispossession (p. 82).

Derrida links Levinas's thought with the possibility of 'dismantling and dispossession'.

Even as he does so, however, he points out that this 'process' is 'inconceivable'.

Levinas explains why. He emphasizes that '[w]hat remains constructed after the deconstruction is, certainly, the stern architecture of the deconstructing discourse which employs the present tense of the verb "to be" in predicative propositions' (Levinas 1991, p. 5). We cannot deconstruct philosophy without constructing a philosophical 'architecture' with which to do so. Derrida's work is bound to use the very 'logocentric language' it is supposedly against and, even after the deconstruction, this 'architecture' remains intact.

Jonathan Tiplady points out that 'whatever the deep questions deconstruction puts to it, presence does not just disappear after Derrida' (Tiplady 2007, p. 160). The effects of presence '[seem] to pre-survive whatever is said about them in a more critical or deconstructive vein' (p. 160).

The metaphysics of presence does not go away. There could be no deconstruction that did not reaffirm presence.

Derrida – employing the term 'Greek thought' in order to designate the metaphysical tradition dating back to the Ancient Greeks – explains that

> Levinas exhorts us to a second parricide [of Greek thought] [. . .] But will a non-Greek ever succeed in doing what a Greek in this case could not do, except by disguising himself as a Greek, by *speaking* Greek, by feigning to speak Greek in order to get near the king? And since it is a question of killing a speech, will we ever know who is the last victim of this stratagem? Can one feign speaking a language? (Derrida 1978b, p. 89; italics in original).

To get close enough to Greek thought to destroy it, Levinas must impersonate the Greeks. In impersonating them, however, he renders himself indistinguishable from them. Levinas is brought back to the philosophy he would move beyond; the break, impossible, is but a dream conjured by and implicated within the tradition it would reject.

Paul Davies explains that '[t]he words that mark the limit of the philosophical horizon . . . are names, philosophical names, asserting the possibility of philosophy's continuing to name whatever confronts it' (Davies 1991, p. 210).[4] The break is compromised from the outset.

Thus, no philosopher will ever step outside philosophy.

Levinas asks again, '[a] new break in the history of philosophy?' and answers in the negative. The 'break', he admits, 'would also mark [philosophy's] continuity' (Levinas 1991, p. 3).

Derrida writes that '[m]etaphysical transcendence is *desire*' (Derrida 1978b, p. 92; italics in original). The emphasis encourages us to realize that this transcendence will remain always a desire, never fulfilled.

The project is flawed. And, for Levinas, '[o]ne might well be tempted to infer an argument from this use of logocentric language against that very language, in order to dispute the produced deconstruction' (Levinas 1991, p. 5). Spurred by this contradiction, we could reject deconstruction *tout court.*

But this remains merely a temptation; 'in following this path, one would risk missing one side of the signification which this very inconsequence bears' (p. 5). The contradiction is too productive to dismiss.

Derrida writes, 'Levinas's metaphysics in a sense presupposes – at least we have attempted to show this – the transcendental phenomenology that it seeks to put into question. And yet the legitimacy of this putting into question does not seem to us any less radical' (Derrida 1978b, p. 133).

> The project is flawed, but, both Derrida and Levinas tell us, necessarily so. Derrida explains,'[w]e are not denouncing, here, an incoherence of language or a contradiction in the system. We are wondering about the meaning of a necessity: the necessity of lodging oneself within traditional conceptuality in order to destroy it' (Derrida 1978b, p. 111).

It is, for Levinas/Derrida, in this already-compromised attempt that Derrida/Levinas's work is most interesting.

In both cases, we both agree and disagree. The movement Levinas and Derrida identify is 'correct'; these works are most productively read with this tension (between a move-beyond and an always-within) in mind.

However, we may still want to object. Levinas/Derrida proceeds as though Derrida/Levinas were not aware of the tension within his work. Yet, as many have pointed out, Levinas/Derrida is fully conscious of the 'objection' Derrida/Levinas proposes. Bernasconi makes this point 'for' Levinas. He explains that '[w]hat Derrida records in "Violence and Metaphysics" are certain necessities which appear to impose themselves on discourse. But can they be described as Derrida attempts to do, in terms of a betrayal of Levinas's intentions by his philosophical language as if Levinas had somehow been defeated?' (Bernasconi 1988, p. 38). Derrida implies that Levinas did not '[know] that that was what he was doing' (p. 127). But Bernasconi reckons he did. An awareness of the 'limitations' is already there in Levinas's work: '[a]lready in *Totality and Infinity* Levinas shows himself to be fully aware of the difficulty of rupturing a tradition' (p. 129).

Equally (although not responding explicitly to Levinas), Derrida's best readers point out that he has never claimed to reject metaphysics or presence outright. My (current) favourite explanation is offered in a footnote by Jonathan Tiplady who points out that deconstruction is not distinct from and does not break with metaphysics; instead, it 'recognises the irreducibility of metaphysics' (Tiplady 2007, p. 160).

For Tiplady, deconstruction attempts 'to think *with* and not just against' presence. He therefore suggests that it 'might even be described as a type of reinvented falling in love with presence. Which is also to say, a taking account of, an ethical and failing becoming-conscious of what that falling in love might entail. Be attentive to the consequences of love, but also its inevitability' (p. 160). Tiplady, moving rapidly from the notion of presence to the thought of falling in love, emphasizes both the 'inevitability' and the 'failing' of this falling in love, an inevitable failure of a 'never altogether avoidable falling in love. Metaphysics is always falling in love, and falling in love always metaphysical' (p. 160).

Blanchot (who, as a philosopher who writes about Levinas and whose work is often conflated with Derrida's, is well suited to marshal this debate) explains,

> [t]he desire that one might call metaphysical is a desire for what we are not in want of, a desire that cannot be satisfied and that does not desire union with what it desires. It desires what the one who desires has no need of, what is not lacking and what the one who desires has no desire to attain, it being the very desire for what must remain inaccessible and foreign – a desire of the other as other, a desire that is austere, disinterested, without satisfaction, without nostalgia, unreturned, and without return (Blanchot 1993, p. 53).

We desire a presence that 'presents itself but cannot be seized' and we desire it only so long as it 'slips away from every grasp' (p. 61). Made present, it would no longer be the presence we desire.

Which is to say, the metaphysics of presence includes already its own deconstruction. The moment with which 'deconstruction' is aligned is inscribed within presence; it has 'always already *infiltrated*' it (Derrida 1997b, p. 163; italics in original).

Derrida declares that '[o]ur discourse irreducibly belongs to the system of metaphysical oppositions' (Derrida 1978b, p. 20).

Derrida stresses that 'one always inhabits, and all the more when one does not suspect it' (Derrida 1997a, p. 24; italics in original). We cannot forget that 'all the defining concepts, all the lexical significations, and even the syntactic articulations, which seem at one moment to lend themselves to this definition, or to that translation, are also deconstructed or deconstructible, directly or otherwise' (Derrida 1991, p. 274). No single concept of deconstruction could conclude the thought that inspires it.

We cannot think presence and deconstruction apart; Derrida suggests that '[d]econstruction is also the idea of – and the idea adopted by necessity of – this *différantielle* contamination' (Derrida 1992a, p. 39).

Derrida makes it clear that deconstruction is not an identifiable 'movement' distinct from the 'metaphysics of presence'. Deconstruction *is* not; rather, it '[inhabits]' structures *'in a certain way'* (Derrida 1997a, p. 24; italics in original). Deconstruction takes place within the metaphysics of presence and, as such, could never take place without it.

We return again to 'Violence and metaphysics' and 'Wholly otherwise'. By stating that Derrida/Levinas intends to break with the metaphysics of presence but fails, Levinas/Derrida misreads Derrida/Levinas's intentions. But he does so for the sake of his argument (the 'his' is deliberately unclear, by the way. Derrida, similarly keen to pose a dilemma of ownership, also plays this trick when he writes that 'Levinas confirms Heidegger in his discourse' (Derrida 1978b, p. 142). I'll return to Derrida on Levinas's reading of Heidegger shortly).

In an echo of the afore-mentioned argument, Derrida, in *Of Grammatology*, outlines Heidegger's reading of Nietzsche; Heidegger reads Nietzsche's work as 'a breakthrough', which, although '[attempting] a step outside of metaphysics', 'still [utilizes it] in a certain way' (Derrida 1997a, p. 19).

Derrida stresses that this limitation is not an '"incoherence"' but a 'trembling', a necessity rather than a fault (p. 24). Nonetheless, he resists the urge to defend Nietzsche's work: 'rather than protect Nietzsche from the Heideggerian reading, we should perhaps offer him up to it completely' (p. 19). To best read Nietzsche, one must *'accentuate* the "naïveté"' of such a project even, perhaps, beyond the naïveté with which Nietzsche pursued it (p. 19; italics in original).

In a similar manner, the notion of (failed) intention employed by both 'Violence and metaphysics' and 'Wholly otherwise' keeps open the notion of desire, of an impossibility we could never simply *not want*. It plays out this most fundamental of realizations despite (or perhaps because) falsely ascribing to Levinas/Derrida a naïveté not properly his own.

We therefore suspect that the misreading is both conscious and deliberate. Derrida and Levinas do not offer a critique *per se*; Derrida/Levinas seems (although we cannot be sure), rather than directly to misread Levinas/Derrida's work, to be ventriloquizing those who misinterpret it. The exclamatory sentences with which 'Wholly otherwise' is strewn parody the reading it offers; the interpretation of Derrida's work as '[s]uspension of truths!' hailing a '[s]trange epoch!' is strained and over-wrought. Levinas, we suspect, does not sincerely believe the interpretation he offers.

Why, then, does he not say so? What does this tell us about ethics and deconstruction? And about their relationship with misreading?

Misread intentions

In a second strand of thought in 'Violence and metaphysics', Derrida plays out this theme of misreading.

Levinas, reading Hegel, Heidegger and Husserl, posits a series of insights, which, he implies, arise from his own reading. Levinas positions himself against these philosophers and claims to move beyond their thought. Derrida, however, repeatedly points out that his thesis is already there to be read in their work:

> Levinas is very close to Hegel, much closer than he admits, and at the very moment when he is apparently opposed to Hegel in the most radical fashion (Derrida 1978b, p. 99).
>
> Did not Hegel say this too? (p. 98)
>
> This last question, which indeed could be Levinas's question to Husserl, would demonstrate that as soon as *he speaks* against Hegel, Levinas can only confirm Hegel, has confirmed him already (p. 120).
>
> Levinas henceforth will move toward a thought of original difference. Is this thought in contradiction with Heidegger's intentions? (p. 90)

The objections Levinas claims to derive from these thinkers do not, Derrida shows, properly belong to him. The critique Levinas performs cannot stand as such.

And neither can Derrida's 'critique' of Levinas. In a third strand to 'Violence and metaphysics', Derrida accepts that the questions he poses are already given to him by Levinas. The 'objections' he voices are already there to be read *in* and as Levinas's own work: 'we will attempt to ask several questions. If they succeed in approaching the heart of this explication, they will be nothing less than objections, but rather the questions put to *us* by Levinas' (p. 84; italics in original).

Again, the point is repeated:

> if our commentary has not been too unfaithful, it is already clear that there is no element of Levinas's thought which is not, in and of itself, engaged by such questions (p. 109).

let it be said, for our own reassurance: the route followed by Levinas's thought is such that all our questions already belong to his own interior dialogue, are displaced into his discourse and only listen to it, from many vantage points and in many ways (p. 109).

Levinas performs a similar return at the end of 'Wholly otherwise'. His aim, he writes, has been to underline 'the primordial importance of the questions posed *by* Derrida'. He rejects 'the ridiculous ambition of "improving" a true philosopher', attempting instead to 'express the pleasure of a contact made in the heart of a chiasmus' (Levinas 1991, p. 8; my italics).

The reading Levinas/Derrida offers is not his own but is to be found already in the work of Derrida/Levinas. Derrida formalizes this situation in 'Force of law' and wonders what it might mean. He offers a reading of Walter Benjamin's *Zur Kritik der Gewalt* only to admit that his deconstruction is effected already by Benjamin's text: 'this deconstruction is in some way the operation or rather the very experience that this text, it seems to me, first does itself, by itself, on itself. What does this mean? Is it possible? What remains, then, of such an event? Of its auto-hetero-deconstruction? Of its just and unjust incompletion?' (Derrida 1992a, p. 30) Benjamin's text 'deconstructs' itself.[5] What injustice might Derrida have performed by claiming such a reading as his own?

This concern is echoed by Paul de Man (but now directed against Derrida) in his review of *Of Grammatology*. He states (responding to Derrida's claim that 'the concept of the supplement is a sort of blind spot in Rousseau's text') (Derrida 1997b, p. 163) that 'Rousseau's text has no blind spots' (De Man 1971, p. 139). For de Man, '[w]hat happens in Rousseau is exactly what happens in Derrida: a vocabulary of substance and of presence is no longer used declaratively but rhetorically, for the very reasons that are being (metaphorically) stated' (pp. 138–9). Rousseau is fully aware of the supplement and its workings: 'Rousseau was not deluded and said what he meant to say' (p. 135). De Man gives back to Rousseau the reading Derrida performs.[6]

He thus poses what Bernasconi identifies as a 'question of ownership': with or to whom does this (deconstructive) reading belong? (Bernasconi 1991, p. 155) And to whom do we attribute the 'non-deconstructive' approach?

I've just instituted a division between a 'deconstructive' and 'non-deconstructive' reading, which, I'm sure you can see, is bound to be problematic. But I also think it's useful, to an extent, to illustrate our dilemma. I'll be employing it, contingently, for a little while yet. Using it, but remembering it's flawed; ready already to let go of it.

(Not everyone is. Simon Critchley, to pick a victim at random, is perhaps guilty of holding too tightly onto it when he writes that 'a moment of blindness in a logocentric text becomes the trace of an alterity that exceeds logocentrism' (Critchley 1989, p. 94). For Critchley, certain texts are *inherently* logocentric. The 'trace of . . . alterity' is posited as its opposite value, which belongs, presumably, to a privileged few: to Derrida, or to Critchley).

The distinction arises, I expect, from *Of Grammatology*, in which Derrida sets up two moments of reading. First, there is 'what [the writer] commands', which Derrida calls 'doubling commentary'. The first moment, for Derrida, 'should no doubt have its place' but 'this indispensable guardrail has always only *protected*, it has never *opened*, a reading' (Derrida 1997b, p. 158; italics in original). We therefore need, secondly, a move beyond or outside. Derrida explains that 'the reading must always aim at a certain relationship, unperceived by the writer, between what he commands and what he does not command of the patterns of the language that he uses' (p. 158).

Derrida writes that '[t]o produce this signifying structure obviously cannot consist of reproducing, by the effaced and respectful doubling of commentary, the conscious, voluntary, intentional relationship that the writer institutes in his exchanges with the history to which he belongs thanks to the element of language' (p. 158).

We are invited to identify (as de Man and Critchley do) the first moment as the dominant (or logocentric) interpretation. The second moment of 'what [the writer] does not command' is aligned with a notion of 'deconstruction' and established as the reading more 'properly' Derrida's.

However, the seemingly simple dominant notion of 'what [a writer] commands', the first moment of reading, is more complex than this schema allows. Derrida *seems* to say that it would be possible to reproduce the 'conscious, voluntary, intentional relationship that the writer institutes'. But, knowing Derrida's work, we read this claim cautiously.

If we turn to *Limited Inc* Derrida qualifies his claims. The term 'doubling commentary' was, he admits, 'perhaps' applied 'clumsily' (Derrida 1988, p. 143).

He writes, 'I used these words [doubling commentary] to designate what, in a very classical and very elementary layer of reading, most resembles what traditionally is called "commentary"' (p. 144). The phrases 'most resembles' and 'what is traditionally called' are much more cautious, and more convoluted, than the statements made previously.

The text continues in this vein: 'the concept that I was aiming at with the inadequate expression of a "doubling commentary" is the concept of a reading–writing that, counting on a *very strong probability* of consensus concerning the intelligibility of a text . . . *seems* only to paraphrase, unveil, reflect, reproduce a text, "commenting" on it without any other active or risky initiative' (p. 146; first italics mine, second italics in original).

He adds, '[w]hat must be understood is not what this or that French word means to say *naturally* or *absolutely,* beyond all possible equivocation, but rather, first, what interpretations are probabilistically dominant and conventionally acknowledged to grant access to what Rousseau thought he meant and to what readers for the most part thought they could understand, in order, second, to analyze the play or relative indetermination that was able to open the space of my interpretation, for example, that of the word *supplément*' (p. 144; italics in original).

The phrases 'very strong probability', 'seems', 'probabilistically dominant and conventionally acknowledged' render Derrida's language equivocal and hesitant. A doubling commentary is by no means self-evident; it is very strongly probable, but by no means certain, that a reading performed as such represents the 'consensus'. There remains a possibility of error even at this first level of reading. Derrida explains that even '[w]ith the best intentions in the world (and this is why one must be careful in assigning responsibilities and culpabilities) a "codifying" theoretician can fail in this *duty*' (p. 138; italics in original).

Thus, 'the essential and irreducible *possibility* of *mis*understanding or of "infelicity" must be taken into account in the description of those values said to be positive' (p. 147; italics in original).

The doubling commentary is 'not a moment of simple reflexive recording that would transcribe the originary and true layer of a text's intentional meaning, a meaning that is univocal and self-identical, a layer upon which or after which active interpretation would already begin' but is '*already* an interpretation', a '*quasi*-paraphrastic interpretation' (pp. 143–4).

And, as 'already an interpretation', it 'belongs' as much to Derrida and to deconstruction as the second moment. It cannot be simply attributed to 'logocentrism' or 'the metaphysics of presence', to 'Rousseau' or 'the dominant tradition of Rousseau commentary' but is always (at least in part) an interpretation forwarded by Derrida in the interests of his second moment of reading.

This realization perhaps poses a problem to the way in which academic discourse often proceeds. It is customary, in academic work, to legitimize what one does in opposition to someone else (who is 'wrong'). Derrida, in contrast, forces us to consider the way in which we might 'own', and be responsible for, both moments of reading.

For example, in my composition chapter, I wanted to show that 'the act of "ourselves writing" remains elusive' even in those texts that privilege it. Writing is not an isolated moment and cannot be rendered purely present.

Barthes, for example, lauds the 'perpetual present of ourselves writing'. I, by contrast, can show that there is no such present; writing's presence is always compromised by the moment of reading.

I can only show that writing's presence is compromised if I first infer that there is such a presence. I conjure this pure presence already knowing I am going to disprove it; my first reading is determinedly blind. It is somewhat feigned, constructed in the service of the second moment of reading that is to follow. But there can be no second reading without it.

I could no doubt attribute this first reading to someone else. To Barthes, perhaps. Or to one or another of his readers. My chapter would then be more coherent, less contradictory.

But this would be disingenuous. The first reading is also my own. And it is only because I am able to read this first moment that the second becomes available to me.

Sedgwick considers this dilemma explicitly, and illuminates it further, via her theorization of strong and weak reading. In her essay 'Paranoid reading, reparative reading', Sedgwick delineates a sort of divide between paranoid, or strong, reading and reparative (weak) reading. The first section of her essay outlines 'the present paranoid consensus' of a 'monopolistic program of paranoid knowing' (Sedgwick 2003, p. 144). Under this the paranoid 'regime', she argues, '[t]he vocabulary for articulating any reader's reparative motive toward a text or a culture has long been so sappy, aestheticizing, defensive, anti-intellectual, or reactionary that it's no wonder few critics are willing to describe their acquaintance with such motives' (p. 150). Sedgwick invites us to challenge these assumptions; she believes 'there are important phenomenological and theoretical tasks that can be accomplished only through local theories and nonce taxonomies' (p. 145). Sedgwick asks us to reject a strong or paranoid reading and to favour the weak or reparative instead.

This summary is, however, a 'strong' reading of Sedgwick's essay. Accordingly, it suffers from the very 'tautology' with which Sedgwick aligns a paranoid stance. I just claimed that Sedgwick privileges weak reading. Yet if we too eagerly propose a weak reading as 'better' than the strong one, it, thanks to the very logic it would contest, 'wins'; it becomes strong.

Yet it's not exactly wrong to propose this reading. It is there to be read and Sedgwick acknowledges it when she admits that 'the preceding section of the present chapter' may fairly be characterized as '[a] strong theory (i.e., a wide-ranging and reductive one)'. However, she also suggests that we might see it differently from other strong theories, reading it as an approach 'not mainly organised around anticipating, identifying, and warding off the negative affect of humiliation'. It '[resembles] paranoia in some respects but [differs] from it in others' (p. 145).

Sedgwick's essay not only contains a strong stance, but it also asks us to think about the function of that stance, and about the way in which it might differ from other instances of paranoia. Its paranoid outlook exists in order to pose a dilemma to our reading, to invite a reparative response.

Sedgwick's text invites both a strong and a weak reading. Writing about Miller's *The Novel and the Police,* Sedgwick, having identified its paranoid argument, admits,

> the very breadth of reach that makes the theory strong also offers the space . . . for a wealth of tonal nuance, attitude, worldly observation, performative paradox, aggression, tenderness, wit, inventive reading, obiter dicta, and writerly panache. These rewards are so local and frequent that one might want to say that a plethora of only loosely related weak theories has been invited to shelter in the hypertrophied embrace of the book's overarching strong theory (pp. 135–6).

Sedgwick's work, too, is far more rewarding on a local level than in the strong reading I identified earlier. Even so, it cannot disqualify such a response. A weak theory is, and must somehow remain, weak by virtue of its dependence on a strong one. It is not a case of banishing one to usher in the other, but an ongoing matter of 'changing and heterogeneous relational stances' in which the stance we adopt is always to some extent constituted by (and constituting) the other it is not (p. 128).[7]

This brings us back – from a detour led by my own particular desires and interests – to 'Violence and metaphysics' and an observation made by Bernasconi. 'In order to generate a double reading', Bernasconi explains, Derrida 'tends to concern himself with certain reductive readings offered by various commentators' (Bernasconi 1988, pp. 35–6). 'Violence and metaphysics', notably, does not do this:

when Derrida wrote 'Violence and Metaphysics' it was the first major discussion of Levinas; he could find no foil for 'another reading'. Derrida's reading of Levinas might therefore seem artificial, as if he had to place Levinas 'within metaphysics' in order to develop his own reading which would generate another text 'outside'.

There is no one, Bernasconi points out, to whom Derrida can attribute the first reading; it also appears to be his own. This results in an 'irony': 'Derrida's readers tend to opt for the former reading, which . . . they then identify as Derrida's' (p. 36). By voicing both readings, Derrida's essay opens itself to misreading; its readers may opt for the 'wrong' interpretation, identifying the 'former reading' as Derrida's. Such readers misconstrue Derrida's intentions (but again, how can we be truly certain what Derrida intended?).

However, Bernasconi continues and points out that

> this attempt to divorce the two readings and set them up in opposition to each other would be to mistake what it means to give a double reading. The second reading is not Derrida's own; it is not opposed to a disowned reading. Derrida's reading is always a reading which embraces duplicity and this is a consequence of the collapse of the notion of a 'text in itself' and the emergence in its place of the notion of the text as the history of its operation, its readings (p. 36).

The first reading cannot be fully 'disowned' or entirely 'opposed' to the second reading. Both moments are fundamental to Derrida's work.

Derrida offers us a first and a second reading and asks us to read their relationship. This strategy is, however, risky. We all too easily opt for *either* the first *or* the second reading and fail to take both into account. Derrida's work remains open to misreading.

But therein lies its value; without this risk, there would be no chance of success.

This possibility of misreading is not coincidental but inherent in 'double reading'. The 'error' the readers of 'Violence and metaphysics' commit points to deconstruction's very condition.

Derrida writes, '[l]anguage must be allowed this freedom to betray so that it can surrender to its essence, which is the ethical. The essence for once, and this is unique, is delivered over to probability, risk, and uncertainty. On this basis, the essence of essence remains to be rethought beginning with responsibility for the other, and so forth' (Derrida 2007a, p. 158). As I explain in my next section, the essence of ethics for both Derrida and Levinas is resituated; the essential has not yet happened and is not guaranteed. We might call it reading. As such, the *possibility* of misreading remains fundamental. As does the notion of intention, as clumsy as it may seem.

A philosophy of the future

As I explained in my first section, the qualities we are after – the supplement, the break with philosophy conjured by the beginning of 'Violence and metaphysics' and 'Wholly otherwise', the trace, ethics, deconstruction – place us in a double bind. They would lie outside or beyond language and, as such, all language betrays them. Derrida explains, '[a]s soon as one attempts to think Infinity as a positive plenitude (one pole of Levinas's nonnegative transference), the other becomes unthinkable, impossible, unutterable' (Derrida 1978b, p. 114; my italics). We cannot definitively summon the 'unthinkable-impossible-unutterable'.

Wittgenstein, in a letter to Ludwig von Flicker, muses on his *Prototractatus* and claims that '[t]he book's point is an ethical one'. He continues, 'I once meant to include in the preface a sentence which is not in fact there now but which I will write out for you here because it will perhaps be a key to the work for you. What I meant to write, then, was this: my work consists in two parts: the one presented here plus all that I have *not* written. And it is precisely this second part that is the important one'. He concludes, '[i]n short, I believe that where *many* others today are just *gassing*, I have managed in my book to put everything firmly into play by being silent about it' (Wittgenstein 1971, p. 16 quoted in Greisch 1991, p. 73; italics in original). Somewhat abruptly, Wittgenstein reiterates the realization Derrida and Levinas offer: ethics cannot be conceptualized; it is not that which we could *mean*. Our writing will always miss ethics and is therefore as effective only as silence.

Wittgenstein's preference for silence is, however, articulated with a great deal of irony; it functions only once broken. We are not aware of his silence (in its specificity) until he points it out.

Levinas points out, '[o]ne can see nothing without thematization, or without the oblique rays which it reflects back, even when it is a question of the nonthematizable' (Levinas 1991, p. 6). The 'nonthematizable' for which we quest will occur only *through* thematization, appearing in it as an uncertain or undecidable presence. We must work *with* thematization's inevitable betrayal.

This is, as Blanchot claims, a 'game of thought' that 'cannot be played alone' (Blanchot 1993, p. 216).

Derrida writes, '[t]he trace of this interruption in the knot is never simply visible, sensible, or assured. It [*Elle*] does not belong to discourse and only comes to it from the Other' (Derrida 2007a, p. 164). Levinas's ethics relies for its presentation on another reading. Ethics cannot be written or guaranteed; Levinas's philosophy is subject to the other.

Deconstruction and ethics alike require a particular reading if they are to work. Levinas points out in 'Wholly otherwise' that '[t]he path toward these pathless "places" ("*lieux*"), the subsoil of our empirical places, does not, in any case, open itself to the vertigo which we get from those who – dreadfully well-informed, prodigiously intelligent, and more Derridian than Derrida – interpret his extraordinary work with the assistance of all the key-words at once, without having or leaving time to return to the thinking of which those words are contemporary' (Levinas 1991, p. 6). The value of Derrida's work lies not in the words it uses (in its said), but in the never-quite-inscribed thought 'of which those words are contemporary' (its saying).

Yet, Derrida admits, '[y]ou are never forced to read or recognize this trace' (p. 165). It is fundamental that we read the work of Derrida and Levinas in the spirit of its saying, yet nothing could impel us.

Derrida explains in 'At this very moment' that

> one must, even though nobody constrains anybody, read his work, otherwise said, respond to it and even answer for it, not on the basis of what one understands by *work* according to the dominant interpretation of language, but according to what *his* work says, *in its manner*, of the Work, about what it is, otherwise said, about what it will have had (to be) as work in the work (Derrida 2007a, p. 177).

Blanchot writes that Levinas creates

> – A speech that is other than any speech already said and thereby always new, never heard: to be precise, a speech beyond hearing and to which I must nonetheless respond.
>   – Such, then, would be my task: to respond to this speech that surpasses my hearing, to respond to it without having really understood it, and to respond to it in repeating it, in making it speak (Blanchot 1993, p. 65).

We must respond to a speech other than the speech that does not permit understanding. We must locate whatever in this speech cannot appear.

Admitting '[y]ou don't even know how, at this moment, *one must* hear this "one must" [*il faut*]', Derrida writes, '[h]ow difficult, probably impossible, to write here, to describe what I seem to be on the verge of describing' (Derrida 2007a, pp. 171, 173; italics in original).

Derrida must work out a way 'to give to [Levinas] the very giving of giving, a giving that would no longer even be an object or a present said' (p. 148). He writes, '[p]*erhaps* Levinas calls us toward this unthinkable-impossible-unutterable beyond (tradition's) Being and Logos. But it must not be possible either to think or state this call' (Derrida 1978b, p. 114; my italics). Derrida's 'perhaps' guards against the betrayal of uttering, thinking or making possible the other as 'positive plenitude'. *Perhaps* Levinas 'calls us toward' the other, but nothing could mark this call.

Derrida writes '[n]*early always with him*, this is how he fabricates the fabric of his work' and 'in his text there is, *perhaps*, a supplementary nodal complication, another way of retying without retying' (Derrida 2007a, pp. 152, 165; my italics). Derrida poses a series of questions implying, but never stating, that Levinas writes the other:

> How, then, does he write? . . . What does he do, for example and par excellence, when he writes in the present, in the grammatical form of the present, to say what does not present itself and will never have been present, the *present said* only presenting itself in the name of a Saying that overflows it infinitely within and without, like a sort of absolute anachrony of the wholly other that, although incommensurably heterogeneous to the language of the present and the discourse of the same, nonetheless leaves a trace there, a trace that is always improbable but each time determinate, this one, and not another? (Derrida 2007a, p. 150)

The second of these sentences is so long we almost forget its interrogative opening; the question answers itself only to re-pose itself as a question at its close. It almost but does not quite state that Levinas's writing traces the other.

Tempted though he is, Derrida knows he must not state the 'unthinkable-impossible-unutterable' he detects in Levinas's work. We cannot, without betraying it, ascribe to the work the 'unthinkable' for which we so much want to praise it; it must remain undecidable.

Critchley is again too certain. He writes that 'Levinas's writing *enacts* what was called above a "spiralling movement" (*AE* 57/*OB* 44), in which language oscillates enigmatically, or undecidedly, between the Saying and the Said' (Critchley 1999, p. 123; my italics). For Critchley, Levinas's writing *does* what Derrida is careful to suggest it is possible only *to read* in his work.

Derrida's reading, if it is to remain faithful to Levinas's work, cannot simply present the trace. It still remains to be opened by yet another reading; it depends once more upon the 'critique exercised by *another* philosopher' (Levinas 1981, p. 20).

Quite simply, the deconstruction has never yet happened:

> the most rigorous deconstructions have never claimed to be . . . possible. And I would say that deconstruction loses nothing from admitting that it is impossible; and also that those who would rush to delight in that admission lose nothing from having to wait. For a deconstructive operation *possibility* would rather be the danger, the danger of becoming an available set of rule-governed procedures, methods, accessible approaches. The interest of deconstruction, of such force and desire as it may have, is a certain experience of the impossible (Derrida 1992a, p. 30; italics in original).

Yet to come, deconstruction and ethics are '"inherently" nothing at all'. Rather, they call into question the inherent (Derrida 1988, p. 141).

They realize that '[p]hilosophy (in general) can only open itself to the question, within it and by it. It can only *let itself be questioned*' (Derrida 1978b, p. 131; italics in original).

Derrida, even as he interrupts Levinas, begs '[i]nterrupt me' (Derrida 2007a, p. 188).

(Sedgwick echoes this imperative. Contemplating the way in which a reader might respond to one's work she points out that it is, in this respect, 'realistic and necessary to experience surprise' (Sedgwick 2003, p. 146). The unanticipated response best activates the work.)

Levinas explains that '[t]he truth of truths would not therefore be capable of being gathered into an instant, nor into a synthesis where the supposed movement of the dialectic comes to a standstill. The truth of truths lies in the Said, in the Unsaid, and in the Otherwise Said – return, resumption, reduction: the history of philosophy or its preliminary' (Levinas 1991, p. 6). 'Truth' is a desired but always-deferred moment. Deconstruction and ethics cannot be claimed but lie in the hands of the other falling, as Derrida writes in *Spurs,* in the 'interval between several styles' (Derrida 1979b, p. 139).

One is '[s]peaking, finally, only to interrupt oneself and to render possible the impossible interruption' (Blanchot 1993, p. 79). Theory is not masterful; deconstruction and ethics remain to be read.

I suppose we have to concede that it is, rather, up to you.

No, I'm not particularly happy about it either. I've spent a lot of time thinking this through. And now, it seems, I have to relinquish control to you without a single guarantee you'll get it right.

I *can't* leave it to you, not yet. I'm not sure you're ready. I won't ever be, of course, but it can't hurt to explain myself a little more. Two more chapters. First, to enjoin you to tact and, finally, to think 'you' a little more. And then you will, I hope, defy my distrust (you're right – how dare I doubt you?), outdoing me in ways I could never have anticipated.

Surprise me.

4

Tact

We will never be done with ethics; we must continue to engage with the 'ethics of reading' even while knowing that we cannot formulate a fixed code for its practice. We must keep re-formulating it. This chapter opens the question once more, in terms of tact. It will show that in questions of reading tact is fundamental. When we wonder how best to read we ask what the most tactful – touching, respectful – approach might be. In *On Touching – Jean-Luc Nancy,* Derrida suggests '[p]erhaps the law is always a law *of tact*. This law's law finds itself there, before anything. There is this law, and it is the law itself, the law of the law. One cannot imagine what a law would be in general without something like tact' (Derrida 2005a, p. 66; italics in original). Derrida identifies tact as the first imperative we must obey; it and the law are inseparable.

Derrida's announcement does not, however, explain how we might identify or determine tact. Val Cunningham is, in his book *Reading After Theory,* more specific. He describes tact as 'gentle touch, caring touch, loving touch' (Cunningham 2002, p. 155). Tact is allied with contact, intimacy and proximity. Cunningham also argues, however, that tact is

> proper tactility; the gentle touch of the right-minded communicant. Tact as proper behaviours before the tended, the offered sacrament; tact as due attention, a proper attending to; a tenderness of touch; tender attention. Tact as that approach with the right hands, the attentively tendered hand of the attentive body, of the body tending towards, the body approaching near, coming carefully close up to the object to be received (p. 156).

In this quotation, the phrases 'tending towards', 'approaching near' and 'coming carefully' all imply an inclination to touch, which never, in fact, makes contact. Cunningham's language demands reservation and restraint; tact's 'proper behaviour' commands distance.[1]

Tact thus attains, not only in Cunningham's work but also elsewhere, two contradictory senses; its exact quality remains unclear. To consider the dilemma in which it therefore places us, I examine three novels in which proximity and distance are thematized and considered: A. S. Byatt's *Possession*, J. M. Coetzee's *Slow Man* and Philip Roth's *The Human Stain*. In the first section of my chapter, I consider tact as touch by examining a distrust of distance and a desire for proximity, which is expressed in all three of my chosen texts. A longing for intimacy is repeatedly expressed. I will show, however, that this wish remains unfulfilled; distance is never fully banished. Non-contact persists at contact's heart. In the second section of my chapter, I will consider an inverse desire, also displayed in these texts, *for* a proper and respectful distance. This wish conjures tact in the second sense I outlined earlier. This desire is, however, also thwarted; the potentially seductive power of distance threatens always to return it to the intimacy it would banish. Each of tact's senses is undone by the other; we can declare neither as its proper sense.

Tact's demand is impossibly contradictory. Derrida gestures towards this fact in the passage I quoted earlier. By arguing that tact precedes the law, Derrida alludes to the bind in which it places us: we will remain unable to formulate a law *of* it. Cunningham's *Reading After Theory* never acknowledges the contradiction by which it is beset. In *On Touching*, however, Derrida accepts and works with this impossibility, as I too will attempt to do in my chapter's third section.

I have already pointed out that Roth's *The Human Stain* and Coetzee's *Slow Man* employ the themes of intimacy and distance on which I will focus in my first two sections. They are, in addition, lauded for their discussion of the 'ethics of fiction' – a category closely aligned with my notion of tact. Jens Martin Gurr argues that the appearance of the author-character, Elizabeth Costello, in *Slow Man* poses an 'ethical issue', which begs the questions 'what about the human costs of writing fiction, what about the *ethical* status of the writer?' (Gurr 2007, p. 104; italics in original). John Lanchester, too, suggests that the novel presents us with 'a question of ethics, touching on the morality of making people up, and then devising trials and torments for them, designed to expose and test their deficiencies. Is there anything of ethical content to be said about the fortunes of these imaginary people? Does making things up have an effect on the maker, and on the reader?' (Lanchester 2005, p. 6). Van der Vlies declares that 'Costello is the embodiment of a writer's conscience, voicing Coetzee's questions about the formal, aesthetic and ethical demands of fiction' (van der Vlies 2005, p. 9). For all three of these critics, the novel, and Elizabeth Costello in particular, demand that we ask what the 'ethics' of fiction might be. In relation to *The Human Stain*, too, Debra Shostak argues that Zuckerman has to 'confront . . . the ethical consequences of his choices' (Shostak 2004, p. 264).[2]

These formulations inform us implicitly what 'ethics' is and is meant to be; Lanchester invokes an 'ethical *content* to be *said*' while for der Vlies Costello '[voices] questions'. For both of these critics, ethics are spoken – a constatively delineated and formal code thematized by the text; these formulations posit 'ethics' as a realm demanding explicit answers and formulations. The first and second sections of my chapter will, however, challenge the assumption that such thematization is possible; they will show that the statements that these novels make concerning distance and contact are undone by and in our experience of the text. My chapter's final section therefore suggests that the 'ethical' possibility of these novels cannot be confined simply to that which they would say; we must (in line with a shift proposed by Levinas) rethink 'ethics' as a 'saying' or in terms of that which happens when we read these texts. John Kerrigan points out that '[b]eing interested in tact would involve more than noticing just how inappropriate Mrs Bennet's [*sic*] behaviour is in *Pride and Prejudice*. It would mean thinking about the conventions that shape the interaction between authors, narrators and characters, and deciding how far critics should respect them' (Kerrigan 2002, p. 21).

Tact as touch: A desire for proximity

To elucidate tact's quality, I begin by examining an example of supposed tactlessness: literary theory as it is portrayed in both Cunningham's *Reading After Theory* and in many of the responses to Byatt's *Possession*.[3] Cunningham contends that tact is 'the missing element in Theory's misconstruings and misreadings' and accuses it of 'tactile failures' (Cunningham 2002, p. 155). By examining more closely the terms of this critique – which is expressed, too, by *Possession*'s readers – I outline, in this first section of my chapter, a concept of tact, which, opposing itself to a too-distant theory, relies on notions of touch, intimacy and proximity.

Byatt's *Possession* juxtaposes two interrelated narratives. The first revolves around two theoretically savvy twentieth-century academics, Roland and Maud, who study the (fictional) nineteenth-century poets Randolph Henry Ash and Isabel LaMotte. At the beginning of the novel, Roland discovers a letter written by Ash to LaMotte; the document, by linking these two previously unrelated figures, demands further investigation and explanation. Roland and Maud embark on a quest to discover the particulars of Ash and LaMotte's relationship and gradually piece together the novel's second narrative strand. As they do so, they too fall for each other.

These parallels invite us to compare the periods represented by the novel's two narrative strands. In most accounts, the twentieth century fares poorly. Jackie Buxton claims that '[i]n comparison to the engaged Victorian poets, the contemporary academics appear not only anaemic, but also decidedly repressed' (Buxton 2001, p. 98). Maud and Roland are, for Lundén, unable 'to feel, to understand love as a feeling' (Lundén 1999, p. 118). The cause of this repression and anaemia is, it transpires, theory. Roland and Maud are, unlike Ash and LaMotte, 'theoretically knowing' (Byatt 1991b, p. 423). They do not however benefit from but are, according to Tim Gauthier, 'hampered' by this knowledge (Gauthier 2006, p. 25); their lives are, for Lundén, 'emotionally deficient' as a result (Lundén 1999, p. 97). The protagonists of *Possession* display, for Buxton, an 'unwillingness to become passionately involved' because burdened by 'a sexualized knowledge so devoid of passion that it has only produced a kind of sexual exhaustion' (Buxton 2001, p. 99). These critics express a belief, formulated explicitly by Cunningham's work, that 'Theory has done its very best to deny and obliterate' 'the human relationship' (Cunningham 2002, p. 141).

This critique of theory intersects with an anxiety that recurs throughout Byatt's work concerning academia in general. Jacqueline in *A Whistling Woman* echoes the afore-mentioned assertions when, for example, she worries that 'her choice of work [as an academic] had deflected or distorted her unthinking life' (Byatt 2002, p. 414). At one point she announces to her friend Luk, '"I must be mad, I should have listened to you, I don't know how I got myself so cocooned in my *self*, I want to be able to do the things – people do – I want to live, not just to think"' (Byatt 2002, p. 169; italics in original). Jacqueline's exclamation suggests that too much thinking has prevented her from doing. Tim Gauthier argues that Byatt's work 'contends that the overintellectualization of our existence has moved us progressively away from the "real". In fact, Byatt reserves her most damning criticism for academic writing and theory, whose shallowness and artificiality have contributed to literature's growing distance from anything concrete, or "things" or "facts" as she often labels them' (Gauthier 2006, p. 26).

A similar belief is expressed by those who write about Byatt's work; Kathleen Coyne Kelly declares that

> Byatt's characters have always been introspective, couching their very real dilemmas in the language of literary allusion and philosophical musings. Readers of her earlier novels who have criticized Byatt for creating such characters feel that too many intellectual layers distance readers from her books and insulate her characters from a real engagement with their lives (Kelly 1996, p. 80).

Kelly argues that the 'intellectual' language in which Byatt's characters couch their 'dilemmas' impedes the proper engagement of the reader. We find, both in and in relation to Byatt's work, an assumption that thought and intellectualism act as a barrier to sympathy and understanding.

This belief is thematized, too, in Coetzee's *Slow Man*. The novel's author-figure, Elizabeth Costello, enters in order to inform its protagonist, Paul Rayment, that he, like Jacqueline, has distanced himself too much from 'life'. She tells him, for example, that "'[l]ife is not an exchange of diplomatic notes. *Au contraire*, life is drama, life is action, action and passion!'" (Coetzee 2005, p. 227). Costello echoes Jacqueline's belief that excessive thought ought to be avoided. She dismisses Paul's ponderings as tactics of avoidance and declares that "'one does not need to under-stand before one takes action, not unless one is excessively philosophic'" (p. 137). Paul's desire to 'understand' is, she implies, 'excessive'. It is, moreover, hopeless and will lead only to paralysis or inaction. Intimacy and contact are distinct from, and cannot be grasped by, 'the theoretical apparatuses' (Lundén 1999, p. 92).

Each of the afore-mentioned examples proposes two categories – the theo-retical (or academic) and the emotional, or 'real' – and presents them as both discrete and incompatible; thinking and living are separate and mutually exclu-sive pursuits.[4] 'Life' or the 'real' is composed of 'desire, emotions and intuitions' which are immediate and intimate; it 'cannot be theorized, or intellectualized, only felt' (Lundén 1999, p. 119). Theory, by contrast, is aligned with distance; Cunningham disparages theory for its 'unclose, its distant, railed-off reading' (Cunningham 2002, p. 157). He argues that *theoros*, theory's etymological route, means spectator and that 'theory becomes spectator work, what onlookers and audiences do' (p. 16).[5] Theory is performed from afar, by those who are outside, not involved in, the 'action'. Derrida, in his essay 'Some statements and truisms about neo-logisms, newisms, postisms, parasitisms, and other small seismisms', also contemplates the term theory and acknowledges Cunningham's interpreta-tion as the word's 'ideal' meaning (unlike Cunningham, however, he proceeds, as I will show later, to highlight the impossibility of this ideal). Derrida's essay was given originally as a paper at a conference entitled 'The states of "theory"'. Derrida wonders why it is that the conference's organizers have placed quotation marks around the word theory; the gesture, he suggests, signals an almost exces-sive caution. He concludes, however, that the word ought always, in its 'proper sense', to be bounded in this way.

To place a word between quotation marks, Derrida explains, is to attempt to mention it without using it.[6] The quotation marks, he notes, 'function as small clothespins meant to keep at a distance, without really touching them, clothes which, whether dirty or still wet, won't be freed from their clothespins and really touched until they are properly clean and dry' (Derrida 1990, p. 77). He conjures similar images elsewhere. In *On Touching*, for example, he speaks of 'discretely and silently approaching the word as if it were contaminated in advance, touching it with the quotation marks as if they were tweezers' (Derrida 2005a, p. 304) while in *Spurs* he writes of suspending 'truth' 'between the tenter-hooks of quotation marks' (Derrida 1979b, p. 57). The images Derrida employs all imply an attempt not to touch; quotation marks are compared to objects such as tweezers, which interpose themselves between the object and s/he who would (not) touch it. Quotation marks touch 'without *really* touching'; they ensure that the word (in this case 'theory') is held at arm's length. Derrida makes it clear that this distancing is apt; theory, too, ought only to mention and never to touch. The operation applied *to* theory by the conference's organizers is also theory's proper operation.

The afore-mentioned examples show us, moreover, that intimacy and distance are not equal categories. Distance infuriates; the distance for which theory and thought are by-words is presented as damaging. LaMotte's cousin Sabine asserts this view forcefully when she announces 'I do not believe all these *explanations*. They diminish' (Byatt 1991b, p. 355). This is evident as Roland and Maud begin to read Ash and LaMotte's letters. Roland finds that Maud 'had decided that they should each read the letters of the poet who interested them, and that they should agree conventions of recording their observations on index cards according to a system she was already using in the Women's Resource Centre'. Roland dislikes this idea; he 'objected to this, partly because he felt he was being hustled, partly because he had a vision, which he now saw was ridiculous and romantic, of their two heads bent over the manuscripts, following the story, sharing, he had supposed, the emotion' (p. 129). Roland longs for an intimate reading experience in which he might experience the 'emotion' of the letters while Maud, in contrast, argues for a rigorously scholarly approach.

Roland finally dismisses his idea as 'ridiculous and romantic'. The novel, however, continues to privilege it. Maud is curt: '[h]e pointed out that by Maud's system they would lose any sense of the development of the narrative and Maud retorted robustly that they lived in a time which valued narrative uncertainty, that they could cross-refer later, and that anyway, they had so little *time*, and what concerned her was primarily Christabel LaMotte' (pp. 129–30; italics in original). Maud's dismissal of Roland's proposal is brash and pragmatic. The reader, however, sympathizes with (and most likely shares) Roland's 'romantic' desire to experience the narrative of the letters.

We long to touch. *Possession* again makes this point in the scene in which Lady Bailey reads Maud and Roland one of LaMotte's letters. The experience is unsatisfactory: 'Lady Bailey's reading was slow and halting; words were miscast; she stumbled over *hoc genus omne* and Arachne. It was like frosted glass between them, Roland and Maud, and the true lineaments of the prose and the feelings of Ash and LaMotte' (pp. 87–8). The stumblings of Lady Bailey's reading interpose a barrier, described as 'frosted glass', between the academics and a 'true' understanding of LaMotte's prose. They long instead to get closer to the letters and to lay their hands on them so as to read them 'properly'. These moments establish the 'real' as a privileged category. In light of the comments Elizabeth makes in *Slow Man*, John Lanchester asserts that 'Coetzee insists on the primacy of feeling' (Lanchester 2005, p. 6).[7]

Proximity is desired. To achieve this moment of contact, these texts suggest, they must transcend theory absolutely; they must abolish the distance that endangers this longed-for touch. According to its critics, *Possession* is successful in its transcendence of distance and indeed offers us access to this non-rational realm. Towards the end of the novel, for example, Roland abandons his scholarly pursuits and instead sits in Maud's house composing lists of words: '[h]e was writing lists of words. He was writing lists of words that resisted arrangement into the sentences of literary criticism or theory' (Byatt 1991b, p. 431). This moment, for Gauthier, indicates 'Roland's transformation . . . from textual critic to poet' and 'is Byatt's most explicit rejection of the current theoretical propensities of academe' (Gauthier 2006, p. 34). At this point, Gauthier argues, 'words have (re)gained their potency in the sense that they mean something to Roland emotionally. He can feel the language without necessarily having to intellectualize it' (Lundén 1999, p. 110). Gauthier compares this scene to another of Byatt's novels, *The Biographer's Tale*, in which its protagonist-academic also abandons the scholarly for a more artistic writing pursuit: 'I have become addicted to writing – that is, to setting down the English language, myself, in arrangements chosen by me, for – let it be admitted – pleasure. I have become addicted to forbidden words, words critical theorists can't use and writers can' (Byatt 2001, p. 250). Here, too, Gauthier contends that 'we are dealing with the concept of language as pure communication, pure correspondence between the word and the thing being described, something clearly out of the reach of theoretical language' (Gauthier 2006, pp. 30–1). The suggestion that Roland is able to 'feel' the words he writes implies a physical and emotional proximity. Gauthier celebrates both of these scenes as instances at which 'theoretical language' is overcome and a greater intimacy achieved.

Jackie Buxton makes a similar claim with respect to *Possession*'s final chapter. At this point in the novel, the narrative switches; rather than hearing about Ash and LaMotte from the perspective of their twentieth-century interpreters, the novel offers us an omniscient third-person account of the moment at which Ash meets his daughter, Maia. Buxton claims that '[w]hat Byatt presents here is not a textual construction, but a living human being, a materiality as opposed to a discursive trace. Maia Thomasine Bailey is something of the past that is not merely an inscription, but is emphatically corporeal, an undeniable product of her parents' (literary) liaison' (Buxton 2001, p. 100). Buxton, like Gauthier, lauds this scene as a moment of the 'real' at which the distances of 'inscription' and 'discursive trace' are suspended in favour of the concrete and 'corporeal'.

The claims made by Buxton and Gauthier for *Possession* are echoed in *The Human Stain*. In this case, however, they are voiced by a character within the novel: Nathan Zuckerman. At the end of the novel, Zuckerman claims (in phrases that invoke Kant) '[t]his was not speculation. This was not meditation. This was not the way of thinking that is fiction writing. This was the thing itself' (Roth 2001, p. 350). Zuckerman aligns the episode with the 'real'; he does this also at an earlier point in the novel. When Coleman loses his temper with his lawyer, Primus, in *The Human Stain* and calls him 'lily-white', Zuckerman announces '[h]ow one is revealed or undone by the perfect word. What burns away the camouflage and the covering and the concealment? This, the right word uttered spontaneously, without one's even having to think' (p. 84). Zuckerman, much like Roland in *Possession*, links the 'perfect word' uttered 'spontaneously' to the 'truth'; Coleman is, he declares, 'revealed' at this moment.

Zuckerman's assertion is, however, undermined by Primus' reaction. For Primus, who is unaware of Coleman's history, there is no revelation, only confusion; to him, Coleman's accusation is absurd and meaningless. He exclaims to his wife '"why *white*?"' (Roth 2001, p. 82; italics in original). When compared directly to this reaction, Zuckerman's statement appears naïve and overstated; a disjunction emerges between Zuckerman's declaration and the reader's understanding.

The claims made for the other moments I just outlined are equally dubious. These episodes are not as unequivocally 'real' and immediate as their critics claim but are undercut by an irony that is most apparent in *The Human Stain*. The final scene of the novel – when Zuckerman announces '[t]his was not speculation. This was not meditation. This was not the way of thinking that is fiction writing. This was the thing itself' – is problematic. Zuckerman (a fictional character) declares, in fiction, 'this wasn't fiction writing'. The irony is compounded shortly after the comment I cited above when Les Farley asks

'What's the name of one of your books?'
'*The Human Stain.*'
'Yeah? Can I get it?'
'It's not out yet. It's not finished yet.' (p. 356)

In contrast to Zuckerman's claim that this is 'the thing itself', this conversation possesses, for the reader, an eerily unreal quality; the book we are reading is cited within its covers; one of its characters purports to be its author. Zuckerman's assertions are possible only as and within fiction; his claim to the real is undercut.

I noted earlier the way in which Elizabeth Costello in *Slow Man* admonishes Paul, telling him that his excessive contemplation has removed him from the real of 'life'. Lanchester, I pointed out, reads this as an advocation for the 'primacy of feeling'. The novel, however, encourages us to read Costello's remarks sceptically. These opinions are, importantly, voiced by the novel's author-figure and are, as such, subject to a similar irony to that I just outlined in relation to *The Human Stain*. Elizabeth decides '"[n]o, the more I listen the more convinced I am that the key to your character lies in your speech. You speak like a book"' (Coetzee 2005, p. 231). Paul, of course, is the 'slow man' and so *is*, indeed, a book, as is *Elizabeth Costello*. Elizabeth offers her comment as a criticism of Paul's character; the reader, however, realizes that neither she nor Paul could speak any other way. Paul makes this clear: '[h]e presumes these remarks about the real are in some sense aimed at him; he presumes they are made with irony. What their point might be he cannot guess' (Coetzee 2005, p. 242).

The irony is less explicit in the final chapter of *Possession*; nonetheless, the scene is equally troubled. As I have already pointed out, the novel offers us a third-person omniscient view of its nineteenth-century protagonists, which contrasts with most of the rest of the novel. For most of *Possession* we learn about Ash and LaMotte via their poems and letters as they are read and interpreted by Maud and Roland; the nineteenth century is revealed to us through the twentieth. However, this revelation is not absolute; the academics point out time and again that interpretation has its limits. Our understanding is tainted by twentieth-century concerns; we will never fully or objectively know the nineteenth century. Gauthier points out that Byatt 'protests, through her characters and their necessary blindness, that the past can never be entirely known' (Gauthier 2006, p. 56).

Given these comments, the third-person narration with which the novel concludes is clearly problematic. Gauthier highlights the issue, writing that

> Byatt attempts to have her historical incompleteness and eat it too. She protests, through her characters and their necessary blindness, that the past can never be entirely known. At the same time, however, she presents a second plot, one available to her readers only, in which history is presented as a coherent and entirely comprehensible entity (Gauthier 2006, p. 56).

Possession, Gauthier points out, conditions us to suspect any account in which history appears 'coherent' and 'entirely comprehensible'. The novel's final episode presents us with a version of events in which all seems, however, 'entirely known'. It is, Gauthier notices, at odds with the rest of the novel; it too neatly fulfils our desire to know. Gauthier accuses Byatt of attempting 'to have her historical incompleteness and eat it too'. But perhaps this scene cannot be so easily dismissed. *Possession* shows that we cannot fully know the past. However, it also demonstrates, through Roland and Maud, that a strong desire *to know* persists, even when we cannot. Their investigations are driven by a longing to know what happened and we, too, share this desire. The book's final chapter appears at first to fulfil this craving for knowledge. However, it is *too* neat; it strikes a false note. Gauthier certainly spots it, and I am sure other readers would too. This scene, we realize, could not possibly derive from the evidence known by Roland or Maud; only fiction could invent it. The chapter is at odds with the claims made by the rest of the novel, but this is clear to the reader; the novel does not get away with it. We become conscious of its impossibility; the reader soon realizes the impropriety of its omniscient view.

A closer examination of Roland's word list also reveals the flaw in the assertions made by the novel's critics:

> He wrote: blood, clay, terracotta, carnation.
> He wrote: blond, burning bush, scattering.
> He annotated this, 'scattering as in Donne, "extreme and scattering bright", nothing to do with scattergraphs.'
> He wrote: anemone, coral, coal, hair, hairs, nail, nails, fur, owl, isinglass, scarab.
> He rejected wooden, point, link, and other ambivalent words, also blot and blank, though all these sprang (another word he hesitated over) to mind. He was uncertain about the place of verbs in this primitive language. Spring, springs, springes, sprung, sprang (Byatt 1991b, p. 431).

I noted earlier Gauthier's claim that Roland transcends academic concerns at this moment. Even on the most obvious textual level, however, Gauthier's assertion is inaccurate; as scholarly as ever, Roland 'annotate[s]' his list with a reference to Donne. The passage undermines Gauthier's declaration in more subtle ways, too. The tone of the passage is sombre; the repetition of the simple phrase 'he wrote' is portentous. Roland creates his word lists seriously; he appears to share Gauthier's belief that this is an important and transcendent moment. For the reader, however, the product of Roland's labours is laughable. Roland links words on the basis of their sound. Hence, Donne's 'scattering bright' reminds him of the word 'scattergraphs' and he feels bound to point out that the quotation does not, in fact, have anything to do with them. For the reader, the qualification is redundant. It never would have occurred to us that 'scattering bright' *was* to 'do with scattergraphs'. The very possibility strikes us as absurd; Roland's project is, for the reader, somewhat ridiculous. Roland's serious attitude towards his task, therefore, contrasts with the reader's experience of it; the discrepancy lends the scene a comic quality.

For the reader, words do not become pure and potent; Roland does not unequivocally occupy a non-theoretical realm or achieve a moment of pure contact. He aspires to such a touch, but does not achieve it. Roland's lists do not imply a moment of transcendence; instead, the novel gently mocks his attempt to achieve such spontaneity, pointing towards the ultimate naivety of any desire to occupy unequivocally the 'real'.[8]

In each of these examples distance interposes itself, tainting the pure proximity we desire. Touch, as I have outlined earlier, emerges in opposition to distance and is figured as its death. Contact would thus be the reduction of distance to zero; it is the 'death of *between*' (Derrida 2005a, p. 2; italics in original). The paradoxes of Zeno and Aristotle inform us, however, that no matter what distance we begin with this absolute cancellation is impossible. J. M. Coetzee's *Diary of a Bad Year* explains this point neatly; its narrator points out that

> Before the arrow can reach its target, says Zeno, it must get half-way there; before it can get half-way it must get a quarter of the way; and so forth: $1, \frac{1}{2}, \frac{1}{4}, \ldots \frac{1}{2}^{N}, \frac{1}{2}^{(N+1)}, \ldots$ If we grant that the series of markers it needs to pass on its way to the target is infinitely long, then how can the arrow ever get there? (Coetzee 2008, p. 94)

The series never reaches zero; the distance between the objects becomes infinitely small but they would, in theory, never touch.

This model thus admits what Derrida describes as the 'hiatus of noncontact at the heart of contact'. Derrida continues, arguing that 'this spacing makes for the trial of noncontact as the very condition or experience *itself* of contact' (Derrida 2005a, p. 221; italics in original). Both Roland in *Possession* and Zuckerman in *The Human Stain* note this inevitable and paradoxical failure; the closer we get, the more acute distance becomes. In *Possession*, Roland 'thought about Randolph Henry Ash. The pursuit of the letters had distanced him from Ash as they had come closer to Ash's life' (Byatt 1991b, pp. 469–70). Similarly, once Zuckerman uncovers Coleman's secret, he finds that 'I couldn't imagine anything that could have made Coleman more of a mystery to me than this unmasking. Now that I knew everything, it was as though I knew nothing, and instead of what I'd learned from Ernestine unifying my idea of him, he became not just an unknown but an uncohesive person' (Roth 2001, p. 333). Both Roland and Zuckerman stress that they have become closer to their subjects' lives than ever before; however, these moments emphasize a gulf. Roland finds himself 'distanced' from Ash while Coleman becomes for Zuckerman an 'unknown' and 'uncohesive person'.[9] Michal Ben-Naftali explains that '[t]here will always be, there has always already been, a space left untouched, untouchable, the recognition of which may be even more intensely felt during the very rare graceful moments of encounter' (Ben-Naftali 1999, p. 663). Non-contact, or distance, always persists at the heart of contact; touch, which begins with the thought of distance, can never transcend it completely.

By presenting this always-compromised contact, the texts I discuss here provoke a number of questions. The impossibility of absolute touch and of intimacy forces them to wonder, for example, what the 'real' might be. In *Slow Man*, Paul Rayment wonders '[w]hat would it take to make Marijana see him as the real thing? What is the real thing? Physical desire? Sexual intimacy? They have been intimate, he and Marijana, for some while now – for longer than some love affairs last, start to finish. But all the intimacy, all the nakedness, all the helplessness has been on one side' (Coetzee 2005, p. 172). In its traditional sense, intimacy cannot be all 'on one side'; the 'side' implies the continued existence of the very between to which intimacy opposes itself. If, however, this between is never overcome, Paul's one-sided intimacy is perhaps as good as any.[10] The reader makes realizations such as this one as a result of – although not necessarily in concordance with – the determined, yet compromised, statements these novels make concerning the 'real'. I show in more detail in my final section that, through their failure, an alternative possibility (which is all the more touching because identified by the reader) is indirectly gleaned.

The ongoing interdependence of distance and contact has implications, too, for the model of close reading to which I alluded earlier. The examples I examined from *Possession* and *The Human Stain* demonstrate that attempts to isolate the real are both problematic and naïve. Close reading cannot, therefore, be the moment of perfect feeling Cunningham claims; we cannot separate from thought and theorization a 'pure' and intimate experience of the text. Isobel Armstrong argues that '[t]he task of a new definition of close reading is to rethink the power of affect, feeling and emotion in a *cognitive* space. The power of affect needs to be included within a definition of thought and knowledge rather than theorized as outside them' (Armstrong 1995, p. 403; italics in original).[11] We must accept that, just as distance and proximity remain bound, so too do thought and feeling; close reading – and the thought of tact on which it relies – must be reconsidered on this basis. I return to this challenge too in my chapter's final section. First, however, I examine the concept of distance in order to subject it to a similar scrutiny to that I have already applied to touch, thus reiterating and reinforcing the logic I have already outlined while revealing the way in which tact also occupies an entirely contradictory sense to the one just shown.

Leaving the other space: Tact as proper distance

As I explained earlier, Cunningham criticizes theory for its too-distant, railed-off stance. However, this is not the only charge he levels against it; he accuses it too of 'interpretative excess, excess of readerly kindness, the too-heavy readerly embrace that smothers, the too-freely heaped-up load of interpretation that just buries the text it's built on' (Cunningham 2002, p. 79). Theory foists upon the text an unwanted intimacy; contradicting his earlier claims, Cunningham now argues that theory is dangerous because it is too close. Again, however, Cunningham suggests tact as the solution: '[t]rue readers don't paw and mammock, don't abuse, the text. True readers are tactful' (p. 157). Tact, in this case, implies a respectful distance; it suggests a hands-off approach that avoids uncouth pawing and mammocking. I consider, in this second section of my chapter, this alternative sense of tact as distance. I show that it, like the model of tact as touch discussed earlier, is problematized and undone by the ongoing interrelation of proximity and distance. Finally, in the third section of my chapter, I will consider how we might unite these two contradictory – and equally impossible – senses; neither grasps tact, but by reading them side by side we might yet touch upon it at a tangent.

The relationship between Leonora Stern and Maud in Byatt's *Possession* reinforces the belief expressed by Cunningham that too great a proximity may be damaging. Leonora, Franken explains, 'is a caricature of a lesbian feminist who follows every theoretical trend there is, in A. S. Byatt's words, and who invades Maud Bailey's life, wreaking havoc there' (Franken 2001, p. 89). The particular 'havoc' Leonora wreaks is explained by Maud herself: '"[s]he is – she is – invasive. An expert in intimacy. She reduces my space. I'm not very good with that sort of thing"' (Byatt 1991b, p. 270). Maud's hesitant start ('she is – she is') and short, uncertain sentences contrast with her usual coherence and thus convey her unease. The source of her discomfort, she points out, is Leonora's proximity; 'intimacy' loses its usual positive connotations, becoming instead a particularly threatening craft in which Leonora has become 'expert'. She is *too* close; too much intimacy is as undesirable as its lack. For Kathleen Coyne Kelly, this idea runs throughout the novel as a whole; she argues that '[t]here is a clear continuum of feeling, from sexual and physical possession to academic absorption, throughout the novel. Excessive possession leads to the objectifying of the other, whether the other is a human being or a text' (Kelly 1996, p. 93). Kelly argues that, at a certain point, possession becomes 'excessive'; like Maud, she implies that one must leave the other space.

A similar wariness is expressed by Nathan Zuckerman in *The Human Stain*. Zuckerman, we discover, has become a recluse; Hamilton notes that 'Zuckerman is not the man he used to be. Nowadays, he is more spectator than participant' (Hamilton 2000, p. 37). Nathan recounts to us his 'determination to concern myself, in whatever time *I* have left, with nothing but the daily demands of work, to be engrossed by nothing but solid work, in search of adventure nowhere else – to have not ever a life of my own to care about, let alone somebody else's' (Roth 2001, p. 43; italics in original). Zuckerman has distanced himself from the world and from life in order to focus solely on 'work'. Throughout the course of the novel, however, this resolve is undone, as Zuckerman finds that 'Coleman Silk's life had become closer to me than my own' (Roth 2001, p. 344). This experience is not, however, entirely pleasant; he describes it as an 'obsession', which is both all-consuming and inescapable (p. 344). Debra Shostak argues that '[w]ith the pleasures of knowing and telling . . . Zuckerman experiences the fall into history, into the contingencies of one's own and others' making, causing him to confront the uncontrollable real' (Shostak 2004, p. 264). The real is unnervingly 'uncontrollable'. Zuckerman finds that his friendship with Coleman denies him the ability to 'live apart from the turbulence and intensity' he has fled. 'I did no more than find a friend', he writes, 'and all the world's malice came rushing in' (Roth 2001, p. 45). Zuckerman is understandably wary of an intimacy that admits an undesirable 'malice' and 'turbulence'.

The narrator of Coetzee's *Slow Man* also evinces this distrust of the too-close. The theme emerges most explicitly in his relationship with Elizabeth Costello. When Elizabeth first arrives in Paul's flat she is out of breath:

> 'Bad heart,' she says fanning herself. 'Nearly as much of an impediment as' (she pauses to catch her breath) 'a bad leg'.
>
> Coming from a stranger the remark strikes him as inappropriate, unseemly (Coetzee 2005, p. 80).

For Paul, Elizabeth contravenes the rules of politeness and propriety; her comment about his 'bad leg' assumes a greater intimacy with his situation than he would expect from a 'stranger'. Later in the novel, Paul finds Elizabeth's notebook; he reads a few pages but then stops, explaining that

> [h]e is not sure he wants to know more. Something unseemly about this writing, the fat ink sprawling carelessly over the tramlines; something impious, provocative, uncovering what does not belong in the light of day.
>
> Is the whole notebook like that: a provocation, an affront to decency? (p. 121)

The comments Paul makes here express more forcefully the criticism he articulates when he first meets Elizabeth; her writing is 'unseemly' and an 'affront to decency' because it places in the 'light of day' what does not belong there. It is too explicit and too direct. In *Possession*, Ash, too, evinces this opinion when he apologizes to LaMotte: "'[f]orgive this baldness. I am truly trying to discover your wishes. We left in so exalted a state – I wish decisions could arise naturally – but you see how it is"' (Byatt 1991b, p. 275). By apologizing for it, Ash establishes 'baldness' as undesirable; it would be better if he and LaMotte could come to a decision 'naturally', without having to address the question obviously. Thus, each of these characters expresses a feeling, as Derrida explains, that '[w]hat is closest *must* be avoided, by virtue of its very proximity. It must be kept at a distance, it must be warned. It must be turned away from, diverted, *warned*' (Derrida 1987b, p. 263; italics in original).

An example from *Possession* suggests why this too-closeness may be problematic. Roland and Maud find a diary written by Sabine, LaMotte's cousin, in which she declares that 'I can't so describe my father's eyes, nor his hair, nor his stoop. He is *too* close. If you hold a book too close to your face, in poor candlelight, the characters blur. So with my father' (Byatt 1991b, p. 342; my italics). Sabine explains that she is 'too close' to be able to describe her father; she cannot attain the distance necessary to see him clearly and properly. To be too close, she implies, is disorientating. The example of a book held too close to the face makes this especially clear. The characters of such a book 'blur'; they can no longer be read.

This theme is explored at greater length in the opening pages of *The Human Stain* as we are introduced to the novel's protagonist, Coleman Silk. Coleman recounts for Zuckerman the events that led to his resignation and, he believes, to the death of his wife. When working at Athena College, Coleman remarks one day on the persistent absence of two students from his class: '[d]oes anyone know these people?' he asks, '[d]o they exist or are they spooks?' (Roth 2001, p. 6). The students, it later transpires, are black, and interpret Coleman's comment as a racial slur. They issue a complaint, which the college upholds. As we hear this story we learn, too, that Coleman is writing a book about the incident. It is apparent, moreover, that he is still very angry. In fact, Zuckerman observes the 'near impossibility of his tearing himself free from his bitterness' (p. 18).

Mark Schechner notes that 'Coleman Silk knows his own life only through the fogs of indignation and grief, the fog of self-intoxication, the fog of self-loathing, the fog of self-misunderstanding, the fog of occluded desire, the fog of self-forgetfulness' (Shechner 2003, pp. 190–1). The fog metaphor, like Sabine's image of a blurred character in a book, implies obscured or imperfect vision; Coleman, Schechner suggests, has lost the ability to consider events objectively. Zuckerman is therefore certain that the quality of Coleman's book will not be high. He writes, 'I'd heard stuff like that from him frequently during these last two years, ravings about black anti-Semitism and about his treacherous, cowardly colleagues that were obviously being mainlined, unmodified, into his book' (Roth 2001, p. 16). Zuckerman implies that the 'unmodified' transcription of these thoughts will make for a bad novel; writing requires transformation. Coleman finally concurs; having read over his 'completed' book he abandons the project: '"[b]ut I read it and it's shit and I'm over it. I can't do what the pros do. Writing about myself, I can't maneuver the creative remove. Page after page, it is still the raw thing. It's a parody of the self-justifying memoir. The hopelessness of explanation"' (p. 19). Coleman admits that his book fails; 'still the raw thing', it is unable to execute the 'remove' necessary for creation to take place.

Coleman's experience reveals the dangerous distortions that result from remaining too-close. Conscious of this danger, the texts I am examining here all express a desire for distance. As I explained in the first section of my chapter, the nineteenth- and twentieth-century narratives of *Possession* invite comparison. Often, I pointed out, the twentieth-century protagonists are criticized for their lack of intimacy. Equally – and yet contradictorily – they are disparaged for their poor command of distance; the nineteenth-century characters are, apparently, also to be lauded for their reticence. Johnson, for example, argues that 'the theme is the contrast between the Victorian and modern worlds . . . this work celebrates the Victorian age, with its reassuring structures, decent reticences, and solid bourgeois comforts. Byatt's convincing imitations pay tacit homage to these old values and comparative certitudes' (Johnson 1991, p. 33). The Victorians are, Johnson argues, superior because masters of an indirect propriety. Roland concurs; he lauds Ash in terms similar to those employed by Johnson: '[h]e thought he knew Ash fairly well, as well as anyone might know a man whose life seemed to be all in his mind, who lived in a quiet and exemplary married life for forty years, whose correspondence was voluminous indeed, but guarded, courteous and not of the most lively. Roland liked that in Randolph Henry Ash' (Byatt 1991b, pp.7–8).

Roland likes that Ash is 'guarded' and that he will never know him more than 'fairly well'; aspects of his character will always remain unspoken. Jenkyns celebrates Byatt's novel in similar terms; he explains that 'Byatt is wise enough not to tell us everything; Christabel keeps some of her secret, including the nature of her feelings for Blanche Glover, and that is as it should be' (Jenkyns 1990, p. 213). Jenkyns praises *Possession*'s tact in letting Christabel's 'secret' be.[12] Jenkyns' comment implies a decidedly non-tactile model of tact, which is echoed by Cunningham when he writes that '[w]hat I shall end up praising as readerly *tact* would . . . respect the integrity of literary texts . . . by letting literary texts speak in their own voice' (Cunningham 2002, p. 86). Cunningham invokes a model of reading in which texts might 'speak in their own voice' and which is echoed both by *Possession* and those who comment upon it. *Possession* announces that '[t]here are – believe it – impersonal readings – where the mind's eye sees the lines move onwards and the mind's ear hears them sing and sing' (Byatt 1991b, p. 471) while Hadley declares that '[a] proper approach towards the past is one that understands it on its own terms, rather than merely co-opting it into the present' (Hadley 2008, p. 66). Jenkyns also echoes Hadley's declaration, announcing that 'we can apprehend the past rightly only by letting it work in its own natural way, absorbing so much that is precious into the mysteries of privacy and oblivion' (Jenkyns 1990, p. 214).

All three of these writers invoke an 'impersonal' or objective mode of reading in which the reader steps back and allows the text (or history) to speak or sing 'on its own terms' or 'in its own natural way'. Cunningham, somewhat paradoxically, again employs the term 'close reading' to invoke this experience. Armstrong points out, however, that we might more aptly call this 'distance reading, not close reading'. Its basis, she explains, lies in 'an account of the text as *outside*, something external which has to be grasped – or warded off. Despite the antipositivist language of so much modern criticism and theory, the text is seen as *other*: it is object to a Kantian subject who stands over against the world in a position of power' (Armstrong 1995, p. 403; italics in original).[13] Armstrong highlights a paradox concealed by the term 'close reading'; it proposes a model of interpretation in which the text in fact remains untouchable. It thus reiterates a model of self and other that we, after Derrida and Levinas, understand to be problematic.

All three of these examples nonetheless echo the belief that it is best to read in this tactful, distant, impersonal manner. As I will show in the paragraphs that follow, however, their narratives demonstrate that it may not in fact be possible to do so. *Possession*, for example, notes in relation to Beatrice Nest's reading of Ellen Ash's diary that

> As is common with extended acquaintance with any task, topic or human being, Beatrice had an initial period of clear observation and detached personal judgment, during which she thought she saw that Ellen Ash was rambling and dull. And then she became implicated, began to share Ellen's long days of prostration in darkened rooms, to worry about the effect of mildew on damask roses long withered, and the doubts of oppressed curates (Byatt 1991b, p. 115).

Beatrice attempts to remain distant and detached, but finally finds that she has become 'implicated' in Ellen's life; the novel records a process by which Beatrice, too-immersed in the diary, comes increasingly to share Ellen's opinions and perspectives. The other characters in *Possession* gently mock Beatrice for this partiality. As Roland and Maud become increasingly obsessed with the lives of Ash and LaMotte, however, the reader notices that they, too, have forsaken 'clear observation' and 'detached judgment'. The novel subtly suggests that this increasing loss of objectivity may be the inevitable result of all academic and 'extended acquaintance'.

This inevitability becomes clear if we return once more to the question of 'theory'. As I explained in my first section, critics of Byatt's *Possession* distance themselves from theory; they dismiss it as both dangerous and damaging. They reject theory as too distant. We are presented with a concept of theory which must – to borrow a phrase of Derrida's – be '*distanced* precisely because it is too *distant*' (Derrida 1987b, p. 368; italics in original). The semi-repetition of 'distanced' and 'distant' in this phrase draws attention to the double bind in which Byatt's critics are caught; they revile theory as distant and yet, by distancing themselves from it, validate the distance they fear. Their distancing-attempt is thus doomed to failure.

The claim that *Possession* distances theory centres and relies on the idea that the novel somehow rejects its twentieth-century plot. Buxton, for example, argues that '[f]or all its postmodern gestures, *Possession* is first and foremost a "straight" narrative, a realistic fiction' (Buxton 2001, p. 98). For Buxton, *Possession* is 'truly' a straight, realistic narrative whose post modern gestures serve only to critique post modernism. Byatt, Buxton claims, 'is using postmodernism – or, at least, post-structuralism – against itself' (Buxton 2001, p. 99). Buxton implies that the novel is able – to recall the categories, which I outlined earlier, highlighted by Derrida – to mention post-structuralism without using it or while holding at a distance. An example from another of Byatt's novels, *The Biographer's Tale*, illustrates, however, that the matter may not be so simple. *The Biographer's Tale*, like *Possession,* is a novel which thematizes – and apparently rejects – theory. Its protagonist, Phineas G. Nanson, evinces a desire to '[abandon] . . . post-structuralist semiotics' and repeatedly satirizes the theory he finds within the university at which he works (Byatt 2001, p. 114). In the opening pages of the novel, for example, he sits in 'one of Gareth Butcher's famous theoretical seminars' and explains that:

> We'd been doing a lot of not-too-long texts written by women. And also quite a lot of Freud – we'd deconstructed the Wolf Man, and Dora . . . All the seminars [. . .] had a fatal family likeness. They were repetitive in the extreme. We found the same clefts and crevices, transgressions and disintegrations, lures and deceptions beneath, no matter what surface we were scrying (pp. 1–2).

Phineas dismisses these 'theoretical seminars' as 'repetitive' and reductive, suggesting that they boil every text down to the 'same clefts and crevices'. Later in the novel, too, he rails against theory when he declares that 'I have resisted the temptation to insert several pages of Foucault. One of the reasons why I abandoned – oh, and I *have* abandoned – post-structuralist semiotics, was the requirement to write page upon page of citations from Foucault . . . in support of the simplest statement' (Byatt 2001, p. 114; italics in original).

Phineas cites post-structuralism but claims repeatedly not to use it. Despite his avowed dismissals, the reader realizes, however, that Phineas has not abandoned theory as absolutely as he might have hoped. The style of the first passage above recalls 'quite a lot of [the] Freud' it would reject; the terms 'symptomatic', 'repetitive' and 'fatal family likeness' all invoke psychoanalysis. Equally, the second passage is followed by a lengthy description of the Foucault Phineas has apparently not inserted. Theory thus appears time and again as Phineas's central concern even as he professes no interest in it. Paradoxically, moreover, Phineas spends more time worrying about 'post-structuralist semiotics' than, for example, Foucault to whom the phrase would be anathema.

We could argue, too, that *Possession* is very much a 'post-modern' or 'post-structuralist' novel; it never fully banishes theory. By citing post-structuralist theory, Byatt's novels implicate themselves within its scene and invite us to read them as its products.[14] To distance themselves from theory, these novels must first admit it. To elude theory entirely, they would have to distance themselves yet again, excluding not only theory but also a critique of theory which always allows its return. Even then there is no guarantee that 'theory' would not reappear once more. A further step is always required, as Derrida points out in 'To speculate' when he writes that '[i]t is exactly *there* (where? *there*), in the paralysis of this further step that always has to be taken away, it is there (but why there? why not one more or one less step? Where, there? *there*, answers life death)' (Derrida 1987b, p. 369; italics in original). 'Absolute' distance is always 'there' – permanently one step further away; we can never gain enough distance from this (supposedly too-distant) theory.

In his essay 'To speculate – on Freud', Derrida demonstrates that one is always, and necessarily, implicated in and by that on which one would merely comment. In his essay, Derrida analyses a passage from *Beyond the Pleasure Principle* in which Freud contemplates the 'speculative assumptions' at which he has arrived (Freud 2003, p. 45). Speculation, Derrida points out, indicates 'a mode of research, a theoretical attitude'; Freud highlights the method that his writing employs. Derrida, however, interrogates the word beyond this 'proper' sense; he behaves as though Freud not only '[speaks] *speculatively* of this or that' but is also 'speaking *of* speculation' (Derrida 1987b, p. 283; italics in original). Derrida claims – and demonstrates that – in what Freud writes 'something must derive from the speculation of which he speaks . . . speculation is not only a mode of research named by Freud, not only the oblique object of his discourse, but also the operation of his writing, the scene (of that) which he makes by writing what he writes here' (p. 284).

Derrida shows that Freud's speculative remarks also remark upon speculation. We find that 'the related is related to the relating' (p. 304). Derrida, notes, moreover that as a result 'one does not gain an auto-reflective transparency, on the contrary' (p. 391). This inevitable self-reflexivity means that there is no purely 'speculative' statement; there is no comment which that merely speculates or maintains itself at an absolute distance. Thus, the pure distance with which theory is aligned is not, in fact, possible. As I explained earlier, Derrida suggests in 'Some statements and truisms' that theory, in its 'proper sense', ought always to be bounded by quotation marks; properly, like these marks, it implies a distant stance in which we mention but do not use. I also suggested, however, that Derrida's formulations imply a further complexity. As I have shown earlier, this 'proper' sense remains elusive; theory and quotation marks alike fail to achieve it. The quotation marks cannot suspend the word absolutely; although they attempt not to touch, they do not succeed. A residual contact persists. Offering yet another quotation-mark metaphor, Derrida argues that 'two pairs of pegs hold in suspension a sort of drape, a veil or a curtain. Not closed, just slightly open' (Derrida 1989a, p. 31). The quotation marks attempt to bound and contain the word, but remain slightly open; the word threatens to escape the veils between which it is placed. It is not, in fact, possible to mention a word without using it; the distance with which theory is allied is inevitably compromised.

As Paul de Man points out in *The Resistance to Theory* '[n]othing can overcome the resistance to theory since theory *is* itself this resistance' (De Man 1986, p. 19; italics in original). Every attempt at theory fails, resists theory.[15] There is no strictly 'theoretical' statement; it is not possible to mention a word without using it. Roland realizes this when he speaks of '"desire, that we look into so carefully"' and admits '"I think all the *looking-into* has some very odd effects on the desire"' (Byatt 1991b, p. 267; italics in original). It is not possible to 'look into' desire without having an effect on that desire; we cannot attain distance enough to speak of it without altering it.

We find that, just as there is no pure proximity, a residual touch always problematizes distance. This realization emerges gradually for the reader of *Possession* through his/her understanding of Maud and Roland's relationship. In *Possession*, Johnson argues, 'the moderns, disillusioned and revolted by their own sexual lives, long for chastity and simplicity' (Johnson 1991, p. 33). Maud is described as 'most untouchable' while Roland 'wanted secrecy and privacy' (Byatt 1991b, pp. 48–9). This desire for 'chastity and simplicity' is most memorably encapsulated by the discussion that Roland and Maud have about a 'clean empty bed in a clean empty room':

'At my life, at the way it is – what I *really* want is to – to have nothing. An empty clean bed. I have this image of a clean empty bed in a clean empty room, where

nothing is asked or to be asked. Some of that is to do with – my personal circumstances. But some of it's general. I think.'

'I know what you mean. No, that's a feeble thing to say. It's a much more powerful coincidence than that. That's what I think about, when I'm alone. How good
it would be to have nothing. How good it would be to desire nothing. And the
same image. An empty bed in an empty room. White.'

'White.'

'Exactly the same.'

'How strange.'

'Maybe we're symptomatic of whole flocks of exhausted scholars and theorists.
Or maybe it's just us' (Byatt 1991b, p. 267; italics in original).

The white of the room the scholars imagine invokes sterility; Maud links the
image to a sense of exhaustion and a wish to 'desire nothing'. The exchange in
which this is revealed, however, is one of the first in which the reader senses the
possibility that Maud and Roland might desire each other. This joint longing
for distance and isolation results in a paradoxical and peculiar intimacy; the
thought that 'maybe it's just us' isolates Roland and Maud from the world, but,
in doing so, places them as a pair closer together.[16]

Maud and Roland's celebration of distance is paradoxically seductive; this is
again apparent in a later conversation:

They were not touching. They were sitting amicably close and not touching.

'Oddly,' said Maud, 'if we were obsessed with each other, no one would think we
were mad.'

'Val thinks we are obsessed with each other. She even said it was healthier than
being obsessed with Randolph Ash.'

'Leonora thinks I've rushed away in response to a telephone call from a lover.'

Roland thought, all this giddy clear-headedness is dependent on our not being
obsessed with each other (p. 332).

Roland and Maud's conversation appears at first to be 'clear-headed' and objective. However, Roland's final comment transforms it; indirectly, he introduces
the idea that he and Maud might, in fact, be 'obsessed with each other'. The
reader, of course, has intuited this long before; now, however, Roland finally suggests that he too may be conscious of the fact. In light of Roland's comment, we
re-read his and Maud's exchange as a coy flirtation; it occurs to us that they are
perhaps using the opinions of Val and Leonora in order covertly to suggest to
each other that they could become 'obsessed' lovers.

Roland and Maud thus seduce each other indirectly and from a distance. *Possession* implies, moreover, that these conditions are necessary. The narrator notes, for example, that '[i]t was important to both of them that the touching should not proceed to any kind of fierceness or deliberate embrace' (p. 424). Later we are told that

> Neither was quite sure how much, or what, all this meant to the other.
> Neither dared ask (p. 424).

To ask, the narrative implies, would be to shatter the distance the pair have carefully maintained; they must avoid the direct question and the 'deliberate embrace' if they are to sustain the indirection which constitutes their flirtation's success.

In *The Human Stain*, Delphine Roux, sitting in a library and scanning it for eligible men, finds that '[t]he ones who make eye contact with her are automatically the ones she doesn't like'. In contrast, 'the ones who are lost in their books' she describes as 'charmingly oblivious and charmingly desirable' (Roth 2001, p. 200). An encounter with Prince the crow later in the novel recalls this moment. When Prince refuses to respond to Faunia's attention the other girl in the barn advises Faunia that

> 'If he knows you're trying to get him, he usually stays out of reach, but if he thinks you're ignoring him, he'll come down.'
>   They laughed together at the humanish behaviour (p. 239).

It is possible to gain the affections of the crow only by distance and (feigned) disinterest. *The Human Stain* is bemused, but nonetheless acknowledges, that distance is the most effective seduction.

Derrida thus writes, in a passage in *Spurs* which ventriloquizes Nietzsche (a process which itself raises questions of touch. *Spurs* gets very close to Nietzsche and his views on women but at the same time it maintains a reserve as the reader wonders, does Derrida agree? Or is he in fact parodying Nietzsche's point of view?) that

> A woman seduces from a distance. In fact, distance is the very element of her power. Yet one must beware to keep one's own distance from her beguiling song of enchantment. A distance from distance must be maintained. Not only for protection (the most obvious advantage) against the spell of her fascination, but also as a way of succumbing to it, that distance (which is lacking) *is necessary. Il faut* la distance (qui faut).) It is necessary to keep one's distance (*Distanz*)! Which failing us, we fail to do. Such might also be the advice of one man to another: a

sort of scheme for how to seduce without being seduced (Derrida 1979b, p. 49; italics in original).

As we learn through these novels, distance may be seductive. Towards the end of *Possession*, for example, Maud explains to Roland "'[e]ven you – drew back – when we met. I expect that, now. I use it'" (Byatt 1991b, p. 506). Roland's drawing back is the 'very element' of Maud's 'power'. Derrida thus tells us that it is imperative that we keep our distance 'for protection'. The success of this move cannot, however, be guaranteed; distance would also be the means by which one 'succumbs' to the seduction one would resist.

In *Possession*, Maud hides her hair under a headscarf, fearful of the attention it might bring. By concealing it, she attempts to erase its interest. However, her attempt fails, as Roland explains: "'[b]ecause if anyone can't see it they think and think about it, they wonder what it's like, so you attract attention to it'" (Byatt 1991b, p. 271). Against her intention, Maud finds that her attempt to distance herself from her hair's seductive potential has backfired; her very act of distancing becomes a further seduction, rendering her (hidden) hair an even greater attraction. We cannot absolutely separate 'genuine' withdrawal from that which begs intimacy and interest.

We cannot distinguish between 'true' distance and that which aims to seduce; it is always possible that the distance we encounter is in fact a coy plea for intimacy. A possible proximity and closeness lies at the heart of all distance, provoking a confusion which Delphine in *The Human Stain* best embodies. As I explained earlier, Delphine falls for those 'who are charmingly oblivious and charmingly desirable'. There is, however, a great deal of pathos in this scene; Delphine finds that 'the ones who are lost in their books, who are charmingly oblivious and charmingly desirable, are . . . lost in their books' (Roth 2001, p. 200). The men who are desirable because 'charmingly oblivious' are, unfortunately, unreachable. Moreover, and more tragically in terms of the novel's plot, Delphine's application of this logic causes her to mis-read Coleman Silk: '[t]he first time they met, in his office, he had seemed so remote, so judging, that she found herself paralyzed with fear until she realized that he was playing the seduction against the grain. Was that what this Dean Silk was up to?' (p. 187). Delphine's logic is not entirely flawed; as my reading of Roland and Maud's relationship in *Possession* has shown, it is entirely possible that Coleman's 'remote' and 'judging' demeanour (words which recall Roland's description of Maud when he first meets her) is an attempt to play 'the seduction against the grain'. The novel shows, however, that Delphine is incorrect. The contamination of distance by proximity makes error as possible as it makes seduction. The ongoing infiltration of intimacy into distance, and vice versa, demands that we negotiate a profound ambivalence, as I will show in the next and final section of my chapter.

Touching on tact at a tangent

I have now outlined two contradictory senses of tact. I showed, in my first section, that tact aligns itself with touch and contact. In my second section, I demonstrated a very different sense of tact as distant propriety. I have illustrated, however, that each sense of tact is undone by the other: a distant non-contact persists at the heart of contact; distance is undone by the possibility of an intimacy it can never wholly eschew. We find that

> what is going on no longer concerns a distancing rendering this or that absent, and then a rapprochement rendering this or that into presence; what is going on concerns rather the distancing of the distant and the nearness of the near, the absence of the absence or the presence of the present. But the distancing is not distant, nor the nearness near, nor the absence absent or the presence present (Derrida 1987b, p. 321).

We are faced with a series of distancing moments which never fully distance and instants of contact which never wholly touch. There is – always a step further away – a touch and a distance, but we never attain either absolutely. Neither distance nor touch can escape the other and neither can claim to be tact's proper sense.

Tact instead situates itself *between* these contradictory inflections and demands that we read them together. It thus functions according to a logic with which Geoffrey Bennington aligns the prefix 'inter' in an essay of that name. 'Inter', Bennington explains, possesses two distinct senses:

> *On the one hand,* inter- separates, places between two or more entities, keeps them apart, puts up a frontier, prevents them meeting, joining, mingling, and maybe identifying. Inter-val is perhaps the clearest case of this sense. Inter-calating, inter-posing, inter-polating, inter-mitting all obey this logic. But *on the other hand,* inter- joins, provides a means of communication and exchange. This can go from inter-view to inter-action to inter-course to inter-pretation, and implies just the first sense of inter-: here the hap or difference is not being established or reinforced, but diminished, overcome or denied (Bennington 1999, p. 103; italics in original).

'Inter' can function either as a mark of separation (or distance) or as a mark which joins (or places in contact). As my analyses have shown, we cannot, however, fully discriminate one sense from the other; Bennington suggests that '"inter" finds its own truth in the sublation of its two contradictory senses' (p. 104).

This 'sublation' of 'contradictory senses' is not, however, simple. *Possession* informs us of this fact via Beatrice Nest's experience of Ash's poetry. 'Reading those poems', we are told, 'she obscurely knew, offered her a painful and as it seemed illicit glimpse of a combination of civilised talk and raw passion which everyone must surely want, and yet which no one, as she looked round her small world, her serious Methodist parents, Mrs Bengtsson running her University Women's Tea Club, her fellow-students agonising over invitations to dance and whist – no one seemed to have' (Byatt 1991b, p. 114). Beatrice makes it clear that what is most desired is a 'combination of civilised talk and raw passion'. However, Beatrice's realization is 'painful' and leaves the reader with a sense of pathos. 'No one' is of course able to successfully unite such contradictory approaches; the 'combination' which 'everyone must surely want' is, the reader realizes, impossible. Beatrice, for one, knows it only 'obscurely' and is afforded only an 'illicit glimpse'.

Marcel Cornis-Pope echoes Beatrice's sentiments when he argues that '[a] esthetic experience relies on a paradoxical, "impossible" combination of absorption and self-consciousness, participation and critical distance' (Cornis-Pope 1992, p. 26). Cornis-Pope's 'aesthetic experience' is very close to what I have been discussing here as tact or close reading. It, too, conjures a certain approach, or 'experience', which is marked by both 'participation' and 'critical distance'. According to tact's rule, Derrida writes, 'one must touch without touching. In touching, touching is forbidden: do not touch or tamper with the thing itself, do not touch on what there is to touch' (Derrida 2005a, p. 66). He repeats this injunction throughout *On Touching*. A little later he writes

> Between two given orders – yes, given as given as much as ordered (do touch
> but *do not* touch, in no way, do touch *without* touching, do touch *but* do watch
> out and avoid any contact) – it in effect installs a kinship that is at the same time
> *conjunctive* and *disjunctive*. Worse than that, it brings into contact both contra-
> dictory orders (do do and do not do), thus exposing them to contamination or
> contagion (pp. 67–8; italics in original).

Derrida's complex and sometimes confusing formulations – 'do touch but *do not* touch', 'do do and do not do', 'touch without touching' – make the counter-intui-tive nature of tact's imperative clear. It is embodied, too, by Jenkyns' declaration in relation to *Possession* that 'the way to possession is through dispossession'

(Jenkyns 1990, p. 214). How are we to touch without touching or possess without possessing? If there is indeed a touch that does not touch, how are we to understand contact? What does a dispossession that leads to possession say about both? Cornis-Pope, like Beatrice, highlights the 'paradoxical' and 'impossible' nature of this demand. Derrida, a little less scholarly, declares simply 'it is madness' (Derrida 2005a, p. 68).

We can thus see that the 'questions of ethics' I outlined in my chapter's introduction will not be so simple as to have a constative, voice-able answer. The interrogation is itself fraught, as we realize if we examine more closely that which the novels' characters ask. In *Slow Man*, Paul says to Elizabeth:

> 'Are you writing a book and putting me in it? Is that what you are doing? If so, what sort of book is it, and don't you think you need my consent first?'
>
> She sighs. 'If I were going to *put you in a book*, as you phrase it, I would simply do so. I would change your name and one or two of the circumstances of your life, to get around the law of libel, and that would be that' (Coetzee 2005, pp. 88–9; italics in original).
>
> 'It would not be proper. My wife would not thank me for offering her up as a minor character in one of your literary efforts. But if it is stories you want, I will tell you a story from the period of my marriage that does not involve my wife. You can use it to illustrate my character, or not, as you wish' (Coetzee 2005, pp. 199–200).
>
> 'And are you sure,' he replies icily, 'that you are not seeing complications where they do not exist, for the sake of those dreary stories you write?' (Coetzee 2005, p. 157).

All three of these statements interrogate the propriety, or impropriety, of Elizabeth's writing project; the second even announces explicitly that 'it would not be proper'. The first and second quotations allude to a decision Elizabeth must make: Is it right for her to include certain facts or characters? Should Paul, and his wife, be 'put in' a book or not? The third quotation refers to a slightly different dilemma; in this case, Paul questions Elizabeth's interpretation of events and implies that it may be skewed 'for the sake of' the work she is composing. Despite their differences, however, all three of these declarations are founded on the same assumption: the book Elizabeth is writing is based on Paul's life and its propriety hinges on the way in which she chooses to portray it; the 'ethics' of her project centre around issues of transformation and representation.

A similar logic emerges in *The Human Stain* as Zuckerman maps his error-strewn path to the uncovering of Coleman's secret. Zuckerman repeatedly informs us that he has 'got it wrong' and, moreover, that getting it wrong is inevitable.[17] Zuckerman is surprised, for example, to discover that Coleman has a tattoo and therefore describes it as '[a] tiny symbol, if one were needed, of all the million circumstances of the other fellow's life, of that blizzard of details that constitute the confusion of a human biography – a tiny symbol to remind me why our understanding of people must always be at best slightly wrong' (Roth 2001, p. 22). Zuckerman alludes to a process of interpretation, which one can get 'wrong' or, by implication, 'right'. Zuckerman invites us to contemplate whether getting it wrong might have ethical consequences for the novel he is writing.

Both Paul and Zuckerman offer what appears to be a valid and straightforward interrogation of the fiction's ethics. However, the form in which these questions are presented to us problematizes them profoundly. The interpretation and transformation to which the two characters allude does not of course ever take place; the exteriority to which these questions apparently refer is in fact an illusion they effect. The 'secret' surrounding Coleman Silk, for example, is not uncovered but is produced by *The Human Stain*. Timothy Clark explains in 'Not seeing the short story' that '[w]ith a fictional character, the observations, however acute they seem, become true by the simple virtue of being made. The language can only describe what it has itself posited and in the terms in which it posits it. There is an effect of nice discrimination, but the fine lines are actually drawn by the finger that seems to be merely pointing them out'. The literary, Clark concludes, 'actually conjures up what it seems merely to re-present as already there' (Clark 2004, p. 8). The 'questions' these novels pose are not questions *per se*; they do not interrogate a pre-existing ethical situation but generate the very dilemmas – the very 'ethics' – they appear simply to discuss. Their content is therefore compromised. In *Slow Man,* Paul's wife appears as a 'minor character' at the very moment he tells Elizabeth he won't 'offer her up'; Paul is clearly already 'in' a book even as he asks Elizabeth whether she is planning to put him in one. What happens at these moments is far stranger than the summaries I outlined in my introduction suggest. These novels do not offer a discussion of, but point to the impossibility of thematizing, an ethics of fiction.

This is not to say, however, that we should abandon 'ethics' *tout court* or cease to tend towards tact. Derrida does not dismiss tact; it continues to inform his reading of Nancy and discussion of touch in *On Touching*. However, this text remains mindful of the 'madness' outlined earlier; *On Touching* plays with the '[u]ndecidable play of the metonymy'. Derrida realizes that '[t]o touch, to touch him/it, is possible only by not touching'; his text, if it succeeds, will have offered us an '[e]xperience of the impossible' (Derrida 2005a, p. 298). Ben-Naftali writes that '[d]econstruction . . . chooses tact. It is a discourse of tact, of involvement, which defines its own measure. However, it is also always already impossible' (Ben-Naftali 1999, p. 663).

Derrida offers a commentary on Nancy's work but, even as he does so, he wonders 'how to do it in the right fashion, by touching it without touching it too much, while observing the limits of decency, of duty, of politeness – of friendship?' (Derrida 2005a, p. 303). Derrida repeatedly expresses a desire to touch Nancy's work and to be in contact with it. At the same time, however, his text maintains a reservation. Sarah Jackson's essay 'Dis-tanz', which also turns to Derrida's *On Touching* in order to explore the interplay between proximity and distance I have been considering, identifies this oscillation in Derrida's writing. Jackson writes that 'Derrida's writing is always a dance of distance and *différance*. Yet it is also always an act of reaching toward, of tending, of tendering' (Jackson 2011, p. 168). The hyphen of Derrida's title, for example, institutes a distance between his wish for 'touching' and his subject, Jean-Luc Nancy (this respectful hesitation is repeated, too, in the title 'To speculate – on Freud').

Derrida proposes the figure of the tangent as that which best embodies this simultaneous desire to touch and not to touch:

> *A tangent touches a line or a surface but without crossing it, without a true inter-section, thus in a kind of impertinent pertinence. It touches only one point, but a point is nothing, that is, a limit without depth or surface, untouchable even by way of a figure. Suppose one were to reach there, what would give one the right to touch it?* (Derrida 2005a, p. 131; italics in original)

Derrida points out that a tangent 'touches a line or a surface' but only briefly, 'without a true intersection'. It is, even at the moment of contact, already moving away. The touch it achieves is glimpsed, only, at a single point. The reader experiences it only fleetingly. As Derrida explains in the intimacy of an aside, '(the etymology of *contingency* also points to touching, tact, or contact)' (Derrida 2008, p. 133). The touch that tact demands happens only contingently, as it moves away.

On Touching attempts to replicate this movement in its approach towards Nancy. It is, like many of Derrida's texts, marked by a series of interruptions. The lengthiest of these occurs at approximately the work's mid-point. Derrida ruptures his text both graphically and logically by declaring in italics '[a]*t this point, my discourse was shaping up badly, and everything already had to be started over from the beginning*' (Derrida 2005a, p. 131; italics in original). He repeats this move time and again until finally he suggests that it might be better were we not to read *On Touching* at all: '[l]et's rush towards the ending and recapitulate. I'm now sincerely asking that this book be forgotten or effaced, and I'm asking this as I wouldn't have done – with as much sincerity – for any of my other books. Wipe it all away, and start or start again to read him – Nancy – in his *corpus*' (Derrida 2005a, p. 301; italics in original). Derrida points out that the most tactful and respectful thing to do would be to read Nancy's work itself; all commentary, Derrida implies, is somewhat tactless. Derrida and Nancy appear as distant as they can be. Just as it seems as though Derrida might be coming close to Nancy's work, he dismisses all that he has written before, informing us that it represents a failed attempt and distancing himself absolutely from his project. Then again, we realize that Derrida's injunction is, of course, somewhat insincere; he does not 'wipe . . . away' his entire work and he asks us to forget his book only once we are very close to completing it. Derrida proposes to remove himself from his work; by taking place within this work, his declaration reveals, however, that he is irrevocably bound within it. This distancing-moment realizes a paradoxical and inescapable closeness.

We experience a similar oscillating movement between closeness and distance when we read *Slow Man* and *Possession*. I pointed out earlier that Paul in *Slow Man* champions distance and indirection. Regarding his nurse, the narrator notes, for example, '[h]e does not refer to her as *Marijana* in case it sounds too familiar; in conversation with her he continues to call her *Mrs Jokić*, as she calls him *Mr Rayment*' (Coetzee 2005, p. 30). Paul posits the 'too familiar' as that which ought to be avoided; it is proper that he address 'Marijana' as 'Mrs Jokić'. The remarks Paul makes about his amputated leg repeat this pattern. Paul admits that '[t]o himself he does not call it a stump. He would like not to call it anything; he would like not to think about it, but that is not possible. If he has a name for it, it is *le jambon*. *Le jambon* keeps it at a nice, contemptuous distance' (p. 29). Distraught, Paul would prefer not to think about his stump at all but, given that he must, he chooses to refer to it euphemistically as 'le jambon'. The word, to the reader, seems a somewhat absurd description. But that, Paul explains, is the point; avoiding direct reference to legs, amputation, or stump, this nonsense-word keeps Paul's predicament at a 'contemptuous distance'.

The figures of Beatrice Nest and Ellen Ash in Byatt's *Possession* share Paul's belief that distance is 'nice'. Jenkyns argues that 'Beatrice Nest, the editor of Mrs Ash's journal, is muddy and pathetic, but she is on the side of the angels because she recognises in it the "mystery of privacy", in contrast to the smart omniscience of more successful academics' (Jenkyns 1990, p. 213). By criticizing the 'smart omniscience of more successful academics', Jenkyns suggests that it might be better not to know. At one point in the novel, Ellen composes a letter to LaMotte in which she announces

> 'You must understand that I have *always known*, that my husband told me, long ago, freely and truthfully, of his feelings for you . . .' (Byatt 1991b, pp. 452–3; italics in original).

Ellen's tone is defiant and certain as she declares that her husband told her about his relationship with LaMotte 'long ago'. As the passage progresses it becomes clear, however, that Ellen 'knows' of her husband's affair because she has gleaned it indirectly through 'silence'. We are surprised to learn this; Ellen's initial description of the telling as free and truthful implies a very different, more direct, form of communication. This initial declaration is clearly at odds with the way in which we would usually understand a message inferred through silence. By describing Ash's discretion in this counter-intuitive way, Ellen validates it, offering us a positive description which, she declares, 'would be no more and no less than the truth'. Silence, Ellen implies, can be as open and as honest as any other form of declaration.

However, there is also an ambivalence here. Ellen is ostensibly defiant. It occurs to the reader, however, that this certainty might be a defence. If, indeed, she is proud of her indirect understanding, why does she write as though events occurred otherwise? Why does she announce that her husband has 'told' her about LaMotte when no such telling occurred? Does Ellen's description, in fact, represent what she wished had happened? *Slow Man* concludes its contemplation concerning the way in which Paul addresses *Marijana* with the words '[b]ut to himself he has no reservation about calling her *Marijana*' (Coetzee 2005, p. 30). Paul's admission that 'to himself' he addresses Marijana familiarly establishes a tension: what is permitted and correct is at odds with the way in which Paul secretly desires to speak to the woman who nurses him. The statements in which Paul and Ellen affirm distance in fact conceal a desire for intimacy; their longing for proximity becomes, paradoxically, apparent at the moments at which they beg for distance.

A similar disjunction emerges between Paul's declaration and the reader's understanding in relation to his stump. Paul celebrates the 'contemptuous distance' of the appellation '*le jambon*' as 'nice'; the reader, however, senses the problem Paul's comments mask: such avoidance may be both undesirable and damaging. In each of these examples, it is therefore possible to read these characters against what they ostensibly say; the reader intuits a 'truth' at odds with what the characters would have us believe.

The realizations that we make concerning Paul and Ellen place us in a position of interpretative superiority; we feel as though we have realized something that these characters themselves have not. Later in both novels, however, it becomes clear that Paul and Ellen are in fact conscious of this alternative reading. Ellen continues:

> And if she did write that, it would be no more and no less than the truth, but it would not ring true, it would not convey the truth of the way it had been, of the silence in the telling, the silences that extended before and after it, always the silences (Byatt 1991b, p. 453).

This admission is more sorrowful in tone and less certain about the benefits of silence; Ellen is somewhat less sure about the 'mystery of privacy' than Jenkyns suggests. In *Slow Man*, Paul tells Elizabeth "'[i]n my earlier life I did not speak as freely about myself as I do today, Mrs Costello. Decency held me back, decency or shame'" (Coetzee 2005, p. 156). Paul first attributes his decision not to 'speak . . . freely' about himself to 'decency', thus reiterating a preference for proper distance. Belatedly, however, he admits that the source of his reservation may be a more negative 'shame'. Ellen, too, wonders '[h]ad she done well, or ill? She had done what was in her nature, which was profoundly implicated in not knowing, in silence, in avoidance, she said to herself, in harsher moments' (Byatt 1991b, p. 455). Ellen and Paul both acknowledge the realization made earlier by the reader: the distance they celebrate *may* be proper and polite or then again, it may also be an 'avoidance', the product of cowardice, 'one of those oblique remarks that people make at moments when the real words are too difficult to bring out' (Coetzee 2005, p. 44). Such comments may be 'oblique', an imperfect substitute for the 'real words'.

The characters display a belated comprehension of our earlier realizations. These admissions have a dual effect. On the one hand, they affirm our interpretation; we were correct to note the conflicted nature of Paul and Ellen's desire for distance. On the other hand, however, they undercut our reading; the realization we believed to be at odds with, and more sophisticated than, the understanding of the characters themselves is in fact shared by them. Our interpretation is not 'wrong' *per se* but has failed to take into account to whom it might properly belong; the realization was not so simply our own.[18] Paul and Ellen reclaim our interpretation; we become conscious of certain tactlessness in our earlier reading.

We are left with an awareness of the potential effect of our earlier 'superiority'. Tact, we realize, might be linked to the problem of 'staying in-tact', as

Naftali's hyphen makes subtly apparent (Ben-Naftali 1999, p. 663; italics in original). Who gets to stay intact? And who might be undone as a result?

This has, for this chapter and for the relationship between these books and myself, been an issue from the outset. If, as the critics of these novels protest, these texts deny any connection between theory and closeness this is for me (and for my theory-embracing book) what Sedgwick calls 'an intimate denegation indeed' (Sedgwick 1989, p. 749). Sedgwick employs this phrase in an essay entitled 'Tide and trust' in which she responds to the criticisms that one of her readers, David van Leer, levels against her book *Between Men*. Sedgwick records the wounds his reading inflicts; however, she tries not to defend herself too hastily, lest she wound van Leer in turn. This chapter has demanded a similar balancing act; even as I wish to stay intact (by proving the critics' characterization of theory 'wrong'), I do not desire, in protecting myself, to disavow what these books, and their critics, have to say.

Ellen compounds this dilemma as she expresses an awareness of potential, future readers of her journal, of those who might interpret her situation. The narrator announces, '[s]he sat down to manufacture the carefully edited, the carefully *strained* (the metaphor was one of jelly-making) truth of her journal. She would decide later what to do with *that*. It was both a defense against, and a bait for, the gathering of ghouls and vultures' (Byatt 1991b, pp. 461–2). By depicting her readers as 'ghouls and vultures' against whom she must defend herself, Ellen positions herself as the victim of others' interpretations; she is, she highlights, vulnerable to our reading.

Ellen's anxiety leaves me aware that I, too, am vulnerable; the interpretation I offer is subject once again to another reading. This fact also becomes apparent in Derrida's *On Touching*. I cited earlier the moment at which Derrida points out that the most tactful and respectful thing to do would be to read Nancy's work itself. Ostensibly, Derrida announces that his work has failed; his relationship with Nancy is doomed. At this moment, however, the question of relationship *per se* – and of our relation to the text – is placed into relief. We can either continue to read Derrida's text or we can abandon it and read Nancy's work instead. This dilemma is left to us to resolve; we, as readers, realize that Derrida's text cannot make the decision for us. Derrida's moment of apparent failure thus signals a dependence; the tactful- or tactlessness of Derrida's reading cannot be affirmed by and within his work itself but will be decided later. Derrida thus announces, '[m]y impertinence will be my tact' (Derrida 2005a, p. 131; italics in original). The moment of impertinence in Derrida's text makes the question of tact indirectly apparent; it shows us that it is left to us to judge.

Tact, I have shown in this chapter, exercises a fundamental yet tricky impera-tive. It demands both distance and proximity; it declares that we ought both to touch and not to touch the work that we read. The co-habitation of these two inflections within a single word highlights the extent to which intimacy and distance are, in fact, never discrete; one always informs and undoes the other. Even as we aim to distance ourselves or to touch we must remain mindful of the impossibility of our task. In our failures we may perhaps achieve the paradoxical touching distance or distant touch that tact demands.

You

I have enjoined you to tact, and elsewhere to responsibility, and realized that neither can be known or guaranteed. The appeal can and must be made, but its success is never certain. It must be made again. This chapter of my book considers it a final time by analysing the direct address in which it is formulated. The conclusion to my Deconstruction and Ethics apostrophizes; it addresses itself directly to you. The form may have struck you as unusual. In her book *Relating Narratives*, Adriana Cavarero points out that 'the *you* [*tu*] is a term that is not at home in modern and contemporary developments of ethics and politics' (Cavarero 2000, p. 90; italics in original). Derrida also wishes 'to underscore to what degree philosophical discourse has excluded (one might even say prohibited) this strophic turn of the apostrophe, as well as "thou" and "you", from Aristotle to Kant, from Descartes to Hegel and to Heidegger'. He points out that '[e]ven today, this prohibition extends to many others' and that '[e]xceptions – if any – are rare' (Derrida 2005b, p. 23). 'You' is also 'an uncommon pronoun in modern literature', as Justine Jordan points out in her review of Smith's *Other Stories and Other Stories* (Jordan 1999, p. 33). It is unusual in comparison to what Richardson calls its 'more established and conventional neighbours, the first and third persons' (Richardson 2006, p. 18). Monica Fludernik, in *Towards a 'Natural' Narratology*, discusses it in a chapter on '"odd" personal pronouns' and describes 'second-person fiction' as '[t]he most outstanding oddity in the pronominal realm' (Fludernik 1996, pp. 223, 226).

These comments suggest that the second person is rare, peculiar and seldom used. Not everyone agrees; Richardson argues that 'you' is in fact fairly prevalent. He asserts that '[t]he genealogy of second person fiction is surprisingly rich' (Richardson 2006, p. 17). Richardson concedes, however, that this richness is seldom acknowledged. He points out that 'earlier theorists of narrative either ignored this kind of narration or dismissed it as a curiosity' (p. 21). Jonathan Culler, in *The Pursuit of Signs*, stresses similarly that the apostrophe is employed 'repeatedly and intensely' in poetry but that one can 'read vast amounts of criticism without learning' that this is the case. Criticism 'in some innate hostility to voice, always seeks to deny or evade the vocative' (Culler 1981, p. 136; italics in original).

It is suggested either that philosophy and literature shun the second person or, alternatively, that the second person *is* employed but that critics refuse to acknowledge it. Whichever is the case, it is clear that 'you' provokes discomfort. Derrida, in *The Politics of Friendship*, reflects briefly on the 'flexions and reflections of personal pronouns, between *I, they, we* and *you*'. He explains that

> I feel responsible towards *them* (the new thinkers who are coming), therefore responsible before *us* who announce them, therefore towards *us* who are already what we are announcing and who must watch over that very thing, therefore towards and before *you* whom I call to join us, before and towards me who understands all this and who is before it all: me, them, us, you, etc (Derrida 2005b, p. 39).

A hierarchy emerges; 'I' or 'me' comes first, followed by 'them', 'us' and finally 'you'. Not all pronouns are equal. There is, as Cavarero also points out, an 'intrinsic morality of pronouns'. Our 'curious linguistic code' places the second person pronoun at the bottom; it dismisses it as 'superfluous' (Cavarero 2000, pp. 90–1). Culler argues that the apostrophe is 'embarrassing' and 'that which critical discourse cannot comfortably assimilate' (Culler 1981, pp. 135, 137). Sarah Wood, reproducing in an analysis of Derrida's 'Envois' the apostrophe we find within it, wonders '[w]as there ever such a text as "Envois" for making you say strange things? And for making you unable to say anything?' (Wood 2006, p. 48). The second person of Derrida's text is perplexing and puzzling.

'You' threatens to destabilize criticism. The conclusion of my Deconstruction and Ethics chapter employs it for this very reason; the second person promises to perform a necessary and productive affront. Morrissette suggests that 'narrative "you"' 'although of comparatively late development, appears as a mode of curiously varied psychological resonances, capable, in the proper hands, of producing effects in the fictional field that are unobtainable by other modes or persons' (Morrissette 1965, p. 2). 'The second person' is, for Richardson, 'a playful form, original, transgressive, and illuminating' whose 'ideological possibilities' are 'rich' (Richardson 2006, p. 36).

My chapter in its first section, explores these possibilities by turning to a number of instances in which the second person is both employed and theorized in Derrida's 'Envois', 'My chances' and *The Politics of Friendship* and in

Ali Smith's short stories. Jordan points out that '[m]any of [Smith's] pieces are interior monologues apostrophizing a lover'. In 'The theme is power', for example, 'the lover, even when absent, provides the necessary audience' (Jordan 1999, p. 33). The story is littered with phrases such as 'I tell you', '[y]ou see, this is what I mean' and '[y]ou see, I tell you' (Smith 1999, pp. 124, 126, 132). Smith's work also offers a theorization of the apostrophe's effects; one of the pieces in her collection *The First Person and Other Stories*, entitled 'The second person', ruminates on the pronoun she so frequently employs.

All of the texts I have chosen to consider in this chapter are ones to which I would like to declare love. Love is, of course, closely tied to 'you'; as Peggy Kamuf points out, '[w]hen I say "I love. . ", it is always the declaration of the other at my address'. Love is 'the experience of the sudden or not-so-sudden arrival of the other' (Kamuf 2000, p. 156). And yet, it may not be easy to announce my love. Kamuf asks, '[h]ow is it possible to love a text? That is, how is it possible to say one loves a text, of any and every sort, without that declaration being simply an abuse of language, a stretching of the proper sense of love to the point of breaking?' (pp. 157–8). Kamuf wonders to whom or what I am able to say 'you' and whether I am really able to say it to something as inanimate as a text. 'You' might, she implies, have its limits.

This sense of limitation appears too in response to celebrations of the second person; the rejoicing is not absolute. Morissette cautions that 'certain recent examples' indicate that the second person may 'denigrate' into 'a technical "trick"' (Morrissette 1965, p. 2). Both 'The second person' and Derrida's theorizations reveal, as I will show in my second section, that 'you' is a tricky pronoun; it does not remain still and its address is not guaranteed. As I pointed out in my earlier chapter, we still need to think you further and read you a little more. Something different *might* happen when I address you, but we must remain suspicious of any claim that this direct address is intrinsically or unquestionably beneficial. As with every concept I've discussed thus far, and as I will show in my chapter's third and final section, it requires reading – even, perhaps, a particular type of reading – if it is to remain useful.

You included

Derrida's *The Politics of Friendship* opens by quoting an apostrophe, which, according to Montaigne, 'Aristotle often repeated': 'O my friends, there is no friend' (Derrida 2005b, pp. 1–2). Straight away, the text reflects on the address it has just made. Derrida writes:

> 'O my friends, there is no friend'.
> I am addressing you, am I not?
> How many of us are there?
> Does that count?
> Addressing you in this way, I have perhaps not said anything yet. Nothing that is *said* in this saying. Perhaps nothing sayable (Derrida 2005b, p. 1; italics in original).

Derrida's book first addresses 'you'; in doing so, Derrida points out, it has 'perhaps not said anything yet'. The address perhaps, performing a 'saying' prior to the 'said', highlights a relationality which precedes whatever constative statement it might later make. Smith's 'Text for the day' begins by telling us to '[i]magine Melissa's collection of books' (Smith 1995, p. 19). The first word of the text anticipates the work (of imagination) in which the reader must engage if this story is to succeed. The opening of the text refers not to the fiction that it will tell, but to the reader with whom it is engaged.

Culler, more definite than Derrida, announces that 'apostrophe is different in that it makes its point by troping not on the meaning of a word but on the circuit or situation of communication itself' (Culler 1981, p. 135). Culler declares, and Derrida tentatively suggests, that the second person shifts the emphasis of an account towards its 'circuit of communication'. For McHale '[t]he second person is *par excellence* the sign of relation. Even more strongly than the first person, it announces the presence of a communicative circuit linking addressor and addressee' (McHale 1987, p. 223).[1]

Second-person texts therefore admit both the reader and the act of reading. The final story in Smith's collection *Free Love and Other Stories,* 'The world with love', opens with the words '[o]n a day when it looks like rain and you're wandering between stations in a city you don't know very well, you meet a woman in the street whom you haven't seen for fifteen years, not since you were at school' (Smith 1995, p. 141). The story's protagonist is referred to as 'you'.[2] For McHale, the text therefore invites us to place ourselves in the position of protagonist; to 'project' ourselves 'into the gap opened in the discourse by the presence of *you*' (McHale 1987, p. 224).

We are welcome to identify ourselves, as Margolin points out, as either 'recipients of the narration' or even as 'the hero of the narrated events' (Margolin 1990, p. 437). Fludernik points out that second-person texts 'seem to involve the reader directly' (Fludernik 1996, p. 226). The direct address turns these texts, according to Margolin, from 'the traditional *lecture d'un aventure*, in Ricardou's terms' to '*une aventure d'une lecture*' (Margolin 1990, p. 444).

Jason Edwards, in his book on Eve Kosofsky Sedgwick, repeatedly pauses in order to address his reader. He writes,

> Before starting formally, though, can I ask you a favour? As you read this book, for reasons I'll again explain, can you check in regularly on how you're feeling, where you're feeling it, and for how long? Could you also note down what you're thinking and dreaming about, recalling and registering? Thanks. I promise I'm not just being enigmatic (Edwards 2009, p. 2).

Edwards begs the reader to monitor his/her reaction to the text; he does this, he explains, 'to make you more visible, dear reader' (p. 4). Edwards acknowledges his reader and admits him/her into the text. The reader is, in Margolin's terms, 'not just an observer, but the main agent of these events as well' (Margolin 1990, p. 443). The second person is, therefore, for Margolin, closely allied with 'the wider concerns of literary theory in the 1970s' I outlined in my introduction under the term 'reader-response' whereby 'the thematics of the reader's role has replaced creativity or the text in isolation as the new focus of investigation' (p. 444).

Smith's stories make the 'thematics of the reader's role' their 'focus of investigation' in other ways too. Their narratives frequently revolve around acts of storytelling and thereby thematize and explore the shift to which Margolin refers. I examine them more closely, in the paragraphs that follow, in order to highlight in more detail the implications of this emphasis on the 'reader's role' and to ask, ultimately, whether the second person is indeed capable of acknowledging them. As the narrator of 'The theme is power' does the washing-up s/he tells 'you' '[l]isten to this. This is what happened' (Smith 1999, p. 121). S/he then proceeds to recall a number of episodes from his/her childhood. The second person does not simply listen, however; the narrative is marked by a series of bracketed interruptions:

> (So it happened quite long ago? you say behind me.) (p. 121)

> I pile the bowls and cups up on each other, a bit unsafe. (Don't you feel bad about that man who got beaten up? you say behind me [. . .]) (p. 129)

> But is it connected? I'm a bit lost, are they connected, the story about your father and the story about the woman with the headscarf? you say behind me. You throw your applecore at the bin with perfect aim; in it goes [. . .]) (p. 130)

> (Aha, you say.) (p. 131)

> (Then what happened? you ask.) (p. 133)

The listener interjects in order to comment on and pose a number of questions about the stories the first person tells. A similar situation is portrayed in another of Smith's stories, 'A story of love'. In this text, the first and second persons take it in turns to tell each other stories which, again, provoke enquiries and objections from the character who listens:

> Is this going to be a sentimental story? . . . Is the dog going to die? Because if it is I don't want to hear it (p. 170).

> But that can't be the end, you said. Were they really brother and sister? Why wouldn't he help her? (p. 175).

The speakers are, in both stories, unimpressed by these interventions. By interrupting, the second person implies – and later in 'A story of love' announces explicitly – that the narrator has told only 'half-stories' (p. 174). The narrator is irritated by this implication; s/he is insulted that the listener would think his/her stories lacking or incomplete. The narrator therefore evinces exasperation towards the demands of the listener. In 'The theme is power' the first person tells the second 'quiet . . . I'm thinking' and 'yes, but wait, in a minute' (pp. 129–30). The first person adopts a despairing tone; s/he implies that the second person is both too impatient and overly inquisitive. In 'A story of love' the first person interrupts and it is the second person who retorts:

> Listen, you said. Either I tell you a story or I don't. Make up your mind. And you have to promise here and now to take that story on its own terms.
>   All right, okay. Within reason, I said (p. 170).

Again, the character telling the story dismisses the listener's demands; s/he requires that the first person 'take the story on its own terms' if s/he is to continue. Nonetheless, the first person continues to complain; at the end of the story about the dog s/he announces:

> That's all very well, I said. But it's not the kind of love story I wanted. I wanted something different.
> You want another kind of love in your story? you said.
> Yes, I said, and I want a story that's a story.
> A story that's a story, you said.
> A proper story, I said (p. 171).

In response to this demand for a 'proper story', the second person responds '[r]ight then . . . There was once a child whose mother fell asleep. The end' (p. 172). The first person provides an abrupt and paltry narrative; s/he refuses

Was there ever such a thing? How good it would be to be sure, to have it there in writing, the ultimate experience of anticipation that actually arrives, in person. And he's not writing to me. How very irritating. It's heartbreaking, in fact' (Wood 2006, p. 53). David Wills points out that 'there immediately exist at least two addressees – her and the reader' (Wills 1984, p. 23). The 'you' first refers to us and then does not.

A similar process occurs in 'My chances'. As in *The Politics of Friendship*, an apostrophe appears very close to the beginning of the text; Derrida admits that '[y]ou are perhaps wondering' (Derrida 2007b, p. 344). Again, the text seems to address us. A little later, however, Derrida writes

> Playing now with the apostrophe, I prefer to tell you right away: I do not know to whom I am speaking. To whom is this discourse or lecture addressed here and now? It is indeed to you that I am delivering it, but that doesn't change the situation much. You understand quite well why I say this (p. 344).

Derrida reminds us that he does not know to whom he writes. The you does not address us as directly as it initially seemed; it is less intimate than we supposed. Barthes complains that '[y]ou address yourself to me so that I may read you, but I am nothing to you except this address' (Barthes 1990b, p. 5). Derrida's text distances itself from us.

In 'Envois' Derrida would address himself directly *to* 'you' so as to declare his love. He wonders, however, whether

> when I call you my love, my love, is it you I am calling or my love? You, my love, is it you I thereby name, is it to you that I address myself? I don't know if the question is well put, it frightens me. But I am sure that the answer, if it gets to me one day, will have come to me from you. You alone, my love, you alone will have known it . . . when I call you my love, is it that I am calling you, yourself, or is it that I am telling my love? and when I tell you my love, is it that I am declaring my love to you or indeed that I am telling *you*, yourself, my love and that you are my love. I want so much to tell you (Derrida 1987a, p. 8; italics in original).

Derrida wants so much to tell you 'I love you', but in doing so he finds also that he tells 'you'; the declaration of 'my love' does not simply address itself to you but names 'you' as 'my love'. Derrida therefore finds 'I have called you, yourself. And thereby I have taken your name' (p. 219).

Smith's 'The second person' explores this taking of 'your name'. The story's first-person narrator tells a story to and about a second person. Once s/he has finished s/he tells the second person

That's what you're like.

No it isn't, you say.

I feel you get annoyed beside me.

That's nothing like me, you say (Smith 2008, p. 123).

The first person claims to describe the second. The second person disagrees, however; the 'you' of the first person's story is, s/he claims, 'nothing like' him/her. To exact her revenge she retorts

God, you're saying next to me now. *This is what you're like.*

    You say it in a voice like it's supposed to be my voice, though in reality it's nothing like my voice.

    This is what you're like, I say. I say it in the mimic voice you've just used (p. 125; italics in original).

The first person, claiming that the second person's imitation is 'in reality . . . nothing like my voice', expresses an almost identical objection; s/he, too, does not agree with the way in which the second person represents him/her.

My reaction to the address I encounter in Edwards' *Eve Kosofsky Sedgwick* is somewhat similar. As I explained earlier, Edwards addresses himself directly to you and asks you to 'check in regularly on how you're feeling'. The thing is (and I apologize if this sounds unduly harsh) I find these moments in Edwards' text intensely irritating. *No*, I think, *I'm not going to think about how I'm feeling, not if you're going to patronize me like that.* 'Dear reader' indeed – I don't know what readers he has in mind but *my* reading is certainly not 'more visible' in his text. I feel not addressed, but, like Smith's characters, appropriated, decided in advance.

I experience a similar dissatisfaction when reading the preface to Derrida's 'Envois'. Derrida tells us '[y]ou might read these *envois* as the preface to a book that I have not written' and that '[y]ou might consider [these texts], if you really wish to, as the remainders of a recently destroyed correspondence'. The phrase 'if you really wish to' expresses an 'if you must'-style exasperation. Derrida later tells us that we are 'in a hurry to be determined', too 'decided upon deciding' (Derrida 1987a, p. 4). He cannot understand why we're so set on knowing.

It is 'you' who – much to Derrida's frustration – would 'really wish' to define the nature of the text. Yet this is perhaps unfair. We, the readers, have not at this point made any such demand; we have not even read the 'correspondence' to which Derrida refers – we are still reading his preface. Derrida's 'you' creates an image of us, which fails to correspond to our actual reading. I instinctively disidentify from it and am inclined to assume that he speaks to some other, less patient, audience.

Each of the characters in 'The second person' is similarly irritated and stresses that the 'you' of the other's story is a fabrication; it is not a depiction of his/her 'true' character. The story's second person complains:

> What amazes me about you, you say still looking away, is that after all these years, all the years of dialogue between us, you think you've got the right to just decide, like you're God, who I am and who I'm not and what I'm like and what I'm not and what I'd do and what I wouldn't (Smith 2008, pp. 123–4).

The second person is appalled that the first person would decide in this way who s/he is and likens it to a God-like act of appropriation. S/he argues that the 'I' has treated him/her as 'a fiction you can play with'.

The 'you' of the text becomes a 'fiction', a construct or a character. McHale examines a number of second-person texts and realizes that 'you' either becomes a substitute for the first person 'indicating that a character is "talking to himself"' or, alternatively, that it 'stands in for the third-person pronoun of the fictional character, functioning in a kind of displaced free indirect discourse' (McHale 1987, p. 223). This slippage does not happen only in fictional texts; it is also a feature of the second person when used in everyday speech, as Smith's 'God's gift' and 'No exit' reveal. In 'God's gift' the narrator declares 'I wasn't frightened, I wasn't frightened on any of the flights, since you are only frightened of losing something if you've got something to lose. Not you: one. One is only frightened, etc.' (Smith 1999, p. 4). The pattern is repeated again at the end of the story: '[e]verything you do, everything you see, everything you feel, every single moment, good or bad, that you get. Not you: one. Every single moment, good or bad, that one gets' (p. 12). And in 'No exit', too, the narrator phones 'you' (again a character from whom it appears s/he has recently separated) in order to ask, '[w]hat I was wondering, I say, is whether or not, if you were trapped in there, well, not you, I mean one, someone, anyone, if someone was trapped in there and the door had shut and everybody'd gone home, do you think there'd still be any lights on in there?' (Smith 2008, p. 111) In each of these examples, the narrator corrects his/her use of the pronoun 'you'. S/he has used it (as we often do) when s/he 'really' means 'one'. 'You' functions as a third person impersonal pronoun. Fludernik therefore describes it as 'inherently ambiguous and multi-functional' (Fludernik 1996, p. 223). You is, for Bonheim, a 'Protean shape-shifter' (Bonheim 1983, p. 79). And for McHale it is simply 'shifty' (McHale 1987, p. 223).

This slippage cannot be controlled; it occurs every time I use the word 'you'. Derrida finds that he writes '[e]n train to write *you* (you? to you?)' (Derrida 1987a, p. 32; italics in original). Cixous echoes this equivocation when she announces 'I write you: I write to you and I write you' (Cixous 1998, p. 199). When I write 'you' I do not simply address myself to 'you' but name and create a 'you'. My writing determines 'you' in a certain way. I mentioned earlier that Coetzee describes a writing which is 'at heart' a transaction with the figure-of-the-beloved. Coetzee admits, however, that writing does not only try to please its figure of the beloved, but 'also tries continually though surreptitiously to revise and recreate her as the-one-who-will-be-pleased' (Coetzee 1996, p. 38).

Derrida realizes that

> I apostrophize. This too is a genre one can afford oneself, the apostrophe. A genre and a tone. The word – apostrophizes – speaks of the words addressed to the singular one, a live interpellation (the man of discourse or writing interrupts the continuous development of the sequence, abruptly turns toward someone, that is, addresses himself to you), but the word also speaks of the address to be detoured (Derrida 1987a, p. 4).

The apostrophe is 'detoured'. When I apostrophize, Derrida points out, 'I have [the other] come, he is present for me; I *presuppose* his presence, if only at the end of my sentence, on the other end of the line [*au bout du fil*], at the intentional pole of my allocution'. However, 'my very sentence simultaneously puts him at a distance or retards his arrival, since it must always ask or presuppose the question "are you there?"' (Derrida 2005b, p. 173). The apostrophe therefore 'resembles at one and the same time a *recall* and a *call*' (p. 235; italics in original). This duality is contained in its very etymology. Although we think of it in terms of address and inclusion it derives, according to the OED, from the Greek meaning 'to turn away' (www.oed.com). McLane invokes this duality when she writes '[a] postrophe: apo-strophe: to turn away, outward. Address: to direct oneself toward (thus the prefix "ad")' (McLane 2000, p. 440).

In any second-person text, there is therefore '[a] continuous dialectic of identification and distancing . . . as the reader is alternately drawn closer to and further away from the protagonist' (Richardson 2006, p. 21). Derrida explains in *The Politics of Friendship* that the readers 'are summoned to be spoken to, *da*, then dismissed, *fort*, saying to them, speaking *of them*, that they are no longer there' (Derrida 2005b, p. 173; italics in original).

The apostrophe does not only speak *to* its addresses, but also speaks *of* them. We realize, moreover, that 'between talking *to them* and speaking *of them* there is a world of difference' (p. 172). Both Derrida's text and the second person of Smith's story imply that the act of determination I just outlined is problematic. To show why this is the case I return, in the paragraphs that follow, once more to the reader-response theory I outlined in my introductory chapter. Reader response, as I pointed out earlier, argues that the response of the reader ought to be taken into account and represented by literary criticism. Fish, however, is conscious that the reader he talks about is 'a construct, an ideal or idealized reader . . . *the* reader is the *informed* reader' (Fish 1980, p. 48; italics in original). As has been highlighted by many commentators on Fish's work, this 'ideal' is not neutral but carries with it a number of assumptions. Most notably, Fish's reader is always male. Vincent B. Leitch stresses, moreover, that theories of reader-response 'pushed critical enquiry towards pedagogy, typically locating text and reader in the classroom' (Leitch 1995, p. 33). Fish's reader is someone who 'does everything within his power to make himself informed' (Fish 1980, p. 49). He even envisages his own reader as a 'user-student' for whom his account might function as a 'way of teaching' (p. 67). Elsewhere, Fish writes that '[i]t seems obvious that the efforts of readers are always to discern and therefore to realize (in the sense of becoming) an author's intention' (p. 161). For Iser, too, '[a]n ideal reader would have to have an identical code to that of the author'. The author, therefore, is 'theoretically the only possible ideal reader' (Iser 1978, pp. 28–9). The above examples construct a specific image of who the reader is or ought to be; the notion of the ideal reader establishes in advance the code to which s/he ought to conform.

Fish and Iser find that, in writing about the experience of reading, they construct an image of a particular reader. They cannot do otherwise. This is, Fish realizes, a problem. Reader response argues that the response of the reader ought to be taken into account and represented by literary criticism. Fish is, however, unable to keep this response sufficiently open in his work. He interrupts his analysis in order to ask anxiously '[b]ut what reader? When I talk about the responses of "the reader", am I not really talking about myself, and making myself into a surrogate for all the millions of readers who are not me at all?' (Fish 1980, p. 44). Later he wonders '[w]ho is this reader? How can I presume to describe his experiences, and what do I say to readers who report that they do not have the experiences I describe?' (p. 159). In both of these quotations, Fish becomes aware of the fact that there are readers and responses other than those his text represents. His text enacts certain exclusions; it cannot take into account every perspective. We may find, as readers of Fish's text, that we 'do not have the experiences' he describes. Our reading diverges from that which Fish sets down; the text does not address us. By constructing a particular reader, Fish's text excludes us as readers and thereby negates its own theory; it fails to take into account our experience or response.

Equally, the texts I am examining set out to acknowledge their dependence on an other; they attempt to speak to, and admit, a reader on whom they rely.

However, they find themselves instead speaking *of* this reader. As I explained earlier, the narrator of Smith's 'The theme is power' begins by announcing 'I really need you with me in this story'. S/he admits, however, that 'you're not home. You won't be home for hours yet' (Smith 1999, p. 121). S/he proceeds nonetheless to tell his/her story, complete with the second-person interjections I mentioned in my chapter's first section. After a while the narrator declares 'I turn around. You're not there. I knew that. There's no one here, just me, and my father breathing next door' (p. 133). Later, after the second person complains 'I still don't really get the connection', the first person admits '[w]ell, no. Okay. Actually you don't say anything, you're not home yet. But you'll be home soon, so I imagine your key in the door, you kicking off your shoes and hanging your jacket in the hall, and coming through, stealing up behind me and kissing the back of my neck' (p. 135). The interjections do not, in fact, come from a second person; the dialogue is imagined wholly by the story's first person. There is no second person proper in these texts; the 'reader' is not in fact made present.

The 'I' appropriates 'you' as knowable and identifiable; it assumes, in its confident representation, an ability to recognize the other. Moreover, whenever I think I have recognized 'you' or think '"[o]h, now I know who you are"', Butler argues, 'I cease to address you, or to be addressed by you' (Butler 2005, p. 43). By assimilating you within *my* language, I do a disservice to your quality *as* other; I return you to the same. The text masters whatever 'you' it represents. Derrida suggests that 'the proper name of the other' would 'perhaps . . . come back to and come down to the same' (Derrida 2007a, p. 147). Even when the name we use is 'you' the other finds itself assimilated within the language of an 'I'.

The other, Derrida explains, is not properly other unless left 'to come'. We must, Derrida points out, 'by definition, leave the other to come' (Derrida 2005b, p. 174). Derrida suggests that '[s]omething of [the] call of the other must remain nonreappropriable, nonsubjectivable, and in a certain way nonidentifiable, a sheer supposition, so as to remain *other*, a *singular* call to response or to responsibility' (Derrida 1995b, p. 276). To remain other, the 'call of the other' must elude the appropriation my language performs. Butler suggests that '[a]s we ask to know the other, or ask that the other say, finally or definitively, who he or she is, it will be important not to expect an answer that will ever satisfy' (Butler 2005, pp. 42–3).

The other must remain 'nonidentifiable' and 'nonsubjectivable'. To fully signal their dependence, these texts must address themselves *to* an other they do not yet, and may never, know. For Derrida, *who* is therefore 'the great question'. We must ask '*Who? Who asks the question who? Where? How? When? Who arrives?*'.

Who, Derrida suggests, remains 'irreducible' to a 'what' which would decide the other. 'Who', Derrida realizes, 'withdraws from or provokes the displacement of the categories in which biography, autobiography, and memoirs are thought' (Derrida 2001, pp. 41–2; italics in original). We might, in the wonder of the question *who are you*, remain open to the other.

Who is, however, 'the most difficult question'. As I have already explained there is no *to* which does not also speak *of* the other. Hannah Arendt admits that '[t]he moment we want to say *who* somebody is, our very vocabulary leads us into saying *what* he is' (Arendt 1998, p. 181; italics in original). Even when we want to say *who*, we find ourselves again saying *what*. For both Arendt and Derrida 'who' remains curiously impossible. Derrida places us in a paradoxical bind; he demands that we favour 'who' above 'what' and yet, at the same time, informs us that there is no answer to the question 'who' which does not return us to 'what'.

By presenting the other, these texts betray his/her otherness, as the 'you' of Smith's 'The second person' is aware. As I outlined earlier, s/he objects to the picture 'I' constructs of him/her and to the way in which the first person's address in fact determines him/her. The complaint the second person offers is, however, ironic: the second person is, precisely, a fiction within the story. There is no second person here – no properly other other; both the 'I' and the 'you' originate from the same place and 'The second person' does not voice any perspective but its own. 'The second person' performs the very mastery it attempts to thematize. We find, as Derrida writes in 'Envois', that '[w]e have never yet seen each other. Only written' and that '[t]he other does not answer, is not published' (Derrida 1987a, pp. 68, 96). I can publish 'you' but the 'you' that I inscribe will never be the answer of the 'true' other of my writing. The second person, despite our hopes, fails fully to signal relationality or the other on whom these texts depend.

Over to you

You are fundamental to the work. The second person – by addressing and including a 'you' on whom the work depends – perhaps admits it. We realize, however, that this 'you' also decides or determines the other or the reader to whom the text supposedly opens itself. Derrida writes in 'Envois' that 'I have called you, yourself. And thereby I have taken your name' (Derrida 1987a, p. 219). By calling 'you' Derrida takes the name 'you' for himself; he appropriates the other to whom he would address himself. The other is returned to the same, mastered by and within the text 'I' write.

I can, in light of these realizations, return now to the concerns I expressed in my introduction about declaring love to these texts. Kamuf asks to whom, when announcing one's love for a text, one will address oneself. *I love you, 'Envois'* or *I love you, 'The theme is power'* seem deprived of force; the text cannot answer, cannot be an addressee proper. Kamuf declares therefore that '[w]hen one declares love to a text, one declares it *necessarily* to another within oneself'. I cannot properly declare love to a text. Kamuf asks, '[i]s this, then, a distinction that has to be made between this act and the act of addressing love to another who is *also* other than oneself, a now living person, that is, one who is not only an other within?' (Kamuf 2000, p. 159). The answer is of course no; this failure is not a particular feature of announcing one's love of a text, but the condition of all declarations of love. Kamuf points out that 'a declaration of love is also a declaration that some internalization of the other has begun' and writes that 'perhaps there has never been a declaration of love that did not keep for itself what it wanted the other to have or feel' (p. 160). The 'you' of 'I love you', like the 'you's of my second section, is not wholly other but a 'you' which in some sense belongs to the first person who declares it; 'I love you' will never signify it is proper or ideal sense.

Should we, then, give up declaring love or writing you altogether? Derrida does not think so; he informs us that '[w]hat cannot be said above all must not be silenced, but written' (Derrida 1987a, p. 194). Derrida explains in *The Politics of Friendship* that 'I need' the 'freedom' of the other 'in order to address the other *qua* other'. Derrida explains that he 'would therefore command him to be capable of not answering – my call, my invitation, my expectation, my desire. And I must impose a sort of obligation on him thereby to prove his freedom, a freedom I need, precisely in order to call, wait, invite' (Derrida 2005b, p. 174). In the act of calling or demanding the other's freedom, we exert an obligation, divesting him/her of the very freedom we wish him/her to prove. Nonetheless, we must call the other in order to demand his/her freedom. We cannot *not* call the other; his/her appropriation is both inevitable and necessary.

Derrida wonders, in 'My chances', what his chances are 'of reaching my addressees if, on the one hand, I calculate and prepare a place of *encounter* (and I underscore the word) or if, on the other hand, I hope, as we say in French, to *fall* upon them by accident' (Derrida 2007b, p. 345; italics in original). We cannot, I have shown earlier, fully 'calculate and prepare a place of encounter'. In the very act of calculating and preparing we betray the 'encounter' we desire. Derrida is, however, equally sceptical concerning our ability to '*fall* upon' the encounter 'by accident'. In speaking of chance, he suggests that 'what I say at this moment about chance has more chance of reaching you than if I had delivered it over to chance without speaking about it' (p. 345). In failing to prepare a 'place of encounter', an encounter might yet become possible. Moreover, it is more likely that an encounter will take place this way than if the meeting is left purely to chance.

Even though I am unable to address myself purely and directly to you, our relation might, I will suggest in the final section of my chapter, yet be glimpsed. Derrida explains in 'Envois' that he has 'taken your name'; his writing involves an act of appropriation. Derrida tells us in *The Politics of Friendship*, however, that 'the inaccessibility can be interpreted *otherwise*' (Derrida 2005b, p. 221; italics in original). '*Mais si*' he continues in 'Envois' 'and somewhat in the way, as they say in their system, that a woman takes the name of her husband' (Derrida 1987a, p. 219). Derrida now compares his appropriation to the marriage custom whereby the woman adopts her husband's name. He thereby offers an entirely different slant on my earlier analysis. By giving up her own name and taking the man's instead the woman is marked as her husband's possession. Taking the name is no longer an act of appropriation; the one who takes the name (typically the wife, but in this case Derrida) is appropriated. A very different relation becomes visible; the one who takes the name may also be dispossessed.

I quoted earlier the moment in 'My chances' at which Derrida tells us 'I prefer to tell you right away: I do not know to whom I am speaking'. Derrida's first 'you' addresses us, his readers. In the declaration 'I do not know to whom I am speaking', however, the text ceases to refer to us. I also described my reaction to the moments in Edwards' text when he addresses his readers and argued that, rather than opening itself to reading, the text writes and decides its reader in advance. I am not, I argued, 'more visible' in his text. Equally, I argued that 'A story with love' ceases to address its reader after the first page.

We are dispossessed. However, the rejection is not absolute; our disidentification is not straightforward. Derrida tells us that 'since you find this intelligible, it becomes at least possible to demonstrate that, beginning with the first sentence, my lecture has not purely and simply missed its destination' (Derrida 2007b, pp. 344–5). You might have noticed that, despite my protestations – in fact, in my very protestations themselves – my relation to the text is acute. At the moment in 'A story with love' at which the text's second person is first addressed as 'Sam' we realize that we have made a mistake; we have identified ourselves with a 'you' that was not properly addressed to us. We become aware, at this moment, of the extent to which we previously identified ourselves with the you of the text.

In the instant it ceases to address us, our relation to the text belatedly becomes pronounced; our relation to it becomes *most* evident at the moments at which it dispossess or un-addresses us, as Smith's 'God's gift' illustrates. 'God's gift' opens defiantly as the narrator announces '[t]here are so many things that you don't know about me now' (Smith 1999, p. 3). We deduce that the story takes place sometime after a break-up between the story's narrator and the 'you' s/he addresses. The narrator's 'there are so many things you don't know about me now' marks a temporal and emotional distance between 'you' and 'I'. Announcing that s/he has changed, it implies 'I'm over you'.

The story's opening sentence is followed by the words '[f]or instance': 'For instance. Some neighbouring cat has been bringing me birds, dead or dying, for several days' (Smith 1999, p. 3). The narrator adopts a casual tone; these are not, s/he implies, pieces of information s/he truly wants to tell 'you', but offhand examples chosen at random. The phrase is echoed later in the story when the narrator introduces an anecdote with the phrase 'again for instance' (p. 4). The emphatic 'again' draws attention to these words; the narrator's tone is *pointedly* casual – s/he wants it to be noticed.

The insouciant tone is not genuine, but is clearly a performance; the narrator feigns (or rather, fails to feign) disinterest and in doing so draws attention to a contradiction inherent in his/her tale. The story's opening sentence eschews 'you', reasserting the independence of the 'I'. In its very performance, however, this declaration fails to achieve that which it announces; it addresses the 'you' it would reject. The story announces that it is over you, but as it does, it reveals its need to inform you of this fact and so illustrates its continued reliance on you.

Against its wish, this story finds that it is preoccupied entirely by a 'you' it can neither forget nor banish. This becomes especially apparent at the moments I cited earlier when the narrator declares 'I wasn't frightened, I wasn't frightened on any of the flights, since you are only frightened of losing something if you've got something to lose. Not you: one. One is only frightened, etc' and '[e]verything you do, everything you see, everything you feel, every single moment, good or bad, that you get. Not you: one. Every single moment, good or bad, that one gets' (pp. 4, 12). The narrator alters his/her 'you' to an impersonal (and more seemly) 'one'. Too late, the narrator realizes that the 'you' the 'I' ought to forget has crept back in. These determined corrections render the mistake all the more visible; they draw our attention to the 'you' of the previous phrases. The narrator, determined not to address you, has failed. As the narrator sits in a café in Greece she declares 'I saw the writing painted all along the wall out to the lighthouse, some Greek words I couldn't understand and then the English words, love, and you' (p. 5). These, too, are the words that gradually emerge from this story, even against its narrator's avowed intention. 'God's gift' demonstrates the inability of the 'I' to banish the 'you'.

'God's gift' patterns a contradiction; even as the narrator aims to separate him/herself from 'you' his/her monologue reveals a continued reliance. The 'I' is inscribed against its will by 'you'; the second person is, for the first-person of 'God's gift', bewilderingly inescapable. The second person is, as in Derrida's 'Envois', 'immense' and 'omnipresent' (Derrida 1987a, p. 107). Obsession, Levinas suggests, is a good name for this inevitable return; he explains that 'obsession traverses consciousness contrariwise, inscribing it there as something foreign, as disequilibrium, as delirium, undoing thematization, eluding *principle,* origin, and will, all of which are affirmed in every gleam of consciousness' (Levinas 1996a, p. 81; italics in original). He argues, moreover, that this 'disequilibrium' is key to the way in which we ought to understand the subject. The condition 'God's gift' describes is not, for Levinas, exceptional, but a general condition.

To understand why, we must turn to the theorization Levinas offers of the subject's inauguration. For Levinas, the 'I' 'begins . . . in the accusative'; the 'I' is inaugurated by the answer 'yes, me' to a 'you', which comes before it (Levinas 1996a, p. 88). Althusser, although working with a very different set of notions to those we encounter in Levinas's work (while Levinas rethinks ethics, Althusser focuses on the concept of ideology), depicts a similar scene. The subject, he suggests, is 'interpellated' into being. Althusser famously imagines a scene in which an individual hears a '"[h]ey, you there"' and '[a]ssuming that the theoretical scene I have imagined takes place in the street, the hailed individual will turn round. By this mere one-hundred-and-eighty-degree physical conversation, he becomes a *subject*. Why? Because he has recognised that the hail was "really" addressed to him, and that "it was *really* him who was hailed" (and not someone else)' (Althusser 1971, p. 163; italics in original). For Althusser, 'I' become a subject only once 'I' have turned around in response to the call of the other.

In the accounts of both Levinas and Althusser, 'I' am formed by and as my response to 'you'. Butler – who discusses both of these theories in *Giving an Account of Oneself* – explains that 'I begin my story of myself only in the face of a 'you' who asks me to give an account' (Butler 2005, p. 11). Smith's 'Erosive', for example, opens with the words '[w]hat do you need to know about me for this story? How old I am? how much I earn a year? what kind of car I drive?' (Smith 2003, p. 99). The narrator finds that the story is governed from the outset by a series of expectations; s/he is bound by the questions 'you' might ask and by what you might 'need to know'. The 'other' precedes the story; the thought of 'you' informs it even before it has properly begun.

I mentioned earlier that the listener in 'The theme is power' sits behind the narrator as s/he stands at the sink. 'Envois' presents a similar scene. Derrida contemplates a postcard, which features a picture of Plato standing behind Socrates: '[h]e is in front of Plato, no, Plato is *behind* him, smaller (why smaller?), but standing up' (Derrida 1987a, p. 9; italics in original). The most obvious sense of Derrida's 'behind' positions Plato at Socrates' back, reading over his shoulder that which he writes. However, 'Envois' also stresses a second sense of the word; Plato is also 'behind' the words that Socrates writes; he invents and is responsible for them. Derrida writes that '*Socrates* turns his *back* to plato, who has made him write whatever he wanted while pretending to receive it from him' (Derrida 1987a, p. 12; italics in original). Although apparently receiving Socrates' work, Plato in fact creates it. The reader dictates the text's emergence. Whoever writes or gives an account finds, as Derrida does in 'Envois' that '[y]ou give me words, you deliver them, dispensed one by one, my own' (p. 12). The words that are supposedly 'my own' are in fact delivered and 'dispensed' from elsewhere, by 'you'. Derrida explains that 'whoever writes must indeed ask himself what it is asked of him to write, and then he writes under the dictation of some addressee' (p. 143).

'You' precede me. There is no 'I' without a 'you' which inaugurates it. I mentioned in my first section McHale's claim that the second person 'announces the presence of a communicative circuit' '*more strongly*' than the first person. McHale's assertion cannot be upheld; the 'I', we now see, is equally marked as a sign of relation and may also signal the 'presence of a communicative circuit'. Derrida explains that 'it is the ear of the other that signs. The ear of the other says me to me and constitutes the *autos* of my autobiography. When, much later, the other will have perceived with a keen-enough ear what I will have addressed or destined to him or her, then my signature will have taken place' (Derrida 1985, p. 51). I must, with a somewhat 'paradoxical' thought, wait for the other to '[say] me to me' before 'I' am able to say 'I'. There is, Derrida writes, 'thought for man only to the extent that it is thought *of the other*' (Derrida 2005a, p. 224). Derrida's genitive signals doubly; 'my' every thought is a thought belonging to, and given to me by, the other, and is also and therefore a thought of or about the other.

The self is not, Coetzee explains, 'the unity it was assumed to be by classical rationalism' (Coetzee 1996, p. 37). We are no longer able to maintain a model in which '[t]he subject assumes presence, that is to sub-stance, stasis, stance' (Derrida 1995b, p. 270). We can no longer uphold a notion of the self for which 'everything is intentionally assumed', which 'always assumes what it undergoes' and which 'reappears as the *principle* of what happens to it' (Levinas 1996a, pp. 82, 89; italics in original). The 'alterity that has become internal' makes us, as Butler writes, 'permanently and partially foreign to ourselves' (Butler 2005, p. 98).

If, as Robert Smith points out, the 'other' 'starts the autobiography off', autobiography can no longer remain the category we believed it to be (Smith 1995, p. 118). The text, Derrida points out, 'will not be an autobiography, naturally, but a heterobiography in the sense in which one also says heterosexuality, and so on' (Derrida 1985, p. 79). There is no *auto*biography proper. Caught in a relational scene, my work is neither masterful nor self-sufficient. I am not the unequivocal proprietor of it, as Derrida makes clear when discussing Levinas's work in 'At this very moment'. It is, he claims, no longer possible to name Levinas as the 'subject-author-signer-proprietor of the work [*ouvrage*] . . . he does not *make* a work, he is not the agent or creator of his work' (Derrida 2007a, p. 175; italics in original).

Derrida points out that '[t]he other is in me before me'. He therefore explains that

> 'Leaving room for the other' does not mean 'I have to make room for the other'. The other is in me before me: the ego (even the collective ego) implies alterity as its own condition. There is no 'I' that ethically makes room for the other, but rather an 'I' that is structured by the alterity within it, an 'I' that is itself in a state of self-deconstruction, of dislocation . . . The other is not even simply the future [*futur*], it is, so to speak, the anterior future [*l'avenir avant*], the advance on the future [*avenir*]. Which means that I am not proprietor of my 'I', I am not proprietor of the place open to hospitality. Whoever gives hospitality ought to know that he is not even proprietor of what he would appear to give (Derrida 2001, pp. 84–5).

'You' are not a figure for whom I can choose to make room or not. 'You' come before my ability to write 'I' or 'you'. 'You', Levinas explains, are 'the primary fact of Saying [*Dire*]' (Levinas 1999, p. 93). 'You' precede my ability to thematize or to master 'you' in language. The 'ethical-vocative origin' which founds the work and the subject 'belongs to an "absolute-past"' (Smith 1995, p. 120). 'The invention of the other' must 'have already taken place, before everything, so that its very question may arise, which renders the question obsolete in advance' (Derrida 2007a, pp. 147–8). Whatever 'other' 'I' represent comes too late. My 'you' comes too late. Cixous therefore realizes that 'I will never say enough what (I) my writing owes you' (Cixous 1998, p. 199).

The dependency to which I alluded in my introduction is more profound than it might at first appear. It belongs to a 'rhetorical dimension that is not reducible to a narrative function' (Butler 2005, p. 63). It is a preontological or linguistic relation, a 'precondition' of 'narration' which cannot therefore 'yield to narrative form' (p. 38). Derrida warns that '[t]he disturbance' Levinas's text '*refers to* (the Relation it relates to the Other by linking to it the *récit*) *is* never assured, perceptible, *demonstrable*: neither a demonstrative conclusion nor a phenomenal monstration'. It is, '[b]y definition' 'not a controllable disturbance, it is not readable within the *inside* of logic, semiotics, language, grammaticality, lexicon, or rhetoric with their supposedly internal criteria, because nothing is less certain than the rigorous limits of such an inside' (Derrida 2007a, p. 161; italics in original). The 'disturbance' to which Levinas's text refers cannot be captured by or within language; it does not belong to the realm of the said. Levinas explains that '[t]he approach is not the thematization of any relation but that very relation which resists thematization in as much as it is an-archic' (Levinas 1996a, pp. 92–3; italics in original). The quality of the relationality to which Levinas alludes lies with a telling which cannot be told.

Butler explains that '[t]his exposure . . . cannot be narrated. I cannot give an account of it, even though it structures any account I might give' (Butler 2005, p. 35). Although resistant to narration, this 'exposure' is always inescapably *there*. I pointed out earlier that in 'The theme is power' the second person, when asked by the first for a 'proper story', responds '[r]ight then . . . There was once a child whose mother fell asleep. The end' (Smith 1999, p. 172). I suggested that this abrupt response refuses to mollify or cede to the demands the first person makes. The story does not, however, escape so simply. The comedy we derive from the second person's story lies in the *relationship* it bears to the first person's demands; it is amusing not in and of itself but as an answer to the request for a proper story. The second person's story, produced in and as its resistance to the first person's expectations, continues to cite them. It cannot wholly discard them. The story is still a response to the demands that the listener levels. We thus realize that although the story may choose the manner in which it responds, it cannot choose whether or not *to* respond; it is bound in a relational scene from which it cannot escape. You may equally have spotted the fact that my rejection of Edwards' address cedes to the very request he makes; it indeed records 'how I am feeling' as I read his text. Somewhat infuriatingly, it obliges him even in turning away from him. Derrida explains that, in relation to the call of the other, 'I can *only* answer, have already answered, even if I think I am answering "no"' (Derrida 1995b, p. 261; italics in original). The demand of the other is inescapable.

'The structure', Robert Smith explains, 'is one of an *essential* responsiveness' (Smith 1995, p. 82; italics in original). Given that the 'call to responsibility' is 'anterior to any possible response' and 'dissymmetrical in its coming from the other within us', we cannot *not* respond; 'even a nonresponse a priori assumes responsibility' (Derrida 2004a, p. 83). The subject is, as Cavarero realizes, '[c]*onstitutively* altruistic, rather than by choice' (Cavarero 2000, p. 90; italics in original). We find, somewhat counter-intuitively, that we cannot escape responsibility; it is not that which we can choose or deny.

Derrida therefore realizes in 'Envois' that 'it only depends on you that it is you' and '(everything depends upon you, it is only up to you that your answer destines my love to you)' (Derrida 1987a, pp. 137, 174). It is in the hands of Derrida's readers (in this case me) to decide, even, whether his 'you' addresses us or not.[3] Even (and especially) when I write you, when I address myself to you, it is up to you to decide what I have written – and whether or not I might have written (to) you. Margolin suggests that '[f]rom now on, any adoption by an actual reader of a 'you' token as referring to him or her is strictly optional and ludic, involving a willingness to place him/herself in or occupy a slot which, strictly speaking, is already occupied by nonfactual recipients' (Margolin 1990, p. 438). It is always '[u]p to you [*toi*] first'; even when I supposedly address you, I find that 'I await only one response and it falls to you' – only you can confer my second-person pronoun the right of address (Derrida 1987a, p. 4).

This is not to say that you decide absolutely. Derrida writes, '[t]o be sure, you are the author of the text you read here, that can be said, but you are still in an absolute heteronomy. You are responsible for the other, who makes you responsible. *Who will have obligated you*' (Derrida 2007a, p. 161; italics in original). I casually commented in my analysis of Edwards' text that 'you may have noticed' that my relation to the text was more acute, and more visible, than I at first admitted. You might already, in reading my second section, have noted the point I come finally to make in my third. My admission might, for you, have come too late. In your reading, I was perhaps still bound by the relation I would escape. I cannot simply refuse Edwards' address; you may deny me the ability to do so. My reading is in thrall to yet another 'you'. It remains in an 'absolute heteronomy'.

The texts I have examined here fail to address themselves directly to you; they fail to inscribe the profound reliance to which you subject them. In doing so, however, they might, in fact, make visible the very relationship to which they would allude. I fail to address you because I am bound already, before I even begin to write, in the scene I would invoke. My failure is caught in the logic it attempts to describe. The relation might therefore yet be glimpsed. Yet it cannot be guaranteed; this happening is easily missed. There is 'no promised encounter without the possibility of a *contretemps*' (Derrida 2005b, p. 1). You can always refuse my address. We discover that '[r]esponsibility carries within it, and must do so, an essential excessiveness. It regulates itself neither on the principle of reason nor on any sort of accountancy' (Derrida 1995b, p. 272).

There is an increasing awareness, thanks both to reader-response and to a growing interest in questions of ethics, of the importance of 'you' and the role 'you' play in deciding the work. Smith's stories openly acknowledge this debt, as does Derrida and those who write after him. The use of the second person itself appears to mark the dependence. The texts I have examined here address themselves to an other to whom they are in thrall. However, the 'you' of these apostrophes is not necessarily the other *per se*. These texts, in their confident inscriptions, decide their addressee in a way which might in fact close down the reading they invite. The other is all too easily returned to the same. The apostrophe does not necessarily make you or your reading more visible in the text that is written. We thus realize that the dependence is not one which can be thematized. Our very thematization betrays it, as Levinas's work points out. The possibilities offered by the apostrophe are more indirect, more difficult to discern. This difficulty is fundamental. Derrida explains that 'the determination of the singular "Who?" – or at least its determination as subject – remains forever problematic'. He asserts, moreover, that 'it *should* remain so. This obligation to protect the other's otherness is not merely a theoretical imperative' (Derrida 1995b, p. 276; italics in original). We must continue to represent and to address ourselves to you. At the same time, however, we must remember that which we are told at the end of 'The second person'. The first-person receives a note that reads '[y]ou're something else, you. You really are' (Smith 2008, p. 134). We must remember that 'you' is always something else; it is always something other than that as which we represent it.

Derrida writes that 'I believe there is no responsibility, no ethico-political decision that must not pass through the proofs of the incalculable or the undecidable. Otherwise everything would be reducible to calculation, program, causality, and, at best, "hypothetical imperative"' (Derrida 1995b, p. 273). For Derrida, '[a] limited, measured, calculable, rationally distributed responsibility is already the becoming-right of morality'. It is no longer a responsibility at all. Derrida writes, 'I repeat: responsibility is excessive or it is not a responsibility' (p. 286). It is – excessively – up to you that you are you.

Coda: Desire

Each of my chapters repeats the pattern established by my first. Each takes as its theme a provocation that gets reading and interpretation going: composition, the trace, deconstruction and ethics, tact and you. These are elements we fall for, concepts we desire. Very quickly, however, we realize that we cannot have or grasp these things that we want; they remain elusive.

In realizing this failure, however, something like reading, writing, the trace and so on happen. We experience and glimpse them. We come to know them 'with a knowledge that is not a knowledge at all' (Derrida 1997b, p. 164). They present themselves momentarily, contingently and fleetingly.

These concepts reward our fascination; they prove themselves useful. But the quality we prize does not last. We cannot, in light of the work that we have done, adopt these concepts or guarantee their future use. We cannot embrace them too heartily. Instead, our investigation demands that we start the next chapter all over again; we must repeatedly re-realize these concepts anew. They remain useful only so long as they stay impossible, only so long as they continue to demand reading.

There can, therefore, be no conclusion. Connors, at the end of her discussion of force, notes that 'the calling to account of a conclusion, with its complacent hindsight, cannot quite render either the shock of force's irruption or the forcelessness of the moment of reading' (Connors 2010a, p. 130). The 'calling to account' and 'complacent hindsight' of the conclusion will never capture the experiences of 'shock' and 'forcelessness', which characterize both 'force' and the concepts my book has discussed. The conclusion betrays the qualities the book sets out to create. The 'only possible end' for philosophical discourse is, therefore, according to Levinas, 'interruption' (Levinas 1981, p. 20). If it is to remain true to the concepts it pursues, philosophy's 'end' cannot be closure but an interruption that starts it all over again.

My aim here is not therefore to offer a conclusion, but to perform one final interruption. This, my coda, performs the fall *par excellence*. It falls for love and in love; it is about desire. You may have noticed already that it has fallen for a phrase. Namely, to fall for. There's something cute, albeit slangy about it, don't you think? I picked it up from Ali Smith's *Hotel World* and was straight away seduced by the neatness of its double meaning. It signifies at once to fall for, to fall in love, and to fall for, be duped by. There is something unknowing about desire. It does not know itself well. For Belsey 'we *know* exactly the opposite of what we *desire*, of what we know our desire to be'. Love is, she points out 'at once infinitely and uniquely desirable' and 'conspicuously naïve' (Belsey 1994, p. 73; italics in original).

Nonetheless (or, perhaps, for this very reason) the language of desire is employed repeatedly by those working alongside and after Derrida. Derrida famously writes that 'I love very much everything that I deconstruct in my own manner; the texts I want to read from the deconstructive point of view are texts I love, with that impulse of identification which is indispensable for reading' (Derrida 1985, p. 87). Jean-Luc Nancy goes so far, in his essay 'Shattered love', as to say that thinking and philosophy *are* love. He cautions, though, that '[w]e know nothing more about what this means. We only know, by a sort of obscure certainty or premonition, that it is necessary or that it will one day be necessary to attest this phrase: *Thinking is love*. But philosophy has never explicitly attended this' (Nancy 1991, pp. 84–5; italics in original). Thinking will always 'have said and will have failed to say that it is love – or to explain what this means'. It 'reaches toward it, it does not reach it' (p. 86).

Nancy, by equating philosophy with love, places the unknown at its centre. Exercising a 'double constraint', the very definition Nancy gives refers us to that which cannot be defined (p. 86). The exact nature of love or desire eludes our grasp. Adam Phillips, in *Kissing, Ticking and Being Bored*, suggests that 'obstacles are the clue to desire, that the word is full of meaning'. At the end of his essay, however, he confesses to an 'uneasy feeling, which we all remember from childhood, and which may be pertinent to the subject at hand; the feeling that comes when one endlessly repeats a word only to be left with an enigmatic obstacle as to its sense' (Phillips 1993, p. 98). 'Desire', Belsey suggests 'eludes final definition, with the result that its character, its nature, its meaning, becomes itself an object of desire for the writer' (Belsey 1994, p. 3). For both Phillips and Belsey, the investigation of desire turns us back on ourselves; it subjects us to the experience my book has described over and over. Certainty about desire eludes us, but in looking for it we find ourselves 'uneasy', desiring.

The OED defines desire as '[t]he fact or condition of desiring; that feeling or emotion which is directed to the attainment or possession of some object from which pleasure or satisfaction is expected; longing, craving; a particular instance of this feeling, a wish' (www.oed.com). Framed in terms of expectation, desire is defined in relation to its end or outcome. It looks towards a future 'attainment' or 'possession'. Desire is desire *for* fulfilment, success, certainty, possession. For presence, in other words.

However, desire places this presence in the future; it expects it and, in expecting it, makes it clear that it is not yet here. Desire declares that presence is, at the moment, absent. Although defined in terms of presence, desire's present is all about absence. Desire is, according to Belsey, 'predicated on lack' (Belsey 1994, p. 38).

Put otherwise, something stands between desire and presence. Phillips explains that 'the existence of that extraordinary phenomena, the wish, always implies a prior perception of obstacles. After all, why would we need to wish if nothing were in the way?' (Phillips 1993, pp. 96–7) 'In order to fall in love with someone', Phillips suggests, 'they must be perceived as an obstacle, a necessary obstacle' (p. 90). Phillips outlines an 'apparently inevitable twining of obstacle and desire' (p. 88). It is, he argues, 'impossible to imagine desire without obstacles, and wherever we find something to be an obstacle we are at the same time desiring' (p. 87). For Phillips '[d]esire without something that resists it is insufficient, wishy-washy, literally immaterial' (p. 4).

For Derrida, too, 'non-assurance' and the 'risk of misunderstanding' go 'to make the essence of desire' (Derrida 2005b, p. 220). However, this leads to confusion; we 'never know whether obstacles create desire, or desire creates obstacles. We are never quite sure which it is we are seeking' (Phillips 1993, p. 87).

The second thought – that desire creates obstacles – seems the stranger yet points to a paradox at the heart of desire. If obstacles are necessary for desire, then desire must create obstacles in order to preserve and prolong itself. Belsey writes that '[p]art of the intensity of love is the desire to know the truth of the other's desire, to be *certain*. But, paradoxically, such certainty would be the death of desire' (Belsey 1994, p. 37; italics in original). If certainty, possession and attainment were achieved, desire would no longer exist. Yet this is, supposedly, the very state for which desire longs. Desire desires its own demise. A strange and melancholy thought.

There lies a paradox at the heart of desire: our desire desires fulfilment, but if it were fulfilled it would no longer *be* desire. There is, at the moment of fulfilment, no more desire; the event 'injures desire'. It is '*traumatic*' (Derrida 2002a, p. 159; italics in original). Desire's 'apparent fulfilment is' for Belsey 'also a moment of loss' (Belsey 1994, pp. 38–9; italics in original). The loss of desire. We can therefore never 'have' what we 'desire'. Having (or presence) and desiring are incompatible; presence kills desire. The two cannot exist simultaneously. The attainment desire craves is impossible, because, at the moment it occurs, it is no longer desired and is therefore not 'attainment' *per se*.

Presence, or attainment, is impossible. Yet there is no desire without the thought of this attainment. There is 'desire for presence and intimacy' only so long as 'there is no such thing' and only because there is 'no pure presence' (Derrida 2003, p. 9). Desire, inscribed and constituted by what it will never have or be, is impossible. 'In one sense', Nancy writes, 'and in a sense that will perhaps always conceal the totality of *sense*, assignable as such – love is the impossible, and it does not arrive, or it arrives only at the limit, while crossing' (Nancy 1991, p. 99; italics in original).

This thought returns us to the questions with which we began. Literary study desires the literary, but remains a *literary* study only so long as its desire remains unfulfilled. The REF (which is very much on my mind as I approach the moment at which I send my book out into the academic sphere, to be judged in its light), which demands that we account for the literary in order to guarantee that its study is taking place, misses the point. Were it possible to present and possess the literary in the way it desires, the REF would have the opposite effect to that which it sets out to achieve; it would kill our desire, and so annihilate literary study. We in fact find, however, that we cannot capture the literary in the way the REF would like; we cannot fully answer its demands. Contrary to its aims – and according to a logic it can neither condone nor comprehend – the REF ensures the non-arrival of the literary and functions as the obstacle which keeps our desire for the literary alive.

Notes

Introduction

1 For discussions of the 'unaccountable' nature of teaching see Connors (2006) and Johnson (1982), as well as Bill Readings's chapter 'The scene of teaching' in which he suggests that it is 'interminable' and thus always 'structurally incomplete' (Readings 1996, p. 159). Sarah Wood, too, argues that '[t]eaching cannot defend its procedures with appeals to doctrine. It is unprotected' (Wood 2007, p. 138).

2 Miller points out in 'The critic as host' that '"criticism" is often said to kill "literature"'. Criticism is frequently figured as a 'parasite' which feeds on literature, its 'host' (Miller 1995, p. 278). Miller is, however, sceptical of the divide he proposes; his essay asks 'can host and parasite live happily together, in the domicile of the same text, feeding each other or sharing the food?' (Miller 1995, p. 278).

3 Prince discusses 'metanarrative signs' in an essay of that name in Mark Currie (1995), *Metafiction*.

4 Derrida, to whom I will turn in my chapter's next section, although a very different thinker, nonetheless expresses a similar sentiment to Fish and Holland when he writes that '[l]iterary criticism is perhaps structurally philosophical. What I am saying here is not necessarily a compliment' (Derrida 1992e, p. 53). What this dissatisfaction entails for Derrida is, as we will see, quite different from the conclusions reached by Fish and Holland.

5 Fish employs this revisionary structure throughout his work; for example, he writes of 'the intuition which stands (or, more properly, on which the reader stands)' (Fish 1980, p. 40).

6 Barthes makes a similar claim in *The Pleasure of the Text* when he writes '[o]n the stage of the text, no footlights; there is not, behind the text, someone active (the writer) and out front someone passive (the reader); there is not a subject and object' (Barthes 1990b, p. 16).

7 The novel is an especially apt example here because, as Clare Hanson points out, it too patterns the realizations outlined above. Hanson explains that 'Cassandra, Byatt has said in an interview, is a better writer than Julia, because she sees

writing as artifice. That is, she is aware that language is not transparent, that it has its own, metaphorical life' (Hanson 2000, pp. 127–8). *The Game*, like the claims made by Waugh and reader response, is underpinned by awareness that language is 'artificial' and 'not transparent'.

8   Theorists of metafiction also point to this dual function. Robert Scholes suggests that '[m]etafiction assimilates all the perspectives of criticism into the fictional process itself' (Scholes 1995, p. 29). For Mark Currie, too, metafiction functions 'as a borderline discourse, as a kind of writing which places itself on the border between fiction and criticism' (Currie 1995, p. 2). For Patricia Waugh, metafiction produces a 'formal tension which breaks down the distinctions between "creation" and "criticism"' (Waugh 1984, p. 6).

9   Derrida makes a similar point in 'Psyche: Invention of the Other'. He points out that self-reflexivity is 'more wily than it seems' and that it 'not only does not produce coincidence with or presence to itself but instead projects forward the advent of the self, of "speaking" or "writing" of itself as other' (Derrida 1992d, p. 318).

10 Although revelation is impossible, we cannot abandon the *language* of revelation *tout court*; it remains necessary, for reasons which will become clear later.

11 Royle points out that '[i]n reading . . . we veer: our attention is not constant, our thoughts and feelings shift about' (Royle 2011, p. 28). Barthes also invokes the non-linear nature of reading when he asserts that 'what I enjoy in a narrative is not directly its content or even its structure, but rather the abrasions I impose upon the fine surface: I read on, I skip, I look up, I dip in again' (Barthes 1990b, p. 12). Matei Calinescu draws our attention to the fact that '"[n]ormal" readers skip, skim, swim back and forth' in order to note that, in reading, we are often *re*reading, engaging in a '*partial rereading* or backtracking', 'in order to recall more precisely certain significant textual details, or to take full cognizance of essential narrative information to which one has not paid, for whatever reason, sufficient attention the first time around' (Calinescu 1993, p. 277).

12 This occurrence is of course inevitable; Calinescu points out that 'when I *write* about what the first reading of a literary piece is like (was like, should be like), I cannot but place myself in a perspective of rereading' (Calinescu 1993, p. 7).

13 That said, Derrida expresses an explicit distrust of the concept. He writes, 'I have never wanted to abuse the abyss, nor, above all, the *mise "en abîme"*. I do not believe in it very much, I am wary of the confidence that it inspires fundamentally, I believe it too representative either to go far enough or not to avoid the very thing toward which it allegedly rushes' (Derrida 1987b, p. 304). I will

employ it for the moment in order to illustrate my argument bearing in mind, however, that Derrida's fear of the 'too representative' is well founded, for reasons which will become clear later.

14 Although Ewing is unable to grasp truth, the infinite regress emphasizes his position in relation to it, as his 'I glimpse' and 'I approach' make clear; as it moves away, the infinite regress places his stance into relief. I will return later, in the third section of my chapter, to this relationality and the possibilities it opens.

15 Barthes discovers this when trying to explain the pleasure of reading. He writes that '[o]ne envisions a vast, collective harvest: bring together all the texts *which have given pleasure to someone* (wherever these texts come from) and display this textual body (*corpus:* the right word), in something like the way in which psychoanalysis has exhibited man's erotic body. However, it is to be feared that such a labor would end *explaining* the chosen texts; there would be an inevitable bifurcation of the project: unable to speak itself, pleasure would enter the general path of motivations, *no one of which would be definitive* . . . In short, such a labor would not *be written*. I can only *circle* such a subject'. He concludes that '[n]o "thesis" on the pleasure of the text is possible' (Barthes 1990b, p. 34).

16 My argument here unites Derrida and Levinas. They are, however, very different thinkers. A later chapter will think in more detail about the differences between Levinas and Derrida's work.

17 Derrida repeats his claim that 'what is called literature, in the European and modern sense of the term' is characterized by 'the right to say everything publicly, or to keep it a secret, if only in the form of fiction' in 'The university without condition'. Moreover, he stresses that this conceptualization 'is also what fundamentally links' literature to 'the university, and above all the Humanities'. Derrida envisages an 'unconditional university or the university without condition' governed by 'the principal right to say everything, even if it be under the heading of fiction and the experimentation of knowledge, and the right to say it publicly, to publish it' (Derrida 2002b, p. 205). Again, however, he cautions us not to read these words too keenly; he points out that '[t]his university without condition does not, *in fact*, exist, as we know only too well'. The unconditional university, like the literary, does not properly exist; nonetheless, Derrida continues to think of both as '*in principle*' 'ultimate [places] of critical resistance – and more than critical – to all the powers of dogmatic and unjust appropriation' (p. 204; my italics).

18 Paul de Man claims similarly in *Allegories of Reading* that 'the allegorical representation of Reading' is 'the irreducible component of any text'. Like Bourdieu,

he points out that every text is 'a theorisation of reading'. However, this does not mean for de Man that reading becomes clear or apparent. He writes that '[a]ll that will be represented in such an allegory will deflect from the act of reading and block access to its understanding. The allegory of reading narrates the impossibility of reading' (de Man 1979, p. 77).

19 Derrida does not mean by this that the 'literary' is conferred *solely* and arbitrarily by the reader. He claims that 'literature' is not merely 'projective or subjective' (Derrida 1992e, p. 44) He writes instead '[t]here is therefore a literary *functioning* and a literary *intentionality,* an experience rather than an essence of literature' (p. 45; italics in original).

20 It provokes a 'disquiet', which for Derrida lies at the heart of all responsibility; he writes that '[a] calm and assured responsibility is never a responsibility; it's good conscience' (Derrida 1989b, p. 837). He asserts that '[t]o speak of [responsibility] calmly and as if there were some obvious, commonsense facts available on this subject, *as if one knew* what were and ought to be the "ethical categories," is irresponsibility itself—moral, political, philosophical, intellectual irresponsibility in general' (Derrida 1989b, p. 846).

21 This never-yet is well illustrated by the theorization of the secret Derrida offers in 'Passions: "an oblique offering"'. The secret, Derrida explains, 'remains inviolable even when one thinks one has revealed it' (Derrida 1992c, p. 21). To affirm the secret we would have to reveal it – at which point it would no longer be one; the secret inscribes the promise of a revelation that is forever deferred.

22 Derrida writes that '[o]ne can do a nontranscendent reading of any text whatever' (Derrida 1992e, p. 44).

Chapter 1

1 Wood's 'all the way to writing' translates Derrida's *jusqu'à l'écriture.* Her translation differs from that given by Alan Bass in *Writing and Difference,* which renders Derrida's phrase as '[t]o the point of embracing it [force] as writing' (Derrida 1978a, p. 28).

2 This division between the literary and the philosophical is helpful and illuminating. As I explained in my introduction, however, the opposition is not simple and needs to be approached in a certain way if it is to remain useful. This chapter will show this too; even at this point, however, we must think the terms tentatively, with their difficulty in mind.

3   Barthes therefore announces '*[l]et the commentary be itself a text*' (Barthes 1990a, p. 44) Similarly, Marcel Cornis-Pope demands that we pay attention to criticism as a 'mode of re*writing*' (Cornis-Pope 1992, p. 11; my italics).

4   He reinforces this suggestion later in his essay when he writes that 'the case is by no means common, in which an author is at all in a condition to retrace the steps by which his conclusions have been attained. In general, suggestions, having arisen pell-mell, are pursued and forgotten in a similar manner' (Poe 2009, p. 61).

5   Celia Wallhead notes that Byatt's earlier novel, *Possession* (which I will discuss later in my chapter on tact), plots a similar progression: '[b]y the end of *Possession* (1990), Roland has become "possessed" by the desire to write, and he has become so captivated by words that he moves away from practising literary criticism to composing verse and becoming a poet' (Wallhead 2003, p. 293).

6   Phineas continues, '[b]ut I feel a kind of nausea at this fate for my hero, myself. It doesn't seem very much of an anything. To be addicted to writing is not to want to be, to become, a Writer'. His reluctance to categorize the novel as a '*writer's story*' is well founded; the label over-simplifies that which these novels perform, as I will show later.

7   There are further suggestions throughout the novel that Zuckerman composes the novel that we read. On the novel's opening page Zuckerman tells us that 'like many a *Bildungsroman* hero before [him]' he is 'already contemplating [his] own massive *Bildungsroman*' (Roth 1998, p. 3) and, following a conversation with Lonoff, he tells us '[o]n a clean sheet of paper I finally wrote down what he'd said so as to see exactly what he'd meant. All he'd meant' (p. 57). The novel informs us that Zuckerman composes a *Bildungsroman* and a 'conversation', which must, we assume, be very close to the ones we read in *The Ghost Writer*.

8   The convergence of psyche and technē in Jason's account points to a more general condition Derrida outlines in 'Typewriter ribbon' in his thinking of two concepts, which, at first sight, 'appear to us to be antinomic': the machine and the event. The machine, on the one hand, represents a 'calculable programming of an automatic repetition'; on the other hand, the event 'ought to keep, so we think, some nonprogrammable and therefore incalculable singularity' (Derrida 2002a, p. 72). Derrida explains, however, that repetition (or iterability) founds all signs. He thus concludes that 'no text can be produced without this formal, grammatical, or machinelike element. No text and no language' (p. 153). The separation between the machine and the 'event' of writing and of language cannot be rigorously maintained.

9   Poe invokes this myth in 'The philosophy of composition' when he writes that
    that '[m]ost writers – poets in especial – prefer having it understood that they
    compose by a species of fine frenzy – an ecstatic intuition'. He therefore suggests
    that they 'would positively shudder at letting the public take a peep behind the
    scenes . . . at the wheels and pinions' (Poe 2009, p. 61). Like *Black Swan Green*
    and *Diary of a Bad Year,* Poe is keen to show that composition involves mechan-
    ical 'wheels and pinions'; his essay is, according to Stuart and Susan F. Levine
    'a healthy corrective to over-romantic portrayals of the poetic process' (Poe
    2009, p. 57). When writing about 'The raven', Poe claims that '[i]t is [his] design
    to render it manifest that no one point in its composition is referrible either
    to accident or intuition – that the work proceeded, step by step, to its comple-
    tion with the precision and rigid consequence of a mathematical problem' (Poe
    2009, pp. 61–2). While Poe is no doubt correct to dismiss 'ecstatic intuition' as
    unrealistic, the picture he paints of an entirely mechanized composition strikes
    us as equally unlikely; Stuart and Susan F. Levine suggest that 'Poe exaggerates
    how methodical he was' (Poe 2009, p. 58).

10 The narrator of another Beckett text, *Worstward Ho*, neatly summarizes the
    despair Lonoff feels: 'Ever tried. Ever failed. No matter. Try again. Fail again. Fail
    better' (Beckett 2009, p. 81).

11 Jensen suggests, moreover, that '[t]his incessant self-commentary enacts a flight
    from literature, from cultivated expression, that purposely prevents the reader
    becoming wholly involved in the writing'. Jensen's claim that Phineas's writ-
    ing 'prevents the reader becoming wholly involved' suggests, perhaps, that this
    'writerly' text indeed subjects us to the different experience of reading to which
    Wood refers in the sentences I quoted in my introduction.

12 The notion of revision alerts us to the interrelation of writing and reading,
    which I consider in my chapter's final section; James writes that '[t]o revise is to
    see, or to look over, again – which means in the case of a written thing neither
    more nor less than to re-read it' (James 1962, pp. 338–9).

13 Adono, in his 'The essay as form', argues that this halting progression is the con-
    dition of the essay *per se*. The essay, he argues, is 'exposed to error' and 'becomes
    true in its progress, which drives it beyond itself, and not in a hoarding obses-
    sion with fundamentals' (Adorno 2000, p. 101). As I mentioned in my intro-
    duction, however, this movement is not guaranteed; our reading may return
    the essay all too quickly to the 'fundamental'. The essay 'escapes' this 'hoarding
    obsession' only when subjected to a kind of reading I will attempt in the final
    section of my chapter.

14 I will pick up on the concerns Phineas expresses concerning the second person in my final chapter.

15 This is not the first time my chapter has referred to Beckett (cf. Zuckerman's allusion to *Waiting for Godot* in my chapter's first section). This reappearance is telling; if the scope of my chapter were broader, Beckett's *Trilogy* is certainly a text I could have discussed here.

16 This dilemma also troubles James; he writes that '[t]hese remarks have constituted to excess perhaps the record of what may have put this, that and the other treated into my head' (James 1962, p. 196). The reader may well find this to be the case. For example, when writing on 'The death of the lion', he writes 'I make the most of this passage of literary history – I like so, as I find to recall it. It lives there for me in old Kensington days; which, though I look back at them over no such great gulf of years . . . have already faded for me to the complexion of so long ago. It was a Sunday afternoon early in the Spring' (p. 217). James promises to tell us how the story told in 'The death of the lion' came to him. In doing so, however, a narrative unfolds, which functions, of course, as yet another story.

17 The scene thus alludes to a theme which recurs throughout Roth's novels. Time and again Roth's author-protagonists ask: To what extent ought one (is one able) to represent 'real life' events in fiction? These questions, which are noted by Wilson and Baumgarten are, however, unsettled by their fictional framing. As I explained in my introduction, any statements made about fiction *in* fiction refuse to signify directly or constatively. In this case, Lonoff's suggestion retroactively confers all that has come before as 'real life'; it tells us that the events of which we have just read have not yet been transposed into fiction. We know, however, that this cannot be true.

18 This belatedness is, again, a fact of which James is also conscious; he writes 'I track my uncontrollable footsteps, right and left, after the fact' and 'for the most part we recognise the character of our interest only after the particular magic, as I say, has thoroughly operated' (James 1962, pp. 30, 338). He reflects that, in order to find out the 'origin of one's wind-blown germs themselves', one would 'have to go too far back, too far behind, to say' (p. 43).

19 Barthes alludes to this interrelation when he writes that '[t]he text you write must prove *that it desires me*. This proof exists: it is writing' (Barthes 1990b, p. 6).

20 Cixous' question, in French – '[e]t maintenant comment appeler cet essai?' (Cixous 1991, p. 64) – employs the word 'essai', which occurs repeatedly

throughout the text. Elsewhere, however, it means 'trial' or 'attempt'. The fact that Cixous' *essay* may in fact only be *an essay* (or attempt) alerts us to the readerly dependence I will outline in my following paragraphs; writing, always deferred until the time of reading, attains a provisional quality.

21   James's *The Art of the Novel*, too, promises to offer an account of the gestation and genesis of writing, but find itself instead bound up in questions of reading; the accounts that he offers function as interpretations, as readings, of his fictions.

Chapter 2

1   If space allowed, I could also mention two even more recent books: Kevin Brockmeier's *The Illumination* and Ali Smith's *There But For The* (both published in 2011).

2   A similar process occurs in Mitchell's novels; they, too, Philip Griffiths explains, offer a 'network of seemingly separate yet cleverly interconnected voices' (Griffiths 2004, p. 83).

3   The form is perhaps not as new as Hensher suggests. Nicholas Blincoe describes Mitchell's novels as 'episodic' (Blincoe 1999). The label, which strikes me as valid, sounds somewhat less new than the analysis Hensher proposes. In fact, it recalls much earlier texts. In Edmund Spenser's *The Faerie Queene*, for example, characters appear in certain episodes only to disappear when the perspective shifts before returning or passing by again much later. We could easily read it in light of the logic Mitchell's novels inspire. Or, to offer a perhaps less contentious example, Joyce's *Dubliners*, although written much earlier than the texts I have chosen to discuss, also forces us to consider the distinction between the short story and the novel. Is it best contemplated as a singular text or as a number of discrete fictions? The trend Hensher identifies is not historically specific; the short story and the novel have been blurred before.

4   Of course, the categories themselves are far from neat, as an examination of discussions surrounding the short story reveals. Maud Ellmann, in her essay 'Drawing the blind', notes that '[i]n 1960 Elizabeth Bowen gave a course on the short story at Vassar, in which she asked her students how a short story differs from a novel. The obvious answer is "shortness"' (Ellmann 2004, p. 31). Later, she mentions '[a]nother American writer, Edith Wharton,' who 'argues that the short story differs from the novel in subordinating character to plot' (p. 36). Both Wharton

and Bowen attempt to define the short story by focusing on the way in which it *differs* from the novel; both writers, and Ellmann herself, consider short stories in terms of their *relation to* the novel. William O'Rourke, in his essay 'Morphological metaphors', again reveals this interdependence as he attempts to offer a definition of the short story. He writes that '[t]he greater the space, the more time it takes to comprehend, to see. To see all the parts of the novel requires great distance, there-fore more time, but not so the short story: the reader is always close enough to see a short story whole' (O'Rourke 1989, p. 195). O'Rourke's 'more' offers a definition whose basis is comparative; the short story is measured against the novel. The short story is not a wholly discrete form but finds itself haunted by the novel it is not. The two forms are far from mutually exclusive; the short story is – by its very definitions – inseparable from ideas of the novel.

5   The structure of *The Accidental* is slightly different from the other texts I discuss here. It is divided into three main parts – titled Beginning, Middle and End – each of which is composed of four accounts: given first by Astrid, then Marcus, Michael and finally Eve. Thus, each of its narrators is granted three sections in total rather than the one accorded to each character in *Hotel World, Cloud Atlas* and *Ghostwritten*.

6   Cavendish draws our attention to the fact that the 'tricksy devices' Mitchell's novel employs are not new; it risks appearing outdated. Somewhat ironically, however, the very critical comment Cavendish offers inserts a scepticism, which differentiates the novel from the confident trickiness of 'Postmodernism and Chaos Theory'.

7   It is, of course, ironic that Cavendish invokes the problem with particular lin-guistic flair.

8   Derrida, in his work, employs the word trace precisely because, conjuring the idea of animal tracks and suchlike, it offers itself as such an un-word-like word. Nonetheless, it does not and could not *entirely* escape naming; as I have shown in this section, the thought of the trace may return us once again to the essential. This risk is not, however, an inconvenience but a productive inconsistency with which Derrida's notion of the trace wishes to work, as will become clear later.

9   We might align this practice with structuralist approaches to intertextuality (undoubtedly the concept by which my chapter is underpinned). As Graham Allen explains, intertextuality is not a stable term, but has been understood in radically different manners. A structuralist approach, such as that represented by Genette in *Palimpsests*, facilitates a mode of reading in which one actively

seeks the work's 'intertextual relations'. My chapter will eventually take us closer to a very different approach to intertextuality, which Allen terms poststructural-ist (Allen 2000).

10 This re-reading does not necessarily occur after a completed first reading. Cali-nescu stresses that 'reading and rereading often go together. Thus, under certain circumstances the first reading of a work can in fact be a *double* reading; that is to say, it can adopt, alongside the prospective logic of reading, a retrospective logic of rereading. Such a double reading consists, naturally, of the sequential temporal movement of the reader's mind (attention, memory, hypothetical anticipation, curiosity, involvement) along the horizontal or syntagmatic axis of the work; but it also consists of a reader's attempt to "construct" (note the build-ing, spatial metaphor) the text under perusal, or to perceive it as a "construc-tion" with certain clearly distinguishable structural properties' (Calinescu 1993, p. 19). The attitude of re-reading which Calinescu and Griffiths invoke can take place even in a 'first' reading of the text.

11 Calinescu also finds, from his examination of re-reading, that 'the number of competing but valid global interpretations, or of different but valid critical rereadings of the same text, is theoretically infinite' (Calinescu 1993, p. 168).

12 The uncertainty Attridge expresses here is telling. It forces us to wonder: what would a deliberate allusion be? How could these not be quotations? A mark that could not be cited would not be legible, is unthinkable; language is by nature citational. For Derrida '[t]he call of the supplement is primary' (Derrida 1978c, p. 211–12). 'Derrida's notions of *trace* and *supplement*' are, Wood explains, 'necessary to understand how something happens for *the first time*' (Wood 2009a, p. 112; italics in original). The echoes we encounter in these texts are not exceptional but force us to '[b]e alert to these invisible quotation marks, even within a word' (Derrida 1979a, p. 76).

13 This inability to remember the word repeats itself, even, past the end of the section. Else 'has looked it up once already, but has forgotten' (Smith 2002, pp. 36–7) and in Penny's account, '[i]t is a, I forget the word for it, the woman said. She put her arms out, as if holding something too big for her' (p. 169).

14 The blanks left by Sara's ghost might, at first sight, appear to be absolute absences; we soon realize, however, that we are able to fill them with the 'correct' word. The novel alludes to this ability: both the advert Else reads in the newspaper—'F y cn rd ths msg y cd bcm a scrtry n gt a gd jb' (Smith 2002, p. 45)—and her repeated 'spr sm chn?' invoke our ability to interpret the strange and to render it once again intelligible. Although these 'half words' appear, initially, incomprehensible,

we are able to hear and to read them. Else 'imagines the pavement littered with the letters that fall out of the half-words she uses (she doesn't need the whole words)' (p. 47). We, the readers, easily re-insert the dropped letters – perhaps *too* easily. After all, nothing in the text validates our assumptions; we may be wrong. Moreover, what gaps might we have filled without even realizing we've done so? Anxieties such as these will trace my readings in the following pages.

15 Repetition is allied, too, with the act of committing to memory; Sara's ghost thinks 'dumb waiter dumb waiter dumb waiter'. The echo is at once determined and anxious; she attempts to remember, but the necessity renders us conscious of the possibility that the word will be forgotten again (as indeed it has been by the end of the section).

16 There is, moreover, an oscillation in the first list of examples between naming and not naming. Sara's ghost calls the dumb waiter 'the lift for dishes' and we know by this what she means. For a moment, it has been named. However, it is soon withdrawn; she tells us once again 'it has its own name' – the name previously offered is inadequate.

17 Its statements inflect weirdly in this light. Susan announces, for example, '"[l]et it not by any means come to pass that Cruso is saved, I reflected to myself; for the world expects stories from its adventurers, better stories than tallies of how many stones they moved in fifteen years, and from where, and to where; Cruso rescued will be a deep disappointment to the world"' (Coetzee 1987, p. 34). Susan's statement signifies ironically in relation to our knowledge of Defoe's novel whose very premise is, of course, that Crusoe has been saved and can therefore relate what the novel promotes as his 'surprising adventures'.

Chapter 3

1 For example, Derrida admits in 'Letter to a Japanese friend' that the word deconstruction 'has never appeared satisfactory to me' (Derrida 1991, p. 272). 'I am not sure', he confesses elsewhere, 'that such a thing as "Deconstruction", in the singular, exists or is possible' (Derrida 1992a, p. 56). Later in his letter Derrida is more forceful; deconstruction, he stresses, 'is not a method and cannot be transformed into one' (Derrida 1991, p. 273).

2 Shane Weller cautions, moreover, that for deconstruction there is 'nothing more debilitating, nothing more speech-robbing than a certain kind of affinity' (Weller 2006).

3 For example, the final three sentences of the first paragraph of 'Tout autrement' read '[n]ouvelle coupure dans l'histoire de la philosophie? Elle en
   marquerait aussi la continuité. L'histoire de la philosophie n'est probablement
   qu'une croissante conscience de la difficulté de penser' (Levinas 1976, p. 65).
   Critchley translates this as '[a] new break in the history of philosophy? One
   that would also mark its continuity. The history of philosophy is probably
   only a growing awareness of the difficulty of thinking' (Levinas 1991, p. 3).
   Michael B. Smith, by contrast, renders it as '[i]s this a new break in the history
   of philosophy? It would also show its continuity. The history of philosophy
   is probably nothing but a growing awareness of the difficulty of thinking'
   (Levinas 1996b, p. 55). Smith turns Levinas's two opening questions into full,
   grammatical sentences, thus losing the fragmented quality that Critchley, by
   contrast, preserves.

4 Davies points out a further ambiguity of these words: despite their use and
   origin within philosophy, they continue nonetheless to point beyond it.

5 De Man echoes this sentiment in *Allegories of Reading* when he notes that '[t]he
   deconstruction is not something we have added to the text but it constituted the
   text in the first place' (de Man 1979, p. 17).

6 In defending Rousseau, however, de Man portrays Derrida's reading as an attack
   or critique, thereby misreading Derrida, who is careful to claim that the supplement is only a '*sort of* blind spot': '[t]he concept of the supplement is a sort of
   blind spot in Rousseau's text, the not-seen that opens and limits visibility. But
   the production, if it attempts to make the not-seen accessible to sight, does not
   leave the text' (Derrida 1997b, p. 163). Derrida is not out to critique or oppose
   himself to Rousseau; he does not, in fact, accuse Rousseau of blindness. And
   I have a feeling de Man maybe knows this too. He wonders '[d]oes it matter
   then whether we attribute the final statement to Rousseau or to Derrida since
   both are in fact saying the same thing?' (De Man 1971, pp. 137–8). The question challenges not only Derrida's 'appropriation' but also the 'return' de Man
   performs.

7 Derrida, in 'By force of mourning', points out this 'reciprocal convertibility of
   the strongest or most forceful and the weakest' (Derrida 2001, p. 163). Force,
   he explains 'must thus now be on intimate terms with what is not force, with
   its opposite, with the "without force," a domestic and paradoxically necessary
   commerce being established between them'. He informs us counter-intuitively
   that '[t]he greatest force is to be seen in the infinite renunciation of force, in the
   absolute interruption of force by the without-force' (p. 147).

Chapter 4

1　John Kerrigan, in his review of Cunningham's book, alerts us to the fact that this 'proper behaviour' 'can be derived only from immersion in shared values'. As such, tact 'has genteel associations that are worrying and not incidental': 'it is inherently conservative, and in practice it falls to elites to determine what tact is' (Kerrigan 2002, p. 21). It is an 'anti-intellectual, a not-rocking-the-boat insiderish business, a way of distinguishing the polite from the oiks' (p. 21). We must continue to theorize tact – as I shall do here – remaining conscious of its 'worrying' inflections.

2　The question of ethics emerges too via the censure Zuckerman attracts from many of the novel's critics. Debra Shostak argues, for example, that 'Nathan has experienced a long history in an at-times dubious moral position with respect to others. As a writer, he engages in manifold exploitation. He is perhaps forced to imagine, to fill in the blankness of others, but he thereby enjoys the intense pleasure of creation, of bending the other invisibly to his own pre-dispositions' (Shostak 2004, p. 264). Tim Parrish applies a similar judgement to the novel as a whole, claiming that '[i]n the novel's eerie conclusion, Roth himself acknowledges that his narrative, like Coleman's story, requires a kind of will to transgression' (Parrish 2005, p. 221). Although Shostak and Parrish do not explicitly invoke 'ethics', their invocation of 'exploitation' and 'transgression' recall the questions (in particular those of John Lanchester) posed in relation to *Slow Man*.

3　The critique I will outline in the following paragraphs derives from responses to *Possession* and not from the novel *per se*, which, as I will show later, is more ambivalent concerning the notion of theory than many of its critics suggest.

4　The division is of course problematic, as my chapter will shortly demonstrate. We are conscious straight away, however, that the 'real' is, of course, not immune to theory. It is repeatedly its subject and is discussed, for example, both by Lacan and by Kant, to name but two (very different) thinkers who have considered it.

5　The meaning of *theoros* is not in fact as unequivocal as Cunningham suggests. Francis Cornford points out, for example, that it was used by the Orphics to mean 'passionate sympathetic contemplation' (Cornford 1991, p. 198).

6　I will return to question the distinction between use and mention, which is particularly important in analytical philosophy, later. I will note here, however, that for Derrida quotation marks *attempt* to mention a word without using it. They do not necessarily succeed; the terms in which Derrida describes these marks hints at a contradiction: the ongoing touch of their not really touching.

7   I would stress, however, that the insistence belongs more properly to Elizabeth Costello. *Slow Man,* as I show shortly, does not concur unquestioningly with the attitude she expresses.

8   John Kerrigan alerts us to a similar paradox in Cunningham's *Reading After Theory.* '[W]hether Cunningham manages to slay the dragon of theory with the sword of tactility is', he writes, 'doubtful' (Kerrigan 2002, p. 19). He explains that 'Cunningham's elevation of tact over Theory is unpersuasive. What we mean by the former owes so much to how it is conceived and socially constructed that it cannot stand free of the latter' (p. 22). Tact cannot abstract itself fully from theory; it finds itself theorized, brought back.

9   Sarah Wood describes this touch, which does not touch in and in relation to Raymond Carver's 'Cathedral'. She writes, '[t]he fingers are passive, "touched to every part". But they are also a little cut off. It is not, in any sense, a synechdocal touch; not that the whole man touches the whole woman. It is the tracing of a boundary, a figuration, and at the same time an intense sensation which frag-ments the individuals concerned: fingers, face, nose, neck. As this touch passes across the surface, it is not clear what the fingers are reaching for other than the surface itself, in a partial and addressed touch, which perhaps also takes time to arrive' (Wood 2004, p. 144).

10 Leo Bersani and Adam Phillips' *Intimacy* asks similar questions about the notion, as do the essays in the collection edited by Lauren Berlant of the same title.

11 This is of course one of the projects my book (especially this chapter) under-takes; it is also pursued by the 'Chicago Feel Tank', especially by Rei Terada's book *Feeling in Theory,* as its title makes evident.

12 Jenkyns thus implies, erroneously, that the novel has decided to exclude infor-mation that exists prior to or outside it; he overlooks the fact that the novel cre-ates the very secrets it decides not to tell – creates them, in fact, in its not-telling. I will return to this point in my chapter's final section.

13 Kerrigan also points out that Cunningham 'associates this tactility with a sacramental sense of language' (Kerrigan 2002, p. 19) thus locating it in a realm inaccessible to the 'earthly' reader.

14 Franken thus acknowledges that Byatt's novels offer us a 'sustained ambivalence which structures the critical work in important ways' (Franken 2001, p. 91).

15 The very term 'resistance' embodies the contamination with which we are faced; it invokes a touch that would repel touch, a touch without touching. In its psychoanalytic sense, too, it refers to a defence: that of the repressed in reaction to attempts to bring it into consciousness. It is, however, the very resistance which, in analysis, belies a too-closeness to that which the unconscious would hide.

16 The image that strikes Maud and Roland so forcefully also appears in other novels by Byatt. In *The Virgin in the Garden*, for example, Alexander 'wanted a clean white empty room and silence. He wanted no liquor and no dancing' (Byatt 1994, p. 416) while in *The Biographer's Tale* we are told that '[t]here was nothing in the room but a white bed and a white chest of drawers' (Byatt 2001, p. 186). For someone who has read these other novels, the re-discovery of the image leads one momentarily (in a glimpse, as I outlined in my 'traces' chapter, that can never be more than fleeting) to share Maud and Roland's sense of 'powerful coincidence'.

17 This theme is also present in the other two books in Roth's American Trilogy.

18 The novels are not innocent to the reprimand but perhaps, through the belatedness of Paul and Ellen's admissions, deliberately invite this mis-reading.

Chapter 5

1 My chapter's third section questions McHale's claim that the second person 'announces the presence of a communicative circuit' '*more strongly*' than the first person. This 'communicative circuit' may become just as apparent when I say 'I'.

2 This text is, according to the rules stipulated by Richardson, Fludernik and others, a 'second person narrative'. It is in fact one the few of Smith's stories that properly fits the definition. The other stories that I have mentioned and will discuss blend first-person narration and second-person address and therefore conform less neatly. They illuminate our thinking of 'you' nonetheless.

3 McLane alludes to the dilemma when she asks 'how do you read "you" in this essay? Are you "you" or not? Under what conditions do you become "you"?' (McLane 2000, p. 438).

Bibliography

Adorno, Theodor W. (2000), 'The essay as form' in Brian Patrick O'Connor (ed.), *The Adorno Reader*. Oxford: Blackwell, pp. 91–111.

Akoma, Chiji (2000), 'The "trick" of narratives: history, memory and performance in Toni Morrison's *Paradise*', *Oral Tradition* 15(1), 3–25.

Allen, Graham (2000), *Intertextuality*. London: Routledge.

Althusser, Louis (1971), *Lenin and Philosophy, and Other Essays*. Ben Brewster (trans). London: New Left Books.

Anderson, Hephzibah (2004), 'Time and emotion study' rev. of *Cloud Atlas*, *The Observer* 29 February, 16.

Arendt, Hannah (1998), *The Human Condition*, Margaret Canovan (ed.) (2nd edition). Chicago; London: University of Chicago Press.

Armstrong, Isobel (1995), 'Textual harassment: the ideology of close reading, or how close is close?', *Textual Practice* 9(3), 401–20.

Attridge, Derek (2004a), *J.M. Coetzee and the Ethics of Reading: Literature in the Event*. Chicago: University of Chicago Press.

— (2004b), *The Singularity of Literature*. London: Routledge.

Barthes, Roland (1974), *S/Z*. Richard Miller (trans). New York: Hill and Wang.

— (1990a), 'Theory of the text' in Robert Young (ed.), *Untying the Text: A Post-Structuralist Reader*. London: Routledge, pp. 31–47.

— (1990b), *The Pleasure of the Text*. Oxford: Basil Blackwell.

Baumgarten, Murray and Gottfried, Barbara (1990), *Understanding Philip Roth*. Columbia: University of South Carolina Press.

Bayley, John (2001), 'What happened to the hippopotamuses' wife?' rev. of *The Biographer's Tale*. *New York Review of Books* 17 May, 16.

Beckett, Samuel (2009), *Company; Ill Seen Ill Said; Worstward Ho; Stirrings Still*, Dirk van Hulle (ed.). London: Faber.

Belsey, Catherine (1994), *Desire: Love Stories in Western Culture*. Oxford: Blackwell.

— (1999), 'English studies in the postmodern condition: towards a place for the signifier' in Martin McQuillan (ed.), *Post-Theory: New Directions in Criticism*. Edinburgh: Edinburgh University Press, pp. 123–38.

Ben-Naftali, Michal (1999), 'Deconstruction: Derrida' in Simon Glendinning (ed.), *The Edinburgh Encyclopedia of Continental Philosophy*. Edinburgh: Edinburgh University Press, pp. 654–5.

Bennett, Andrew (1995), *Readers and Reading*. London: Longman.

Bennington, Geoffrey (1999), 'Inter' in Martin McQuillan (ed.), *Post-Theory: New Directions in Criticism*. Edinburgh: Edinburgh University Press, pp. 103–22.

Bernasconi, Robert (1987), 'Deconstruction and the possibility of ethics' in John Sallis
    (ed.), *Deconstruction and Philosophy: The Texts of Jacques Derrida*. Chicago; London:
    University of Chicago Press, pp. 122–42.
— (1988), 'The trace of Levinas in Derrida' in David Wood and Robert Bernasconi (eds),
    Derrida and Différance. Evanston, IL: Northwestern University Press, pp. 13–30.
— (1991), 'Skepticism in the face of philosophy' in Robert Bernasconi and Simon
    Critchley (eds), *Re-Reading Levinas*. London: Athlone Press, pp. 149–61.
Birchall, Clare (2006), *Knowledge Goes Pop: From Conspiracy Theory to Gossip*. Oxford:
    Berg.
Birne, Eleanor (2005), 'The day starts now' rev. of *The Accidental*. *London Review of
    Books* 23 June, 30–1.
Blanchot, Maurice (1982), *The Space of Literature*. Ann Smock (trans). Lincoln; London:
    University of Nebraska Press.
— (1993), *The Infinite Conversation*. Susan Hanson (trans). Minneapolis; London:
    University of Minnesota Press.
Blincoe, Nicholas (1999), 'Spirit that speaks' rev. of *Ghostwritten*. *The Guardian* 21
    August, <http://www.guardian.co.uk/books/1999/aug/21/guardianfirstbooka-
    ward1999.guardianfirstbookaward>.
Bonheim, Helmut (1983), 'Narration in the second person', *Recherches Anglaises et
    Americaines* 16, 69–80.
Broughton, Trev (1999), 'Acts of human kindness' rev. of *Other Stories and Other Stories*.
    Times Literary Supplement 5 March, 22.
Butler, Judith (2005), *Giving an Account of Oneself*. New York: Fordham University Press.
Buxton, Jackie (2001), '"What's love got to do with it?": Postmodernism and *Possession*'
    in Alexa Alfer and Michael J. Noble (eds), *Essays on the Fiction of A.S. Byatt:
    Imagining the Real*. Westport, CT London: Greenwood Press, pp. 89–104.
Byatt, A. S. (1983), *The Game*. London: Penguin.
— (1991a), *Passions of the Mind: Selected Writings*. London: Chatto & Windus.
— (1991b), *Possession: A Romance*. London: Vintage.
— (1994), *The Virgin in the Garden*. London: Vintage.
— (2001), *The Biographer's Tale*. London: Vintage.
— (2002), *A Whistling Woman*. London: Chatto & Windus.
Calinescu, Matei (1993), *Rereading*. New Haven; London: Yale University Press.
Campbell, Jane (1988), 'The hunger of the imagination in A. S. Byatt's *The Game*',
    Critique: Studies in Contemporary Fiction 29(3), 147–62.
Cavarero, Adriana (2000), *Relating Narratives: Storytelling and Selfhood*. Paul A. Kottman
    (trans). London: Routledge.
Cixous, Hélène (1991), 'Sans arrêt, non, etat de dessination, non, plutôt; le décollage du
    bourreau' in Françoise Viatte (ed.), *Repentirs*. Paris: Réunion des musées nationaux,
    pp. 55–64.
— (1993), *Three Steps on the Ladder of Writing*. New York: Columbia University Press.
— (1998), *Stigmata: Escaping Texts*. London: Routledge.

— (1999), 'Post-word' in Martin McQuillan (ed.), *Post-Theory: New Directions in Criticism*. Edinburgh: Edinburgh University Press, pp. 209–13.

Clark, Timothy (1992), *Derrida, Heidegger, Blanchot: Sources of Derrida's Notion and Practice of Literature*. Cambridge: Cambridge University Press.

— (2002), 'Literary force, institutional values' in Elizabeth Beaumont Bissell (ed.), *The Question of Literature: The Place of the Literary in Contemporary Theory*. Manchester: Manchester University Press, pp. 91–104.

— (2004), 'Not seeing the short story: a blind phenomenology of reading', *Oxford Literary Review* 26, 5–30.

Coetzee, J. M. (1987), *Foe*. London: Penguin.

— (1996), *Giving Offense: Essays on Censorship*. Chicago; London: University of Chicago Press.

— (2005), *Slow Man*. London: Secker & Warburg.

— (2008), *Diary of a Bad Year*. London: Vintage.

Connor, Steven (1999), 'The impossibility of the present, or contemporary to contemporal' in Roger Luckhurst and Peter Marks (eds), *Literature and the Contemporary: Fictions and Theories of the Present*. Harlow: Longman, pp. 15–35.

Connors, Clare (2006), 'Teaching rhythms', *Parallax* 12(3), 8–16.

— (2007), 'Derrida and the fiction of force', *Angelaki* 12(2), 9–15.

— (2010a), *Force from Nietzsche to Derrida*. London: Legenda, Modern Humanities Research Association and Maney Publishing.

— (2010b), *Literary Theory: A Beginner's Guide*. Oxford: Oneworld.

Cornford, Francis Macdonald (1991), *From Religion to Philosophy: A Study in the Origins of Western Speculation*. Princeton, NJ: Princeton University Press.

Cornis-Pope, Marcel (1992), *Hermeneutic Desire and Critical Writing: Narrative Interpretation in the Wake of Post-Structuralism*. London: Macmillan.

Critchley, Simon (1989), 'The chiasmus: Levinas, Derrida and the ethical demand for deconstruction', *Textual Practice* 3(1), 91–106.

— (1999), *The Ethics of Deconstruction: Derrida and Levinas*. Edinburgh: Edinburgh University Press.

— (2007), *Infinitely Demanding: Ethics of Commitment, Politics of Resistance*. London: Verso.

Culler, Jonathan D. (1981), *The Pursuit of Signs: Semiotics, Literature, Deconstruction*. London: Routledge & Kegan Paul.

Cunningham, Valentine (2002), *Reading After Theory*. Oxford: Blackwell.

Currie, Mark (1995), *Metafiction*. London: Longman.

Davies, Paul (1991), 'A fine risk: reading Blanchot reading Levinas' in Robert Bernasconi and Simon Critchley (eds), *Re-reading Levinas*. London: Athlone Press, pp. 201–28.

De Man, Paul (1971), *Blindness and Insight: Essays in the Rhetoric of Contemporary Criticism*. New York: Oxford University Press.

— (1979), *Allegories of Reading*. New Haven; London: Yale University Press.

— (1986), *The Resistance to Theory*. Minneapolis: University of Minnesota Press.

Derrida, Jacques (1978a), 'Force and signification' in Alan Bass (ed.), *Writing and Difference*. London: Routledge & Kegan Paul, pp. 1–35.

— (1978b), 'Violence and metaphysics: an essay on the thought of Emmanuel Levinas' in Alan Bass (ed.), *Writing and Difference*. London: Routledge & Kegan Paul, pp. 97–192.

— (1978c), 'Freud and the scene of writing' in Alan Bass (ed.), *Writing and Difference*. London: Routledge & Kegan Paul, pp. 246–91.

— (1979a), 'Living on – border lines' in Harold Bloom (ed.), *Deconstruction and Criticism*. London: Routledge & Kegan Paul, pp. 62–142.

— (1979b), *Spurs: Nietzsche's Styles = Éperons: Les Styles de Nietzsche*s. Barbara Harlow (trans). Chicago; London: University of Chicago Press.

— (1981), 'Outwork, prefacing' in *Dissemination*. London: Athlone Press, pp. 1–66.

— (1982), 'Tympan' in Alan Bass (ed.), *Margins of Philosophy*. Brighton: Harvester, pp. ix–xxix.

— (1985), *The Ear of the Other: Otobiography, Transference, Translation: Texts and Discussions with Jacques Derrida*. Peggy Kamuf and Christie McDonald (trans). New York: Schocken Books.

— (1987a), 'Envois' in *The Post Card: From Socrates to Freud and Beyond*. Chicago: University of Chicago Press, pp. 1–256.

— (1987b), 'To speculate – on "Freud"' in *The Post Card: From Socrates to Freud and Beyond*. Chicago: University of Chicago Press, pp. 257–410.

— (1988), *Limited Inc.* Evanston, IL: Northwestern University Press.

— (1989a), *Of Spirit: Heidegger and the Question*. Geoffrey Bennington and Rachel Bowlby (trans). Chicago; London: University of Chicago Press.

— (1989b), 'Biodegradables: seven diary fragments', *Critical Inquiry* 15(4), 812–73.

— (1990), 'Some statements and truisms about neo-logisms, newisms, postisms, parasit-isms, and other small seismisms' in David Carroll (ed.), *The States of 'Theory': History, Art, and Critical Discourse*. New York: Columbia University Press, pp. 63–94.

— (1991), 'Letter to a Japanese friend' in Peggy Kamuf (ed.), *A Derrida Reader: Between the Blinds*. New York; London: Harvester Wheatsheaf, pp. 269–76.

— (1992a), 'Force of law: the mystical foundation of authority' in Drucilla Cornell, Michel Rosenfeld and David Carlson (eds), *Deconstruction and the Possibility of Justice*. New York; London: Routledge, pp. 3–67.

— (1992b), 'The law of genre' in Derek Attridge (ed.), *Acts of Literature*. New York; London: Routledge, pp. 221–52.

— (1992c), 'Passions: "an oblique offering"' in David Wood (ed.), *Derrida: A Critical Reader*. Oxford: Basil Blackwell, pp. 5–35.

— (1992d), 'Psyche: invention of the other' in Derek Attridge (ed.), *Acts of Literature*. New York; London: Routledge, pp. 310–43.

— (1992e), 'This strange institution called literature' in Derek Attridge (ed.), *Acts of Literature*. New York; London: Routledge, pp. 33–75.

— (1995a), 'There is no *one* narcissism' in Elisabeth Weber and Peggy Kamuf (eds), *Points: Interviews, 1974–1994*. Stanford, CA: Stanford University Press, pp. 196–215.

— (1995b) "'Eating well', or the calculation of the subject' in Elisabeth Weber and Peggy Kamuf (eds), *Points...: Interviews, 1974–1994*. Stanford, CA: Stanford University Press, pp. 255–87.

— (1996), *Archive Fever: A Freudian Impression*. Chicago; London: University of Chicago Press.

— (1997a), 'The end of the book and the beginning of writing' in *Of Grammatology*. Baltimore: Johns Hopkins University Press, pp. 6–26.

— (1997b), '...That dangerous supplement...' in *Of Grammatology*. Baltimore: Johns Hopkins University Press, pp. 141–64.

— (2001), 'By force of mourning' in Pascale-Anne Brault and Michael Naas (eds), *The Work of Mourning*. Chicago; London: University of Chicago Press, pp. 139–64.

— (2002a), 'Typewriter ribbon: limited ink (2)' in Peggy Kamuf (ed.), *Without Alibi*. Stanford, CA: Stanford University Press, pp. 71–160.

— (2002b), 'The university without condition' in Peggy Kamuf (ed.), *Without Alibi*. Stanford, CA: Stanford University Press, pp. 202–37.

— (2003), 'Following theory' in Michael Payne and John Schad (eds), *Life.After.Theory*. London: Continuum, pp. 1–51.

— (2004a), 'Mochlos, or the conflict of the faculties' in Richard Rand and Amy Wygant (trans), *Eyes of the University: Right to Philosophy 2*. Stanford, CA: Stanford University Press, pp. 83–112.

— (2004b), 'Punctuations: the time of the thesis' in *Eyes of the University: Right to Philosophy 2*. Stanford, CA: Stanford University Press, pp. 113–28.

— (2004c), 'The principle of reason: the university in the eyes of its pupils' in *Eyes of the University: Right to Philosophy 2*. Stanford, CA: Stanford University Press, pp. 129–55.

— (2005a), *On Touching – Jean-Luc Nancy*. Stanford, CA: Stanford University Press.

— (2005b), *The Politics of Friendship*. George Collins (trans). London: Verso.

— (2007a), 'At this very moment in this work here I am' in Ruben Berezdivin and Peggy Kamuf (trans), Peggy Kamuf and Elizabeth Rottenberg (eds), *Psyche: Inventions of the Other,* vol. 1. Stanford, CA: Stanford University Press, pp. 143–90.

— (2007b), 'My chances/mes chances: a rendezvous with some Epicurean stereophonies' in Irene Harvey and Avital Ronell (trans), Peggy Kamuf and Elizabeth Rottenberg (eds), *Psyche: Inventions of the Other*, vol. 1. Stanford, CA: Stanford University Press, 2007, pp. 344–76.

— (2008), *The Gift of Death and Literature in Secret* (2nd edition). Chicago: University of Chicago Press.

Derrida, Jacques and Ferraris, Maurizio (2001), *A Taste for the Secret*. Giacomo Donis and David Webb (trans). Malden, MA: Polity.

Derrida, Jacques and Labarrière, Pierre-Jean (1986), *Altérités: Jacques Derrida et Pierre-Jean Labarrière: Avec des Etudes de Francis Guibal et Stanislas Breton*. Paris: Osiris.

Dictionary, Oxford English. Oxford: Oxford University Press. <http://www.oed.com/>

Edwards, Jason (2009), *Eve Kosofsky Sedgwick*. London: Routledge.

Elam, Diane (1992), *Romancing the Postmodern*. London: Routledge.

— (1994), *Feminism and Deconstruction: Ms En Abyme*. London: Routledge.

Ellmann, Maud (2004), 'Drawing the blind: Gide, Joyce, Larsen, and the modernist short story', *Oxford Literary Review* 26, 31–61.

Fish, Stanley (1980), *Is There a Text in this Class?: The Authority of Interpretive Communities*. Cambridge, MA; London: Harvard University Press.

Fludernik, Monika (1996), *Towards a 'Natural' Narratology*. London: Routledge.

Franken, Christien (2001), *A.S. Byatt: Art, Authorship, Creativity*. Basingstoke: Palgrave.

Freud, Sigmund (1975a), 'Childhood memories and screen memories' in Alan Tyson (trans) and Angela Richards (ed.), *The Psychopathology of Everyday Life*. Harmondsworth: Penguin, pp. 45–52.

— (1975b), 'The forgetting of proper names' in Alan Tyson (trans) and Angela Richards (ed.), *The Psychopathology of Everyday Life*. Harmondsworth: Penguin, pp. 5–11.

— (1984), 'A note upon the "mystic-writing pad"' in Angela Richards (ed.), *On Metapsychology*. Harmondsworth: Penguin, pp. 427–34.

— (2003), *Beyond the Pleasure Principle and Other Writings*. John Reddick (trans). London: Penguin.

Gauthier, Tim S. (2006), *Narrative Desire and Historical Reparations: A.S. Byatt, Ian McEwan, Salman Rushdie*. New York; London: Routledge.

Giobbi, Giuliana (1992), 'Sisters beware of sisters: sisterhood as a literary motif in Jane Austen, A. S. Byatt and I. Bossi Fedrigotti', *Journal of European Studies* 22(3), 241–58.

Greisch, Jean (1991), 'Face and reading: immediacy and mediation' in Robert Bernasconi and Simon Critchley (eds), *Re-reading Levinas*. London: Athlone Press, pp. 67–82.

Griffiths, Philip (2004), '"On the fringe of becoming" – David Mitchell's *Ghostwritten*' in Stefan Glomb and Stefan Horlacher (eds), *Beyond Extremes: Repräsentation und Reflexion von Modernisierungsprozessen im Zeitgenössischen Britischen Roman*. Tübingen, Germany: Narr, pp. 79–99.

Gurr, Jens Martin (2007), 'Functions of intertextuality and metafiction in J. M. Coetzee's *Slow Man*', *Anglistik* 18(1), 95–112.

Hadley, Louisa (2008), *The Fiction of A.S. Byatt*. Basingstoke: Palgrave Macmillan.

Hamilton, Ian (2000), '"OK, holy man, try this"' rev. of *The Human Stain*. *London Review of Books* 22 June, 36–7.

Hanson, Clare (2000), *Hysterical Fictions: The 'Woman's Novel' in the Twentieth Century*. Basingstoke: Macmillan.

Head, Dominic (1997), *J.M. Coetzee*. Cambridge: Cambridge University Press.

Hensher, Philip (2005), 'Short and curlies' in *The Telegraph* 17 May, < http://www. telegraph.co.uk/culture/books/3642130/Short-and-curlies.html >

Holland, Norman N. (1968), *The Dynamics of Literary Response*. New York: Oxford University Press.

— (1973), *Poems in Persons: An Introduction to the Psychoanalysis of Literature*. New York: Norton.

— (1980), 'Re-covering "The purloined letter": reading as a personal transaction' in Susan Rubin Suleiman and Inge Crosman Wimmers (eds), *The Reader in the Text:*

Essays on Audience and Interpretation. Princeton, NJ: Princeton University Press, pp. 350–70.

Iser, Wolfgang (1978), *The Act of Reading: A Theory of Aesthetic Response*. London: Routledge & Kegan Paul.

— (1988), 'The reading process: a phenomenological approach' in David Lodge (ed.), *Modern Criticism and Theory: A Reader*. London: Longman, pp. 211–28.

Jackson, Sarah (2011), 'Dis-tanz: 29 tangos', *Oxford Literary Review* 33(2), 167–87.

James, Henry (1962), *The Art of the Novel*. New York: Charles Scribner's Sons.

Jenkyns, Richard (1990), 'Disinterring buried lives' rev. of *Possession*. *Times Literary Supplement* 8 March, 213–14.

Jensen, Hal (2000), 'Unexaggerated lions' rev. of *The Biographer's Tale*. *Times Literary Supplement* 2 June, 23.

Johnson, Barbara (1982), 'The pedagogical imperative: teaching as a literary genre', *Yale French Studies* 63, iii–vii.

Johnson, Diane (1991), 'The best of times' rev. of *Possession*. *New York Review of Books* 28 March, 33.

Jones, Thomas (2006), 'Outfoxing hangman' rev. of *Black Swan Green*. *London Review of Books* 11 May, 34–5.

Jordan, Justine (1999), 'Dropped stitches' rev. of *Other Stories and Other Stories*. *London Review of Books* 1 July, 33.

Kamuf, Peggy (2000), 'Deconstruction and love' in Nicholas Royle (ed.), *Deconstructions: A User's Guide*. Basingstoke: Palgrave, pp. 151–68.

Kearney, Richard (1984), *Dialogues with Contemporary Continental Thinkers: The Phenomenological Heritage: Paul Ricoeur, Emmanuel Levinas, Herbert Marcuse, Stanislas Breton, Jacques Derrida*. Manchester: Manchester University Press.

Kelly, Kathleen Coyne (1996), *A.S. Byatt*. New York; London: Twayne Publishers; Prentice Hall International.

Kerrigan, John (2002), 'Touching and being touched' rev. of *Reading After Theory*. *London Review of Books* 19 September, 19–22.

Kubitschek, Missy Dehn (1998), *Toni Morrison: A Critical Companion*. Westport, CT; London: Greenwood Press.

Lanchester, John (2005), 'A will of his own' rev. of *Slow Man*. *New York Review of Books* 17 November, 4–6.

Leitch, Vincent B. (1995), 'Reader-response criticism' in Andrew Bennett (ed.), *Readers and Reading*. London: Longman, pp. 32–65.

Levinas, Emmanuel (1976), 'Tout autrement' in *Noms Propres: Essais*. Montpellier: Fata Morgana, pp. 81–9.

— (1981), *Otherwise Than Being, or, Beyond Essence*. The Hague; London: Nijhoff.

— (1991), 'Wholly otherwise' in Robert Bernasconi and Simon Critchley (eds), *Re-reading Levinas*. London: Athlone Press, pp. 3–10.

— (1996a), 'Substitution' in Adriaan Theodoor Peperzak, Simon Critchley and Robert Bernasconi (eds), *Emmanuel Levinas: Basic Philosophical Writings*. Bloomington: Indiana University Press, pp. 79–96.

— (1996b), 'Wholly otherwise' in Michael B. Smith (trans), *Proper Names*. London: Athlone Press, pp. 55–62.

— (1999), *Alterity and Transcendence*. Linton: Athlone.

Lowry, Elizabeth (2007), 'Initial contacts' rev. of *Diary of a Bad Year*. *Times Literary Supplement* 24 August, 3–4.

Luckhurst, Roger and Marks, Peter (1999), *Literature and the Contemporary: Fictions and Theories of the Present*. Harlow: Longman.

Lundén, Bo (1999), *Reeducating the Reader: Fictional Critiques of Poststructuralism in Banville's Dr Copernicus, Coetzee's Foe, and Byatt's Possession*. Göteborg, Sweden: Acta Universitatis Gothoburgensis.

Margolin, Uri (1990), 'Narrative "you" revisited', *Language and Style* 23(4), 425–46.

McHale, Brian (1987), *Postmodernist Fiction*. New York; London: Methuen.

McLane, Maureen (2000), '"Why should I not speak to you?" The rhetoric of intimacy' in Lauren Berlant (ed.), *Intimacy*. Chicago; London: University of Chicago Press, pp. 435–42.

Miller, J. Hillis (1987), *The Ethics of Reading: Kant, de Man, Eliot, Trollope, James, and Benjamin*. New York; Guildford: Columbia University Press.

— (1995), 'The critic as host' in David Lodge (ed.), *Modern Criticism and Theory: A Reader*. Harlow: Longman, pp. 277–85.

— (1999), 'Literary study in the transnational university' in *Black Holes or, Boustrophedonic Reading: Cultural Memory in the Present*. Stanford, CA: Stanford University Press, pp. 3–184.

Mitchell, David (1999), *Ghostwritten: A Novel in Nine Parts*. London: Sceptre.

— (2001), *number9dream*. London: Sceptre.

— (2004), *Cloud Atlas*. London: Sceptre.

— (2006), *Black Swan Green*. London: Sceptre.

Morgan, Clare (2004), 'Between worlds: Iris Murdock, A. S. Byatt, and romance' in Corinne Saunders (ed.), *A Companion to Romance: From Classical to Contemporary*. Malden, MA: Blackwell, pp. 502–20.

Morlock, Forbes (2007), 'The institute for creative reading', *Angelaki* 12(2), 5–6.

Morrison, Toni (1999), *Paradise*. London: Vintage.

Morrissette, Bruce (1965), 'Narrative "you" in contemporary literature', *Comparative Literature Studies* 2, 1–24.

Nancy, Jean-Luc (1991), *The Inoperative Community*. Peter Connor (trans). Minneapolis; Oxford: University of Minnesota Press.

O'Rourke, William (1989), 'Morphological metaphors for the short story: matters of production, reproduction, and consumption' in Susan Lohafer and Jo Ellyn Clarey (eds), *Short Story Theory at a Crossroads*. Baton Rouge; London: Louisiana State University Press, pp. 193–205.

Parrish, Tim (2005), 'Becoming black: Zuckerman's bifurcating self in *The Human Stain*' in Derek Parker Royal (ed.), *Philip Roth: New Perspectives on an American Writer*. Westport, CT; London: Praeger, pp. 209–24.

Phillips, Adam (1993), *On Kissing, Tickling and Being Bored: Psychoanalytic Essays on the Unexamined Life*. London: Faber and Faber.

— (1999), *The Beast in the Nursery*. London: Faber and Faber.

— (2002), *Equals*. London: Faber and Faber.

Phillips, John (2010), 'Angel: the telescopic soul or the episcopic gaze' <http://courses.nus.edu.sg/course/elljwp/readingthepostcard.htm>, consulted 6 April.

Poe, Edgar Allan (2009), 'The Philosophy of composition' in Stuart Levine and Susan F. Levine (eds), *Critical Theory: The Major Documents*. Urbana, IL: University of Illinois Press.

Poole, Steven (2001), 'I think I'm turning Japanese' rev. of *number9dream*. *The Guardian* 10 March, <http://www.guardian.co.uk/books/2001/mar/10/fiction.davidmitchell>

Prince, Gerald (1980), 'Notes on the text as reader' in Susan Rubin Suleiman and Inge Crosman Wimmers (eds), *The Reader in the Text: Essays on Audience and Interpretation*. Princeton, NJ: Princeton University Press, pp. 225–40.

— (1995), 'Metanarrative signs' in Mark Currie (ed.), *Metafiction*. London: Longman, pp. 55–70.

Pughe, Thomas (1994), *Comic Sense: Reading Robert Coover, Stanley Elkin, Philip Roth*. Basel: Birkhäuser.

Ratcliffe, Sophie (2005), 'Life in sonnet form' rev. of *The Accidental*. *Times Literary Supplement* 20 May, 19–20.

Readings, Bill (1996), *The University in Ruins*. Cambridge, MA; London: Harvard University Press.

Richardson, Brian (2006), *Unnatural Voices: Extreme Narration in Modern and Contemporary Fiction*. Columbus: Ohio State University Press.

Robbins, Jill (1999), *Altered Reading: Levinas and Literature*. Chicago; London: University of Chicago Press.

Robolin, Stephane (2006), 'Loose memory in Toni Morrison's *Paradise* and Zoe Wicomb's *David's Story*', *Modern Fiction Studies* 52(2), 297–320.

Roth, Philip (1998), *Zuckerman Bound: A Trilogy and Epilogue*. London: Vintage.

— (2001), *The Human Stain*. London: Vintage.

Royle, Nicholas (2003), *The Uncanny*. New York: Routledge.

— (2004), 'Spooking forms', *Oxford Literary Review* 26, 155–72.

— (2011), *Veering: A Theory of Literature*. Edinburgh: Edinburgh University Press.

Scholes, Robert (1995), 'Metafiction' in Mark Currie (ed.), *Metafiction*. London: Longman, pp. 21–38.

Schwenger, Peter (1995), 'Uncanny reading', *English Studies in Canada* 21(3), 333–45.

Scurr, Ruth (2001), 'A ghost with guests' rev. of *Hotel World*. *Times Literary Supplement* 23 March, 7.

Sedgwick, Eve Kosofsky (1989), 'Tide and trust', *Critical Inquiry* 15(4), 745–57.

— (1994), *Tendencies*. London: Routledge.

— (2003), *Touching, Feeling: Affect, Pedagogy, Performativity*. Durham; London: Duke University Press.

Shakespeare, William (1989), 'A midsummer night's dream' in Gary Taylor and Stanley W. Wells (eds), *The Complete Oxford Shakespeare,* vol. 2. London: Guild Publishing.

Shechner, Mark (2003), *Up Society's Ass, Copper: Rereading Philip Roth*. Madison, WI: University of Wisconsin Press.

Shostak, Debra B. (2004), *Philip Roth: Countertexts, Counterlives*. Columbia, SC: University of South Carolina Press.

Skidelksy, William (2005), 'Under the shifty shadow of God' rev. of *The Turning. Times Literary Supplement* 25 March, 21.

Smith, Ali (1995), *Free Love and Other Stories*. London: Virago.

— (1999), *Other Stories and Other Stories*. London: Granta.

— (2002), *Hotel World*. London: Penguin.

— (2003), *The Whole Story and Other Stories*. London: Hamish Hamilton.

— (2005), *The Accidental*. London: Hamish Hamilton.

— (2008), *The First Person and Other Stories*. London: Hamish Hamilton.

Smith, Robert (1995), *Derrida and Autobiography*. Cambridge: Cambridge University Press.

Smith, Terry (2006), 'Contemporary art and contemporaneity', *Critical Inquiry* 32(4), 681–707.

Spacks, Patricia Ann Meyer (1995), *Boredom: The Literary History of a State of Mind*. Chicago; London: University of Chicago Press.

Sterne, Laurence (1976), *The Life and Opinions of Tristram Shandy, Gentleman*. Harmondsworth: Penguin Books.

Tiplady, Jonathan (2007), 'Good air, my only friend, believe', *Angelaki* 12(2), 151–61.

van der Vlies, Andrew (2005), 'The novelist has entered the room' rev. of *Slow Man. Times Literary Supplement* 2 September, 9–10.

Wade, Stephen (1996), *The Imagination in Transit: The Fiction of Philip Roth*. Sheffield: Sheffield Academic Press.

Wallhead, Celia (2003), 'Metaphors for the self in A. S. Byatt's *The Biographer's Tale*', *Language and Literature* 12(4), 291–308.

Waugh, Patricia (1984), *Metafiction: The Theory and Practice of Self-Conscious Fiction*. London; New York: Methuen.

Weller, Shane (2006), 'When the other comes too close: Derrida and the threat of affinity', *Kritikos: An International and Interdisciplinary Journal of Postmodern Cultural Sound, Text, and Image*, no pagination.

Whitehead, Anne (2009), *Memory*. London: Routledge.

Wills, David (1984), 'Post/Card/Match/Book/Envois/Derrida', *SubStance: A Review of Theory and Literary Criticism* 13(2), 19–38.

Wilson, Alexis Kate (2005), 'The ghosts of Zuckerman's past: the *Zuckerman Bound* series' in Derek Parker Royal (ed.), *Philip Roth: New Perspectives on an American Author*. Westport, CT; London: Praeger, pp. 103–18.

Winton, Tim (2005), *The Turning*. London: Picador.

Wittgenstein, Ludwig (1971), *Prototractatus: An Early Version of Tractatus Logico-Philosophicus*. London: Routledge & Kegan Paul.

Wood, Sarah (2004), 'Optic nerve', *The Oxford Literary Review* 26, 139–53.

— (2006), 'Edit', *Mosaic* 39(3), 47–57.

— (2007), 'All the way to writing', *Angelaki* 12(2), 137–47.

— (2008), 'A new international, or what you will', *The Oxford Literary Review* 30(1), 147–60.

— (2009a), *Derrida's Writing and Difference: A Reader's Guide*. London; New York: Continuum.

— (2009b), 'Foreveries', *The Oxford Literary Review* 31(1), 65–77.

Zimmerman, Everett (1987), '*Tristram Shandy* and narrative representation', *The Eighteenth Century: Theory and Interpretation* 28(2), 127–47.

Index

absence   44, 46–7, 54, 63, 66, 70, 74–5,
        78, 86, 131, 169, 180–1n. 14
alterity   27, 87, 96, 149, 163
aphorism   80
apostrophe   141–4, 151, 154, 166
archive   39, 63, 70, 72–7, 86
Armstrong, Isobel   119, 124
autobiography   27, 40, 157, 162

Barthes, Roland   98, 175n. 3
    Pleasure of the Text   38–9, 41, 56,
        151, 171n. 6, 172n. 11, 173n. 15,
        177n. 19
    S/Z   5, 30, 34–5
Beckett, Samuel   46, 176n. 10, 177n. 15
Belsey, Catherine   3, 5
    Desire   168–9
Bennington, Geoffrey,
    'Inter'   131–2
Bernasconi, Robert   91, 95, 99–100
betrayal   17, 91, 101, 103
Blanchot, Maurice   15, 19–20, 24, 31,
        34–5, 50, 87
    The Infinite Conversation   30, 68–9,
        92, 101–2, 104
boredom   38–9, 41, 56
Butler, Judith   17, 148, 156, 161, 163–4
Byatt, A. S Byatt   9
    The Biographer's Tale   32–4, 40, 42–3,
        45, 48, 66, 113, 125–6, 185n. 16
    The Game   7–8, 10, 171–2n. 7
    Possession   25, 109–18, 120–30,
        136–9, 175n. 5, 183n. 3

chance   17, 55, 64, 66–8, 76, 100, 142,
        151, 158–9
citation   55–6, 125, 180n. 12
Cixous, Hélène   30, 32, 43, 47, 51–2, 59,
        148, 153–4, 163
    'Post word'   31, 39, 44, 46
    'Without end'   31, 39, 41–2, 46, 48,
        53–4, 177–8n. 20

Clark, Timothy   1–3, 14, 16, 19–20,
        22, 134
close reading   119, 124, 132
Coetzee, J. M.   148, 154, 162
    Diary of a Bad Year   32–3, 36–7,
        53–5, 117
    Foe   61, 71–5, 84–5, 181n. 17
    Slow Man   108, 111, 113, 115, 118,
        121, 133–4, 136–8, 184n. 7
coincidence   43, 47, 66–7, 172n. 9,
        185n. 16
commentary   29, 52, 94, 96–7, 136,
        175n. 3
conclusion   23–4, 167
Connors, Clare   17, 20, 23, 148,
        167, 171n. 1
conspiracy theory   70, 73
contemporaneity   12, 26
creativity   33, 145
Critchley, Simon   16, 96, 103, 182n. 3
Cunningham, Valentine,
    Reading After Theory   107–11,
        119–20, 123–4, 184n. 8

De Man, Paul   25, 63, 95, 173–4n. 18,
        182n. 5
    The Resistance to Theory   127
Derrida, Jacques,
    Archive Fever   63, 70, 72–4, 76–7
    'At this very moment in this text here
        I am'   87, 89, 92, 100, 102–4,
        149, 156, 163–4
    'Biodegradables'   20, 22, 56
    'By force of mourning'   18–19, 22,
        156–7
    The ear of the other   148, 162–3, 168
    'Envois'   142, 150–4, 157–9,
        161–2, 165
    Eyes of the university   2–3, 87–8,
        173n. 17
    'Force and signification'   29, 54, 58–9
    'Force of law'   93, 95, 104

The gift of death   15
'The law of genre'   50
'Letter to a Japanese friend'   93
Limited Inc   96–7, 104
'My chances'   55, 66, 68, 76, 142,
        151, 158–9
Of Grammatology   17–18, 23, 55, 70,
        75, 78, 92–3, 95–6, 167
On Touching – Jean-Luc Nancy
        107–8, 112, 117–18, 132–5,
        139, 162
'Outwork'   52
'Passions'   174n. 21
The Politics of Friendship   26, 141–4,
        151, 154, 156, 158–9, 166, 169
'Psyche'   172n. 9
'Some statements and
        truisms'   111–12, 127
Spurs   78, 104, 112, 129–30
'There is no one narcissism'   20–1
'This strange institution'   10, 14–15,
        17, 20–2, 27, 55
'To speculate – on Freud'   121, 124–6,
        131, 135
'Violence and metaphysics'   87–94,
        99–101, 103–4
desire   24, 91–3, 118, 127–8, 167–70
différance   2, 87, 135
distance   24, 29, 53, 57, 65, 76, 107–14,
        117–24, 126–32, 135–8, 140,
        151, 154, 160

echo   6, 63–6, 72, 75, 78, 82–5
error   24, 35, 37–9, 41–3, 53–4, 59, 63,
        81, 97, 100, 131, 133
ethics   4, 14, 21, 23–5, 87–105,
        107–9, 133–4, 141, 161, 166–7,
        183n. 2

failure   3, 12, 24, 29, 35, 46, 48, 51–3,
        56–7, 59, 69, 84, 92, 109, 118,
        125, 139–40, 158, 165, 167
Fish, Stanley   4–7, 10–12, 18–20, 155
force   2, 52, 54, 68, 87, 104, 158, 167,
        182n. 7
forgetfulness   74, 78, 81, 122
Freud, Sigmund   57, 76, 80–2, 125–6

Holland, Norman   4–7, 10–12

ideal reader   155–6
impossible   3, 13, 16–17, 22–4, 35, 44,
        48, 53, 58, 68–9, 90, 101–4,
        117, 119, 132–4, 148, 157, 167,
        169–70
infinite logical regress see *mise-en-abîme*
intention   40, 81, 91, 93–4, 96–7, 100–1,
        130, 155, 160, 162
interruption   19, 24, 72, 87, 102, 104, 135,
        145, 167
intertextuality   85, 179–80n. 9
intimacy   107–9, 111–13, 118–21, 123,
        128, 130–1, 135, 137, 140,
        149, 170
introduction   23–4, 87
inverted commas   17, 23, 52, 111–12,
        127, 183n. 6
irresponsibility   21, 174n. 20
Iser, Wolfgang   4, 6, 11, 155
iterability   175n. 8

James, Henry   3, 30–1, 37–8, 176n. 12,
        177n. 16, 178n. 21
justice   20, 22, 95

Levinas, Emmanuel,
        'Wholly otherwise'   70, 89–91, 95,
        101–2, 104, 182n. 3
literary *see* literature
literary criticism   3, 5, 8, 21, 29, 59,
        113, 155
literature   3, 14–18, 20–2, 26–7, 87, 170,
        173n. 17, 174n. 19
love   92, 110, 143, 150–1, 158, 165,
        167–70

memory   27, 69, 75–8, 80–2, 86, 181n. 15
metacriticism   6–7, 10
metafiction   4, 6–10, 34, 171n. 3, 172n. 8
metalanguage   7
metanarrative *see* metafiction
metaphysics of presence   89–93, 97, 100
Miller, J. Hillis   1–3, 13, 171n. 2
mise-en-abîme   10, 13, 50, 53
misreading   35, 93–4, 100–1, 109
Mitchell, David,
        Black Swan Green   32–6, 43, 49–50, 53
        Cloud Atlas   13, 61, 65–8, 71–2, 77–8,
        80–2, 84

Ghostwritten   61–2, 64–7, 70–5, 78, 80, 84
Morrison, Toni,
    Paradise   61–3, 65, 75

Nancy, Jean-Luc,
    'Shattered love'   168, 170
narcissism   20–1
Nietzsche, Fredrich   93, 129
novel   62–3, 178n. 3, 178–9n. 4

objectivity   4–5, 7, 124
other   2, 16–17, 19–20, 22, 87, 102, 120, 143, 149, 154, 156–8, 161–5

paranoia   73, 99
phenomenology   6, 91
Philips, Adam   12, 68–9
    On Kissing, Tickling and Being Bored   168–9
philosophy   15–18, 20–1, 27, 29–30, 89–90, 101–2, 104, 142, 149, 167–8
Poe, Edgar Allan   30–2, 175n. 4, 176n. 9
point of view   85–6
presence   13, 29, 39, 51, 54, 59, 63, 66, 70, 74–5, 78, 90, 92–3, 95, 98, 101, 131, 144, 149, 154, 162, 169–70
present   26, 33, 103, 131, 134
proximity   88, 107–9, 113, 117, 119–21, 127, 130–1, 135, 137, 140

queer   87
quotation marks *see* inverted commas

RAE *see* Research Assessment Exercise
reader-response theory   4–6, 10–12, 18–20, 155–6
real   9–10, 33, 49, 76, 110–11, 113–15, 117, 120, 138
REF *see* Research Excellence Framework
relationality   144, 148–9, 157, 164
repetition   24, 63, 65, 72, 74, 84–5, 88
representation   4, 13–18, 20, 29, 33, 35, 133, 156
rereading   71, 172n. 11, 180n. 10
Research Assessment Exercise   1–2
Research Excellent Framework   1, 20, 25, 170

responsibility   4, 6, 14, 18, 20–3, 25, 56, 100, 141, 156, 164–6
revision   24, 37, 41–2, 45–6, 53, 72
risk   19, 21, 56, 58, 69, 76, 91, 97, 100, 148, 169
Roth, Philip,
    The Human Stain   108, 114–15, 118–22, 129–30, 133–4
    Zuckerman Bound   32, 34, 37, 44, 49
Royle, Nicholas   1–2, 14, 85

said   14–17, 19, 23, 102–4, 109, 144, 158, 164
saying   9, 14–17, 19, 45, 87, 102–3, 109, 144, 154, 163
secret   17, 48, 123, 134, 174n. 21, 184n. 12
Sedgwick, Eve Kosofsky   24, 70, 73, 78, 98–9, 104, 139, 145
seduction   129–31
self-consciousness   4, 7, 10, 34, 132
self-reflexivity *see* self-consciousness
Shakespeare, William,
    A Midsummer Night's Dream   9
short story   62–3, 178n. 3, 178–9n. 4
signature   19, 21–2, 52, 162
singularity   21–2, 175n. 8
Smith, Ali   144, 150
    The Accidental   62–3, 65–6, 75, 78, 80–1, 179n. 14
    'God's gift'   160–1
    Hotel World   61, 64, 66, 76, 78–80, 168, 180–1n. 14
    'The second person'   151–3, 166
    'A story of love'   146–8
    'The theme is power'   143, 145–8, 150, 153, 156, 158, 160–1, 164
strong reading   98–9
style   6, 35, 40, 87, 89, 104, 125
supplement   5, 70, 95, 101, 103, 180n. 12, 182n. 6
surprise   18, 104–5

tangent   24, 119, 131, 135
teaching   1, 3, 155, 171n. 1
theory   4, 7, 24–5, 32, 73, 87, 99, 109–13, 119, 124–7, 139, 145, 183n. 4–5, 184n. 8

touch   18, 24, 107–9, 111–13, 117–19,
           124, 127–9, 131–2, 134–6, 140,
           183–4n. 6, 185n. 9
trace   1–2, 17, 23–4, 59, 61–87, 96,
           101–3, 167

university   1–3, 7, 173n. 17

weak reading   98–9

Winton, Tim,
    The Turning   62–3, 65, 82–3
Wittgenstein, Ludwig   101
Wood, Sarah   1, 12, 180n. 12,
           184n. 9
    'All the way to writing'   2, 29–31, 51,
           56–9, 171n. 1
    'Edit'   31, 42, 47, 50–2, 55–7, 59,
           142, 151

Lightning Source UK Ltd.
Milton Keynes UK
UKOW07f1827060115

244101UK00002B/158/P

9 781472 589729